Klaus-Jürgen Nagel | Stephan Rixen [eds.]

Catalonia in Spain and Europe

Is There a Way to Independence?

 **Nomos**

Die Deutsche Nationalbibliothek lists this publication in the
Deutsche Nationalbibliografie; detailed bibliographic data
is available in the Internet at http://dnb.d-nb.de

ISBN   978-3-8487-1828-3 (Print)
          978-3-8452-5825-6 (ePDF)

British Library Cataloguing-in-Publication Data
A catalogue record for this book is available from the British Library.

ISBN   978-3-8487-1828-3 (Print)
          978-3-8452-5825-6 (ePDF)

Library of Congress Cataloging-in-Publication Data
Nagel, Klaus-Jürgen/Rixen, Stephan
Catalonia in Spain and Europe
Is There a Way to Independence?
Klaus-Jürgen Nagel/ Stephan Rixen (eds.)
229 p.
Includes bibliographic references.

ISBN   978-3-8487-1828-3 (Print)
          978-3-8452-5825-6 (ePDF)

1. Edition 2015
© Nomos Verlagsgesellschaft, Baden-Baden, Germany 2015. Printed and bound in Germany.

Inhalt

Introduction   7
Stephan Rixen / Klaus-Jürgen Nagel

Trajectories of Catalan nationalism and its present discontents   14
Hans-Jürgen Puhle

A "right to decide"? On the normative basis of a political principle and
its application to the Catalan case   28
Jaume López

The Spanish constitution, the Constitutional Court, and the Catalan
referendum   42
Antoni Abat i Ninet

Catalonia's independence – is there a way in international and
European Union law?   52
Hermann-Josef Blanke / Yasser Abdelrehim

Catalonia: a failure of accommodation?   98
Ivan Serrano

Which people? Exploration of the role of immigration in the
secessionist process of Catalonia   115
Núria Franco-Guillén

Language policy and Catalan independence   129
Peter A. Kraus

Fiscal issues of Catalan independence   141
Elisenda Paluzie

Becoming more independent without independence? Strong
federalism with territorial autonomy as an alternative: the case of
Belgium 157
Stephan Rixen

Devolution in the UK – a slippery slope or an alternative to
independence? 169
Markus Möstl

Scottish independence in Europe – a model for others? 182
Florian Becker

The consequences of an independent Catalonia for the German foreign
policy 197
Mario Kölling

Independent Catalonia – a viable new European state? 209
Klaus-Jürgen Nagel

Some conclusions and final reflections 224
Klaus-Jürgen Nagel / Stephan Rixen

Authors 229

Introduction

Stephan Rixen / Klaus-Jürgen Nagel

During the fall of 2014, two well-established nation states of Europe, both EU members, faced important secessionist challenges. In the United Kingdom, the claim for Scottish independence was rejected in an official referendum that took place after the victory of Scottish independentist party, SNP, at the Scottish election. This victory brought the UK government to the negotiation table. In the end, the UK changed the rules of the game and the Scottish people were allowed to decide. In Catalonia, Catalan nationalist parties standing for a referendum on independence also won their parliamentary elections (in late 2012). However, attempts to reach an agreement with the Spanish government failed. Defying the prohibition by the Spanish government and the Constitutional Court, an unofficial consultation on independence was organized. On November 9, 2014, of the 2.3 million participants (about a third of the census), over 80% voted "yes" to becoming an independent state. Participants, however, were aware that this act would have no binding legal consequences. While in the UK a debate on greater devolution started after the decision, in Catalonia, at the time of writing, the deadlock on the "right to decide" remains unbroken.

This book is primarily about Catalonia. However, we will also analyze its case and claim inside both the Spanish and European contexts. We will include some comparative perspective, not only by providing particular chapters on Scotland and Belgium, but by referring to other cases in most of the chapters on Catalonia. The development of Catalan sovereigntism, in fact, has surprised more than one observer, national as well as foreign. On September 11, 1977, the Catalan national holiday, one million Catalans took to the streets of Barcelona to claim autonomy. These were years when, according to pollsters, only ~2% of the population preferred independence to other ways of accommodation (see Martínez-Herrera/Miley 2010: 13). On the same occasion in 2012, 2013, and 2014, even more people participated in marches organized by civil society associations. But they now claimed "a new state in Europe" (2012), or an outright referendum on independence (2013, 2014). According to polls conducted by the Centre d'Estudis d'Opinió, independence is the preferred option of the Catalan people, stopping very short of achieving an absolute majority.[1] This recent and quick change of public opinion in Catalonia is also confirmed by an absolute majority of the Catalan parliament standing for a referendum – and a somewhat smaller, but still clear, majority of MPs that would vote "yes" to independence.

Catalan nationalism has been considered, more often than not, to be just a regionalist movement striving for a Catalanization of Spain and to secure the states' governability when necessary. Controlled by elites, Catalanism, in this record, could easily be pacified by granting some competence or financial autonomy - and be denounced as blackmailing in turn. Catalanism, stemming from the 19th century language movement in favor of the Catalan language, had always been divided between left and right wing parties, and these divisions provided some clues to Spanish forces in need of support. The Catalan population, in great part stemming from Spanish migrants, was and still is in its majority linked to family members and friends living in the rest of Spain. Immigration from outside the state, eg from Latin America, North Africa, and elsewhere, also seemed to dilute ethnic identity. Catalonia's history as an independent polity had ended as early as 1714 when it became fully incorporated into the Bourbon monarchy of Spain. Although Catalonia was the first industrialized region of the peninsula, its leading role in terms of GDP is nowadays contested by other regions, and its economy, though industrialized and export orientated, still depends quite a lot on the Spanish market (see Nagel 2015 forthcoming).

Considering all these links, how could the number of people in favor of a referendum and even those preferring independence grow so quickly; why is the current status of one of the 17 autonomous communities of Spain not acceptable or no longer acceptable to the majority among the Catalan population, in spite of providing some recognition (as a region and nationality), many administrative and some legislative competences, and a co-official status to the Catalan language (albeit strictly limited to the territory)? Ready-made explanations like those provided by media in and outside Spain seem inadequate. An egoistic rejection to share Catalan taxes with other part of Spain does not explain the moment and the speed of the independentist turn. The draining of resources to Madrid and other parts of Spain has had a long history. To consider the economic crisis (which makes the yearly financial deficit of 6-8% of the Catalan GDP less bearable) may provide some insight, but the social composition of sovereigntism and the moment of its growth

---

1   See numbers published in the Catalan daily newspaper "Ara", 1.11.2014, www.ara.cat

seem to indicate that there are other issues at stake. Nation-building activities of Catalan elites that could have used autonomy to indoctrinate children at school or people via the Catalan public media do not provide a satisfactory explanation. About 55% (soon 65%) of the contents of the curriculum of Catalan secondary schools remains under the control of Madrid, and the audience rate of Catalan TV stands between 20 and 30%. These factors cannot be ignored. But they cannot explain the timing and the speed of the turn towards independence.

We have repeatedly insisted on the importance of the political moment (eg Nagel 2013, 2014). In 2003, socialist candidate Rodríguez Zapatero came to Barcelona to help his fellow socialists in their Catalan elections. He promised to help Catalonia to a new, enlarged statute of autonomy, if only the Catalans (in 2013) and the Spanish electors in 2014 would render correspondent majorities, which – to nearly everybody's surprise – happened. A window of opportunity seemed to have opened. As a statute of autonomy is a Madrid law and no constitution of a member state, the Catalan parliament alone could only propose, but not decide such a new statute. In 2005, it agreed a text that was backed by >80% of its MPs. However, the Madrid parliament, with its socialist majority, did not accept this text as it stood (as promised by Zapatero), but watered it down considerably. Nevertheless, the text was passed by a referendum in Catalonia and accepted by the Catalans in 2006. This, however, proved to be only the start of a story, because the conservative opposition and some socialist politicians brought the text to the Constitutional Court, which in 2010 (ie after 4 years of debate) failed against many of its provisions. The long duration of this process (with its corresponding leaks) and the final decision that was interpreted as going against the dignity of Catalonia as it disavowed the result of the referendum and mobilized the civil society of Catalonia. New sovereigntist movements and platforms bypassed the reluctant moderate Convergència party. New leaders proved their value in this process. The Catalan nationalist parties radicalized, and where the leaders did not adapt (like Artur Mas of Convergència), they were exchanged (as in Esquerra Republicana). In spite of the burgeoning economic crisis, the 2012 Catalan election was fought on the issue of a referendum on independence. This political choronology of the upsurge of sovereigntism and independentism is shared by many of the contributors to this book.

But our book also looks into the possibilities of achieving independence. Like most Constitutions, the Spanish one does not provide any right to secede. But can it possibly be inferred from other principles? The European institutions and particularly the Commission lead by Barroso have interpreted the European Treaties as adverse to admitting an independent Catalonia as a member state of the EU, and they have therefore been quite outspoken in rejecting the claim. However, Catalans may feel to have some rights as European citizens, in particular, to be considered by a European government. International Law, while not excluding secession per se, is written by states and its purpose may be to support them and avoid any instability. Can the normative set-ups be interpreted or adapted in more favorable ways to accommodate the will of a majority of the Catalans, if it has been declared? And in case it happens, how should Europe and other states react? Would a Catalan state be in any way dangerous for its minorities, democracy, stability, or public welfare? And what alternative forms of accommodation could and should politicians and citizens analyze when coming to a decision?

This book brings together specialists from different fields, but all the authors deal with the challenges of national diversity to the existing nation-states, the European Union and the state system. Academic disciplines represented herein include Law, Political Science, Economy, Sociology and History. They bring together Catalan academics (working in their country or abroad) and German researchers, living either in Germany or in Catalonia and Spain. Germany's political class and its media (see examples in Nagel, 2014) are particularly critical towards nationalism and separatism, while these phenomena are quite intensively treated in German academy. This provides some reason for bringing these communities together. However, the composition of the authorships of this book also reflects its history, which started at a conference in Bayreuth on May 22th and 23rd, 2014. We want to express our thanks to all those that contributed to organizing this event and its intensive and lively discussions. The chapters of this book were written after these discussions, and many had to update their contributions more than once due to the intensive history of the "process" that has culminated in the unofficial referendum of November 9th, 2014.

This book starts with Hans-Jürgen Puhle's succinct account of the trajectories (in the plural form) of Catalan Nationalism during the 150 years of its history, providing insight on the mostly reformist, interventionist, and, particularly during the last 30 years, law-abiding character of Catalan nationalism. However, it also affirms that these "idyllic" years are now over. From the standpoint of a political theorist, Jaume López discusses the moral issues at stake when a claim for independence is based on a "right to decide", that is, democracy, challenging current views on self-determination based on the nation. As lawyers, Antoni Abat and Hermann-Josef Blanke deal with the juridical possibilities of achieving independence, with Abat mainly analyzing the Spanish constitutional and legal background, and Blanke tackling European and International Law. Abat refers to the Constitutional setting, the judgments of the Constitutional Court, and the dominant opinions, but also refers to some possibilities of interpretations as more favorable for allowing a referendum. Blanke and Abdelrehim insist that there is no right to secession in the Spanish constitution or international law – there is "no way without Madrid" in this interpretation. A secession, if it took place, would then be based on a revolutionary act, in spite of eventual ratification after a successful control of the territory. Inside Catalonia and Spain, conditions for a successful accommodation were favorable, considering the demographic relations to Spain and the dual identities that have prevailed for so many years. Ivan Serrano therefore asks why sovereigntism has surged so strongly, in the end even changing the self-identification of many Catalans. Numbers in hand, he insists on the importance of the failure of the statute of autonomy negotiated between 2004 and 2006, a process that ended only with the sentence of the Constitutional Court in 2010. One of his conclusions is the loss of salience of the identity argument for those that defend Catalan independence, while Spanish identity is of high salience for those that reject it. His data may change the point of view of many that used to see minority nationalisms as driven by ethnic identity, while considering state nationalism as civic. The civic concept of Catalan nationality is also treated in Núria Franco's account of (recent) immigration and independence, in particular, the integrative efforts of the Catalan nationalist organizations that in many ways parallel the Scottish case. Peter Kraus tackles a directly related issue, language. Language was at the core of the historic nationalist movement of Catalonia, and for a long time it has been the most important marker of Catalan identity. However, according to Kraus, language claims are losing salience, while the sovereigntist movement grows – this movement is based on other grounds. After tackling these important issues of Catalan identity and identity construction, Elisenda Paluzie analyses the fiscal issues of Catalan independence. She insists on the size of the fiscal deficit, and sees the financial imbalance upset primarily by the lack of state spending in infrastructures that an underfinanced region could not make good for. This contrasts with the situation of the Basque Country. Many Catalan nationalists would have voted for a similar solution, but this option now seems to be closed. While the economic crisis, in her view, may have accelerated the process, the political crisis on the statute reform had preceded it.

While from a Catalan and particularly from a sovereigntist position (and we hasten to add, also from most Spanish viewpoints), the alternatives of a maximized devolution, federalism, confederalism and consociationalism are now impossible (as they would need a constitutional reform that would have to be supported by both major parties of Spain, without the need for Catalanist support), they do however exist, at least from a theoretical viewpoint. From a law professor's point of view, Stephan Rixen gives a summary of the Belgian mode of strong federalism. In his view, Belgium's institutional setting, backed up by sophisticated constitutional law arrangements, installs a never-ending process of negotiations that have avoided until now formal independence and foster a sort of hidden independence, especially of Flanders. Law professors Markus Möstl and Florian Becker tackle devolution in the UK, Möstl asking whether it will lead to independence, but in a "soft" way, and Becker considering the possible accommodation of an independent Scotland in the EU. As Scotland is a model to which Catalan independentists often refer, this is of utmost importance for the so-called "process" in Catalonia. These contributions may provide useful insights for defenders of negotiated solutions, but they may also increase the envy of those Catalans that, after the experience of the last years, consider the Spanish institutions to be essentially averse to serious and open negotiation. Mario Kölling, from his privileged position as a German expert working in Spain and (also) for Spanish institutions, analyzes the possible consequences of Catalan independence for Germany's foreign and European policy. While it may be unfair to ask too much hindsight of an academic, it may also be true that think-tanks and governments consider the consequences of a possible independence for their country and Europe, in spite of initially rejecting such an outcome. Germany is perhaps the country that has most clearly sided with the position of the Spanish government, and this is of utmost interest here. In the last chapter, Klaus-Jürgen Nagel tries to analyse the "viability" of an independent Catalonia, not only as a national economy, but as a liberal democracy. For him, an independent Catalonia, should it transpire, would most probably be just a normal European state of medium to small size, but not suitable to be taken over by a sole economic interest, and endowed with a civil society and a democratic party system, thereby causing little significant danger to liberal rights of its inhabitants, democracy and peace (thus excluding these reasons for rejecting independence on principle).

References

Martínez-Herrera, Enric/Miley, Thomas: The constitution and the politics of national identity in Spain, Nations and Nationalism 16, 2010, 1, 5-30.

Nagel, Klaus-Jürgen: Katalonien – vom Autonomismus zum Separatismus?, Europa Ethnica 70 (Wien), 2013, 1-2, 32-45.

Nagel, Klaus-Jürgen: Gibt es ein Referendum über die Unabhängigkeit Kataloniens?, in: Europäisches Zentrum für Föderalismus-Forschung Tübingen (ed.): Jahrbuch des Föderalismus 15, Föderalismus, Subsidiarität und Regionen in Europa*, Baden-Baden: Nomos Verlagsgesellschaft 2014, 362-378.

Nagel, Klaus-Jürgen: Catalonia's struggle for self-determination: From regionalism to independence?, in: Fonkem, Michael (ed.): Nationalism and intra-state conflict in postcolonial societies, Lexington Books, 2015, forthcoming.

Trajectories of Catalan nationalism and its present discontents

Hans-Jürgen Puhle

This chapter is *not* about Catalan independence. It will rather focus on the trajectories of Catalan Nationalism, its concepts and movements, with particular interest in changes over time, and in the different stages of Catalanism and Catalan Nationalism throughout 150 years. In the limited space, only a brief summary will be possible and some hints at the basic lines of social background, interests, programs and ideology of the Catalan Nationalists. It will look at their achievements and limitations, internal cleavages and divisions, and possible or impossible alliances with 'Spanish' political forces, as well as with each other. Simplifications – hopefully adequate – will be unavoidable.[1]

1. Initial constellations

Nationalism requires organization. In order to organize a nationalist movement, a concept of a nation is needed, whatever its definition, its dimension, and ultimately its construction. What a nation is, is basically a matter of opinion, even if some plausible and tangible characteristics (often called the 'proto-national minimum') may be required to make the idea sustainable. Usually they are found in language and culture, and the history and the networks behind it, and less in voluntaristic aspirations.[2] The Catalan idea of the nation has been a product of European romanticism of the first half of

---

1 A more extended version of this paper is pre-published as part of a comparative study on Welsh and Catalan Nationalisms in the NISE platform Studies on National Movements (www.nise.eu; 2015). I am particularly grateful to Klaus-Jürgen Nagel and Enric Ucelay da Cal for their critical comments.
2 Cf. H.J. Puhle, 'Nation States, Nations, and Nationalisms in Western and Southern Europe', in: J.G. Beramendi et al. (ed.), Nationalism in Europe. Past and Present (Santiago de Compostela 1994), vol. 2, 13-38; J.J. Linz, 'State Building and Nation Building', in: *European Review*, 1 (1993) 355-369; J. Breuilly, *Nationalism and the State,* 2nd ed. (Manchester, 1993); M. Hroch, *Das Europa der Nationen. Die moderne Nationsbildung im europäischen Vergleich* (Göttingen, 2005).

the 19th century. As in all cases of 'belated' or 'stateless' nations, it was a culturalist concept driven by reifications, drawing more on Herder than Rousseau. It has never been a uniform idea. Since the 1860 s, two different connotations could be distinguished: a more conservative and a more liberal (later a progressive one). These corresponded to the different contexts from which Catalan Nationalism has developed. For the 19th century, at least four strands of movements and ideologies can be identified: first, the broad and rich spectrum of Catalan cultural renaissance (*Renaixença*) since the 1830-40 s, often linked to romantic ideas; second, petty bourgeois federalism and progressivism, around and since the Revolution and the First Republic in the late 1860 s and the 1870 s; third, conservative bourgeois provincialism that later became regionalism; and fourth, clerico-reactionary conservatism, mostly of Carlist origins.[3]

The breakthrough of the Catalanist movement to Miroslav Hroch's phase B around 1880 was due to a characteristic constellation in which several factors came together: cultural and organizational saturation due to the effects of the Renaixença (from the 1830 s onwards), economic prosperity and modernization by the repercussions of full scale industrialization in relevant parts of Catalonia since the 1860 s, on the one hand, and a continuation and intensification of politico-institutional dispossession and frustration, on the other, from the 1830 s through the 1860 s down to the Restauration and the end of the Third Carlist War in the 1870 s.[4]

Catalan Nationalism has been part of what I call the fourth wave out of a total of six waves of contemporary nationalist movements, each defined by a number of macro-regional, developmental and functional similarities. These were the nationalist or regional-nationalist movements of the so-called 'smaller' peripheral nations within the Western and Southern European

---

3 Cf. E. Ucelay-Da Cal, 'History, Historiography and the ambiguities of Catalan nationalism in: *Studies on National Movements*, 1 (2013) 105-159; G. Brunn, 'Die Organisation der katalanischen Bewegung 1859-1923', in: T. Schieder & O. Dann (eds.), *Nationale Bewegung und soziale Organisation* I (München, 1978) 281-571.

4 Cf. M. Hroch, *Die Vorkämpfer der nationalen Bewegung bei den kleinen Völkern Europas* (Praha, 1968) 24-26; M. Hroch, *Social Preconditions of National Revival in Europe* (Cambridge, 1985) 22-30; Puhle, 'Nation States', 28-35, and: Pi i Margall's project for a federal constitution and the 'Projecte de Constitució per al'Estat Català' (1883), in: J.A. González Casanova, *Federalisme i autonomia a Catalunya (1868-1938). Documents* (Barcelona, 1974) 465-493; F. Pi i Margall, *Las nacionalidades*, 2 vols. (Madrid 1972 [1877]); V.Almirall, *Lo Catalanisme* (Barcelona, 1979 [1886]).

states, which have fought for autonomy statutes and federalization of the state more often than for a new nation state of their own. Among them, we can find different intensities and different types.[5] For Catalan Nationalism, we can date the Hrochian thresholds[6] as following: AB around 1880, BC around 1900,[7] and the autonomist equivalent for statehood (NS) in 1932/79, so that the complete formula relating the developmental stages of the national movement to the stages of statewide socio-economic and political development (simplified BR, IR, OW),[8] would look like this: BR – IR – AB – OW – BC – (NS). In my terminology Catalonia would therefore belong to the cases of disintegrated dissociation (because BC comes much behind BR) of a relatively developed society.[9]

2. Divided actors

A characteristic feature of Catalan Nationalism is that it has always been divided, almost from its beginnings, often along class lines, recently more along ideological lines. It experienced its first substantial turnaround when the Lliga Regionalista was established in 1901, triggered by the repercussions and polarizations of the great Spanish crisis around 1898. Before the turnaround, Catalanism had been dominated by anti-centralist and mostly anti-modernist notables of the small towns of the hinterland. It then established itself as a relatively 'modern' Barcelona-centric emancipation movement of the urban bourgeoisie, which had become regionalist because it was strong enough to rule Catalonia, but too weak either to dominate Spain or declare independence, and hence embarked on a tendentially 'imperialistic'

---

5 For details see H.J. Puhle, 'Neue Nationalismen in Osteuropa - eine sechste Welle?', in: E. Jahn (ed.), *Nationalismus im spät- und post-kommunistischen Europa*, vol 1 (Baden-Baden 2008) 162-181.

6 AB transition to cultural nationalism, BC transition to political nationalism, NS 'nation state' (or equivalent).

7 For AB, e.g., 1879 Diari Català, 1880 1. Catalanist Congress, 1882 Centre Català, 1883 2. Congress (political program), 1886 Almirall: *Lo Catalanisme*; for BC: 1886 Almirall: *Lo Catalanisme*, 1891 Unió Catalanista (UC), 1892 *Bases de Manresa* [the political program, part. art. 4, 16], 1897 Centre Català (Almirall), 1898 Spanish crisis (polarization), 1901 Lliga Regionalista.

8 BR bourgeois revolution, IR industrial revolution, OW organisation of working class movement.

9 For comparison, see Puhle, 'Neue Nationalismen', 170.

course (Ucelay da Cal) that tried to follow its own interests at home as well as influence and penetrate Spanish society and politics as much as possible. The Lliga Regionalista under the leadership of Prat de la Riba and Cambó became a modern mass party, equally present in Catalonia and in Madrid politics. It was the hegemonic faction of Catalan Nationalism between 1901 and the mid-1920 s and one of the dominant forces of Catalan politics (besides the Lerroux Republicans); the party's mobilization reached its peak in 1916.[10]

The Lliga dominated wide sectors of the intense networks of Catalan civil society, particularly among the entrepreneurial (Foment), agricultural (IAC-SI) and cultural organizations, but not all of them. There always were dissenters, more radical minority factions, mostly under the umbrella of the Unió Catalanista (UC), particularly the commercial employees (CADCI), and later the tenant winegrowers of the Unió de Rabassaires (UDR 1922),[11] or the many middle class and intellectual initiatives trying to win over more Republican voters and attract workers. Among these groups of the 'Catalanist Left', we can find short-lived enterprises, like the axis Layret/Segui/Companys around 1920, and many organizational endeavours, often small, given to fragmentation and of short duration.[12] The most important ones were the Centre Nacionalista Republicà (CNR 1906/07), the Unió Federal Nacionalista Republicana (UFNR 1910), the Esquerra Catalanista (1914), the Bloc Republicà Autonomista (BRA 1915), the Partit Republicà Català (PRC 1917), Macià's separatist Federació-Democràtica Nacionalista (FDN 1919), and Domingo's populist Esquerra Catalana (1921). There were also the heretic and explicitly nationalist (and no longer regionalist) youth organizations and social catholics of Acció Catalana (AC) that split from the Lliga in 1922. So we better might put Catalan Nationalisms into the plural.

---

10 Cf. P. Vilar, *La Catalogne dans l'Espagne moderne*, 2 vols. (Paris, 1962); E. Ucelay Da Cal, *Nacionalisme i imperialisme catalanista: d'Almirall a Prat de la Riba* (Barcelona, 2012); I. Molas, *Lliga Catalana*, 2 vols (Barcelona, 1972).
11 Cf. M. Caminal Badia, 'La fundació de l'Institut Agrícola Català de Sant Isidre: els seus homes i les seves activitats (1851-1901)', in: *Recerques*, 22 (1989) 117-135; M. Lladonosa i Vall-llebrera, *Catalanisme i moviment obrer: El CADCI entre 1903 i 1923* (Abadia de Montserrat, 1988) [Tesi Doctoral, Universitat Autònoma de Barcelona, 1979]; J. Pomés, *La Unió de Rabassaires* (Barcelona, 2000); A.Balcells, *El problema agrari a Catalunya (1890-1936). La qüestió rabassaire* (Barcelona, 1968).
12 See the comprehensive analysis in K.J. Nagel, *Arbeiterschaft und nationale Frage in Katalonien zwischen 1898 und 1923* (Saarbrücken, 1991).

The internal divisions of the Catalan Nationalists were, of course, a liability for their political influence and weight. The Lliga's strategy of corporate integration failed, due to the limitations of its bourgeois class politics, its many pacts with the Spanish government, and because its room for manoeuvre in the Mancomunitat (1913-24) was insufficient. The party lost votes, split in 1922, and continued discrediting itself through the 1920 s and 30 s.[13] The diffuse 'Catalanist Left' consisted mostly of artisans and intelligentsia trying to reach out to the workers, particularly those organized by the CNT. But whenever they did so, they lost middle-class Catalanists and mostly could not win over the workers either. Until 1917/18, they often became sandwiched between the Lliga and the CNT. This changed in the Second Republic when cooperation increased. On the whole, the 'Catalanist Left' was much more Nationalist than Socialist: Wilson triumphed over Lenin (Ucelay da Cal).[14]

Political separatism that emerged after the First World War was basically tied to middle class interests from the hinterland (and eventually the CADCI) and had no mass basis because it polarized the Catalans by attacking the Lliga and splitting the left. However, at least in retrospective, Macià's Estat Català (EC 1922) should be singled out. It started out separatist, fought the Primo dictatorship, moved back to a federalist position, used populist strategies to make Catalan nationalism more attractive to the middle and working classes, colonized the PRC and others, and became one of the driving forces behind the populist alliance of the Esquerra Republicana de Catalunya (ERC) of 1931, which united separatists (Macià), Republican Catalanists (Companys) and Radical Populists (Domingo), and established itself as the hegemonic actor in Catalanist politics throughout the 1930 s. In 1931, the Esquerra proclaimed a Catalan Republic within an Iberian Federation, even before the Spanish Republic had been proclaimed. The 'Catalanist Left' had taken over Catalan Nationalism, but at a price.[15]

---

13 See B. de Riquer, *Alfonso XIII y Cambó. La monarquía y el catalanismo político* (Barcelona, 2013); Ucelay da Cal, *El imperialismo*.

14 E. Ucelay Da Cal, 'Wilson i no Lenin: l'esquerra catalana i l'any 1917', in: *L'Avenç*, 2, 9 (Oct. 1978) 53-58.

15 See E. Ucelay Da Cal, *La Catalunya populista. Imatge, cultura i política en l'etapa republicana (1931-1939)* (Barcelona, 1982); J.B. Culla i Clarà, *Esquerra Republicana de Catalunya, 1931-2012. Una història política* (Barcelona, 2013).

3. Party politics and pacts

During most of the 20th century, Catalan Nationalism has been dominated by party politics. The exception was the consolidated years of the Franco Regime when Catalanist interests and strategies were coordinated more by culturalist and civil society organizations. Nationalist policies were usually defined by the hegemonic parties (or alliances) that organized and represented the nationalists. Between 1900 and the mid-20 s, this was the Lliga, during the 1930 s the ERC, and for a longer time after the transition of the late 1970 s the Pujolisme of Convergència i Unió (CiU). Despite the differences between these parties there have been a number of interesting continuities in shared beliefs, programmatic preferences, in the articles of the nationalist credo, the use of the movements' traditions (including what Enric Ucelay da Cal has called the 'Catalan Whig interpretation of history')[16], and particularly in the secular shift towards populist politics. The Lliga paved the way, ERC pushed populism to its breakthrough, and Pujolisme (to the chagrin of the resurrected Esquerra) ratified and continued it in an eclectic way, as if CiU were the natural successor of the ERC of the Republic (and of the Lliga). Which it was, in a way.

Another crucial element of the politics of Catalan Nationalists has been , at least until 2012, a modern version of 'pactisme', i.e. a tendency towards (and often a need for) concluding pacts and building alliances with other, mostly non-nationalist political forces, usually ad hoc, and differently on different issues and in different political arenas. Often the differences between Nationalist groups have been defined by their alliances, be it with bourgeois or middle class groups, populist and catch-all parties of all kinds, or the usual factions of the working class movements. Among the last, the special relationships between 'more Catalan' groups of the anarcho-syndicalist CNT (Segui, Trentistes), the Socialists and Communists (USC, PSUC, POUM, eventually the PSC, though less and less) and the 'Catalanist Left' are particularly interesting. Here various additional cleavages (like Monarchy/Republic, Church/State, Right/Left) interfered and partly overlapped with the principal cleavage between Nationalist and Non-Nationalist politics. Classical examples for such 'mixed-cleavage' pacts have been the participation in the conservative Spanish governments from 1899 onwards, Solidaritat Catalana (1906), the alliances for the Mancomunitat (1913), for

---

16 Ucelay da Cal, 'History', 129.

the political transitions and autonomy statutes of the 1930 s, the 1970 s, and after 2000, or the various pacts with Republicans and Anarchosyndicalists after 1917 and in the 1920-30 s, or with Socialists and Communists since the Second Republic, in the Civil War and opposition against Franco (e.g., Coordinadora de Forces Polítiques de Catalunya 1969, Assemblea de Catalunya 1971).[17]

In Spain's new democracy, both Conservative and Socialist governments have often needed the votes of Jordi Pujol's CiU in Madrid (and paid for it). At home in Catalonia, Pujol, when he needed a partner after 1999, preferred to ally himself with the Conservative Spanish Partido Popular (PP), and not (like in the mid-80 s) with his 'leftist' fellow Nationalists of the ERC. And the latter had no major problems to join the coalition governments of the 'Tripartit' led by the Catalan Socialists (2003-2010), the chief rivals of the Nationalists (though with rising internal dissent from 2006 onwards), while at the same time (2004-2006) CiU leaders negotiated an agreement on the new autonomy statute with the Spanish Socialists in Madrid. It was not until the conflict over the new autonomy statute had escalated and CiU had been punished in the elections of 2012 that the Esquerra came back to tolerate a CiU government in Catalonia. In times of Nationalist radicalization and polarization, the space for 'pactisme' seems for the first time to have shrunk. It appeared (at least for the time being) to be confined to the Nationalist camp only.

4. From regionalism to 'autonomism' to separatism

If we reduce the aspirations and options of the significant actors of Catalan Nationalism to four basic types: regionalism, federalism, 'autonomism', and separatism (or independentism), and look at the trajectories of the various movements through the last 130 years or so, we can identify a characteristic trend along those lines. This was from regionalism and federalism through 'autonomism' to separatism and independentism, not without overlaps, double standards, shifts, and many elements of 'die Gleichzeitigkeit des Ungleichzeitigen' that might require some caveats. 'Federalism', for example, has

---

17 Cf. J. Casanova, *The Spanish Republic and Civil War* (Cambridge, 2010); B. de Riquer, *La dictadura de Franco*, Historia de España 9 (Madrid, 2010) 179-245, 547-607; A. Dowling, *Catalonia since the Spanish Civil War. Reconstructing the Nation* (Brighton, 2013); J. Benet, *Catalunya sota el règim franquista* (Paris, 1973).

to be qualified because the notion in some cases might not refer to unifying federal systems like the Swiss, German or North American, but more to loosely coupled confederations like the 'Iberian Federation' in traditional Anarcho-syndicalist or Catalanist terminology, which could be combined with independentism or with regionalism, as in the Bases de Manresa of 1892. New notions of 'asymmetric federalism' have emerged in more recent times.[18]

On the whole, we can clearly distinguish four phases. From the beginnings in the 1880s until around 1917/18 regionalist concepts prevailed as they were embodied in the politics of the Lliga or in the modest institutions of the Mancomunitat (1913-24), even if there were eventual overlaps with federalist positions, Catalonia was more and more seen as a nation, and some dissenting organizations of the 'Catalanist Left' from 1906/1910 on increasingly asked for more institutionalized autonomy and a respective statute. There were no meaningful separatist demands whatsoever.

This changed significantly in the second phase from 1917/18 to the end of the Spanish Civil War in 1939. It was characterized by the disappearance of regionalism, a structural parallelism of separatist and autonomist demands, in which the latter prevailed, and a number of different federalist revivals in both contexts. Separatist aspirations were first voiced by Macià in November 1918, and remained the credo of FDN and Estat Català through 1923 and beyond, although it lost some of its teeth by being ever more blended with federalism and populism, and by a general upsurge of autonomism. The position of the ERC in 1931 was federalist (including some separatists), but it accepted the autonomist compromise of the Statute of Nuria of 1932, although not without a tendency to relapse, as in the October uprising of 1934 when Companys proclaimed a Catalan State that was not to be. The ERC's position was shared by its Socialist ally of the Unió Socialista de Catalunya (USC), which in 1936 became the core of the PSUC, one of its closest partners in a time of war. Also the influential tenant wine-growers of the Unió de Rabassaires (UDR) and the Bloc Obrer i Camperol (BOC) which was more Socialist and Communist than Nationalist (and later

---

18 Cf., e.g., F. Requejo & K.J. Nagel (eds.), *Federalism beyond Federations. Asymmetry and Processes of Resymmetrisation in Europe* (Farnham, 2011).

ended in the POUM), favoured separatism for a time before the final phase of the Civil War and Franco's victory made further discussions pointless.[19]

The third phase from the reinstallation of the Generalitat in 1977 and the Autonomy Statute of Sau (1979) to 2005/06 was the heyday of 'autonomism', and an almost 'idyllic' phase of Catalan Nationalism under the hegemony of Pujolisme, in a new structural context: the Spanish Estado de las Autonomías. Conceived as 'asymmetric' in the beginning, the system has, however, been increasingly 'resymmetrized' by framework legislation and more generalized policies of decentralization, so that it is now deemed insufficient by the Catalan Nationalists and government. Pujol's ruling coalition (CiU) of the liberal CDC and the Christian-Democratic UDC (smaller and less nationalistic) represented an unspecific and streamlined nationalism 'without adjectives'. It paid lip-service to self-determination, remained unclear toward federalism, and behaved loyal to the Estado de las Autonomías actively taking advantage of its mechanisms and opportunities, particularly in educational and cultural matters. 'Pujolisme', in a selective way, embraced the populist heritage of the ERC of the 30 s, and many of the entrepreneurial, missionary and 'imperialist' traditions of the Lliga, defining Catalonia as a principal agent of progress and modernization, for the Països Catalans, and for Spain and Europe. 'Autonomism' also overwhelmingly prevailed in the surveys on the preferences of the Catalans with regard to territorial organization, but separatism was not an issue. Only the small and more radical Republican Esquerra (ERC), after a generational shift of its leadership, set a separatist course again in its new program of 1992, far earlier than others.[20]

This 'idyllic phase' came to an end and a fourth phase began when after 2005 survey preferences began to change, more rapidly so from 2007 on-

---

19 See E. Ucelay-Da Cal & A. Gonzàlez i Vilalta (eds.), *Contra Companys, 1936. La frustración nacionalista ante la revolución* (València, 2012); Pomés, *Unió*; F. Bonamusa, *El Bloc Obrer i Camperol (1930-1932)* (Barcelona, 1974); P. Pagès, *Andreu Nin: su evolución política (1911-1937)* (Bilbao, 1975).

20 Cf. M. Guibernau, *Nacionalisme català. Franquisme, transició i democracia* (Barcelona, 2003); P. Lo Cascio, *Nacionalisme i Autogovern: Catalunya, 1980-2003* (Barcelona, 2008); J. Pujol, *El caminant davant del congost* (Barcelona, 2013); F. Martínez & J. Oliveres, *Jordi Pujol. En nom de Catalunya* (Barcelona, 2005), and: O. Barberà, *Unió Democràtica de Catalunya (1931-2003). Evolució política i organitzativa* (Bellaterra, 2010); J.B. Culla i Clarà (ed.), *El pal de paller. Convergència Democràtica de Catalunya (1974-2000)* (Barcelona, 2001); Culla i Clarà, *Esquerra.*

wards. In only five years (2007-12) 'autonomism' lost about half its support and since then has ended up third behind independentism / separatism and federalism.[21] This corresponded to a decisive new turn of Catalan Nationalism for many reasons: The outcome of the negotiations on the new Autonomy Statute of Miravet (2004-06) was disappointing for the Catalans. Most intended reforms were watered down first by the Spanish Parliament (03/2006), and then, after the statute's ratification by a (still impressive) majority in a referendum (06/2006) and a long process of deliberation, by the Constitutional Court (2010). 'Autonomism' and federalism had not delivered. Hence the majority Nationalists of the CiU, under its leader Artur Mas who took over the Catalan government in 2010, followed the minority ERC in embarking on a separatist course advocating sovereignty, independence and a vague confederation. There did not seem to be a way back to the Estado de las Autonomías as we knew it.[22]

And we can find the corresponding basic thresholds: The five most important ones have been mentioned: the long 1890 s, 1917/18, 1939, the second half of the 1970 s, and 2005/06. To these 'big' thresholds, we may have to add others with high significance, referring to regime change, social conflictivity, and repression. A few thresholds have also reflected the repercussions of macro-processes of social change: The rise of the Lliga around 1900 ratified the consequences and characteristics of industrialization in Catalonia. The precarious consolidation of the ERC in the 1930 s reflected the populist tendencies inherent in democratic mass politics in an uprooted society. And the all-encompassing moderate neo-populist course of Pujol's catch-all CiU after 1980 can only be understood by considering that Catalan society during the transition and afterwards was significantly different from what it had been down to the 1930 s and 40 s. Economic opening, rising investment in industries, services and infrastructure since the late 1950 and the 1960 s had produced a rise in the standard of living, new waves of migration, and triggered comprehensive processes of modernization, urban-

---

21 See the CEO data on the evolution of Catalans' territorial political preferences 2005-2013.

22 See, e.g., the data in *Anuari polític de Catalunya 2012*, Institut de Ciències Polítiques i Socials (Barcelona, 2012), and: F. Requejo & M. Sanjaume, *Recognition and political accommodation: from regionalism to secessionism. The Catalan case*, GRTP Political Theory Working Paper 13, Universitat Pompeu Fabra (Barcelona, 2013); K.J. Nagel, 'Katalonien – vom Autonomismus zum Separatismus?', in: *europa ethnica*, 70, 1-2 (2013) 32-45.

ization and liberalization. Anarcho-syndicalism had practically disappeared, communism was weak, and the more fundamentalist Catholic and Nationalist traditions of the hinterland were in retreat.[23] So Pujol did not hesitate to dance at the fiestas of immigrants from Andalucía, and he succeeded, at least in the polls for the Catalan parliament.

5. *Threats and models for the 21st century*

There is some evidence that also the latest 'big' threshold in the politics of Catalan Nationalism – the turn towards independence and separatism of the last decade – may have to do with other macro-processes of economic and social change, although in a complicated and sometimes contradictory way. I am here referring in particular to a secular process of basic and substantial change in almost all dimensions of social and political group formation and interaction that has occurred in the decades around the turn of the century (hence 'threshold 21'). This process has been triggered and intensified by a constellation of at least six to seven factors:

1. the late repercussions of the 'stagflation crisis' since the 70 s for political and social organisation and regulation, deregulation and liberalisation,
2. the further increase in 'globalisation', global exchange of capital and people, and the protests against it,
3. the implications of the financial, economic and institutional crisis since 2008,
4. the availability of the new electronic media and IT, particularly the internet and the social media which have given new momentum to
5. a comprehensive mediatization of politics and an intensification of the processes of structural change of the public sphere and of the character of the political.
6. A sixth process can be described as the breakthrough of 'populist democracy' on a broad scale, within a favorable ambiente full of windows of opportunity, 'populist moments', and agency.

---

23 For a good synthesis of economic, demographic, social and attitudinal change, cf. (besides all the data collections) B. de Riquer & J.B. Culla, *El Franquisme i la transició democràtica (1939-1988)*, Història de Catalunya VII (Barcelona, 1989) 171-384.

7. For the European context we have to add a seventh process: intensified European integration and institution building, combined with a perceived lack of democratic legitimation and an underdeveloped institutional imagination regarding the future of the Union, and finally the crisis of the Euro and the remedies to cure.[24]

Among other things, this implied for Catalonia a severe economic and social crisis, a disproportional fiscal deficit and public debt, increased immigration and a progressive Castilianization of Catalan society, which produced new identity problems and intensified identity politics in the Nationalist camp that could take advantage of the good conjunctures of populist politics. Even a peacefully and productively integrated Catalan society would be less 'Catalan' in the traditional way conceived in 'ethnic' terms (and hence we also can increasingly find more 'progressive' additional definitions of Catalan 'identity' in more 'civic' terms of democracy and welfare). The new Autonomy Statute negotiated and ratified in 2005/06, beyond its function to remedy the shortcomings of the old one after 25 years, to bring it up to date and develop further the mechanisms of the Estado de las Autonomías, was also meant to address these problems and give some relief to the real and perceived threats to Catalan identity, symbolically, linguistically, institutionally and fiscally. When the Statute, however, was further watered down by the Constitutional Court after its ratification and did neither recognize the plurinationality of the State nor make any significant improvements in self-government, transfer of competences and tax sharing, disenchantment and frustration set in which were further increased by the subsequent intransigence and immobility of the Spanish Parliament and governments in (not) addressing the urgent Catalan problems and needs.

This was the constellation into which a new generation of leaders of the Catalan Nationalists in both parties, ERC and CiU, (and also beyond the parties) could launch a renewed separatist project demanding the 'right to decide', Catalan statehood, and independence, with all the agitation and the visible 'tools for torture' this implies (like the controversial 'unilateral ref-

---

24 For more details of the 'threshold 21' see H.J. Puhle, 'Old and New Populisms in the 21st Century: Continuities and Change', in: A.Ostheimer de Sosa & M. Borchard (ed.), *Populism Within Europe and Beyond Its Borders* (Baden-Baden, 2015, forthcoming).

erendum' as an initial step).[25] Addressing the Catalan discontents and demands within the framework of Spanish institutions would have required that both sides renounce their maximalist positions and compromise on some kind of imaginative and practical models for territorial organization (and national recognition), as had been debated in the first decade of the 21st century, e.g. a gradual reform of the autonomy statutes beyond the status quo, or some kind of federalism, more but not too asymmetric. But as the conservative government in Madrid (like the Socialist opposition) had not been ready for a substantially improved 'Spanish solution' all the way, and the Catalan Nationalists have hence become increasingly disaffected and alienated of it, the project of independence has significantly gained momentum throughout Catalan society. Polarization has increased, and both sides have become radicalized, the Catalan and the Spanish Nationalists, as could be seen in the elections of 2012 (gains for ERC and Ciutadans), and particularly in results from more recent surveys on perceived identities, preferences of territorial organization and voting intentions.[26]

The present quarrels on the modalities of a ('unilateral') referendum, and of 'negotiating independence' more in general, have also contributed to further escalation of the conflict. And considering the present actors, it has become clear that, at a given point, the Catalan Nationalists might have no choice but to commit revolutionary acts if they are to pursue their goals, and the Spanish Nationalists in government might be tempted to send in the police. In this polarized situation, it appears as if Catalan Nationalism has not only changed its character and concept from 'positive' to 'negative', as Enric Ucelay da Cal has eventually observed (2013),[27]and from a saturated and self-conscious to an insecure and complaining Nationalism, but also a number of other important features, constellations and functions:

• Catalan Nationalism is no longer law-abiding or 'idyllic', as during Pujolisme, nor necessarily reformist. It has again become (at least poten-

---

25 Cf. J. Muñoz & M. Guinjoan, 'Accounting for internal variation in nationalist mobilization: unofficial referendums for independence in Catalonia (2009-11)', in: *Nations and Nationalism*, 19, 1 (2013) 44-67.

26 See the data in *Anuari polític de Catalunya 2013*, Institut de Ciències Politiques i Socials (Barcelona, 2013), and: Requejo & Sanjaume, *Recognition*; L. Pérez & M. Sanjaume, 'Legalizing Secession: The Catalan Case', in: *Journal of Conflictology*, 4, 2 (2013) 3-12.

27 Ucelay-Da Cal, 'History', 142-147 (145).

tially) revolutionary, in the sense of being determined to break out of the existing institutional order.

- At the same time, its social base in Catalan society has been broadened because the politics of Catalan Nationalism are no longer dominated solely by the respective political parties. One of the most significant new elements of Catalan Nationalism has been the wide and intense mobilization and organization of civil society following a broad variety of initiatives and associations (e.g., the historic Òmnium and the more recent Assemblea Nacional Catalana [ANC] of 2012), along more participatory, inclusionary (and 'loosely coupled') lines that has enhanced the dynamics of the separatist project and given new momentum to Nationalist politics. 'Independence' also seems to have particularly inspired young people in a similar way 'democracy' did in the 1970 s: for a new beginning, a brighter future, and Catalan 'majoria d'edat'.

- Here some of the consequences of advanced globalization and of the 'threshold 21' come in: On the one hand, the politics of Catalan Nationalism are now framed by the generalized and globalizing trends toward populist democracy. On the other hand, the Catalan scene looks more like others and less 'special', and Catalan Nationalism may appear more unilinear and less sophisticated than before.

- For the same reasons, we can also no longer analyze the politics and interactions of Catalan Nationalism within the container of the Spanish nation state as the only frame of reference, as has been done for many years, although not always. This is not only because Spain, and hence Catalonia belong to the European Union (and many other alliances), but because of globalization and all the 'entangled' and 'reflexive' interdependencies it implies. What happens in Scotland or Québec, the Balkans, Ukraine or Crimea, as also in Brussels, New York and elsewhere may have significant repercussions for Catalonia.

The creation of a new nation state in Europe in the age (and within the constellations) of its demise and 'blurring' would certainly have something ironic about it. Unless it would be a post-nation state, conceived by postnational Nationalists.

A "right to decide"?
On the normative basis of a political principle and its application to the Catalan case

Jaume López

1. Introduction

In the last few years, conceptual and political affirmation of the right to self-determination, especially in a liberal and democratic context, has experienced new treatments, justifications and implications that indicate new patterns, both in the regulatory and argumentative area, and in the strategic and political ones. We may consider the appearance of a new concept, 'the right to decide', as a reflection of these new trends.

The concepts of 'right to decide' and 'right to self-determination' often get mixed up and used interchangeably as if they were synonyms. However, this is not clear, and we might also be talking about two different political principles. The right to self-determination is the only one of the two with an explicit regulatory reflection in international law. This is different in the case of the right to decide, but there are elements with legal basis that may give it legal status in the future. In this sense, the Advisory Opinion of the International Court of Justice on Kosovo's unilateral independence (2010) is a key legal document. In it, the Court reflects and highlights – despite focusing only on the Kosovo situation – the basic principles that served as a legitimizing paradigm in the "third wave" of states' creation in the twentieth century (1900-2008). This document would give these principles *a posteriori* legal and legitimating expression.

In Catalonia, the right to decide became popular as a result of the Right to Decide civic Platform (PDD), through large-scale mobilizations and a later process of non-official consultations on independence organized by the civil society. Between 2006 and 2010, three large demonstrations took place in Barcelona that brought together hundreds of thousands of citizens who demanded (literally) the right to decide for the Catalan people. The concept 'right to decide' was part of the slogans used in these three demonstrations. Its practical exercise was developed by the same civil society that organized 4 waves of non-official referendums on independence between 2007 and

2011. About 885,000 citizens (15% of the population over 16 years old) from 551 towns (60% of the total) participated (Muñoz & Guinjoan, 2013). These consultations were organized without any institutional support – in some cases there was even opposition from some political forces – and required the help of thousands of volunteers.

The demand (and exercise) of the right to decide in Catalonia implies a bottom-up frame change in the Catalan people's demands. In 2007, and for the first time, the then main opposition party – currently forming the Catalan government (the Convergència Democràtica de Catalunya) – accepted it in its political agenda. Since 2012, it has become the key idea that focuses the 'National Transition'. In the institutional ground, three milestones can be highlighted in its political development: 'Catalonia's declaration of sovereignty and right to decide' (23/01/2013), 'National pact for the right to decide' (26/06/2013), and the agreement for the holding of a consultation on November 9th, 2014 (13/12/2013), in which two question were at hand: "Do you want Catalonia to become a state?"; and if so, "do you want it to be an independent state?"[1].

In Catalonia, the importance of the right to decide has left the "right to self-determination" in a political secondary level, although it is mentioned as a more traditional formula to defend the holding of a referendum on independence. In fact, since both demand a referendum, they have often been considered synonyms.

But are these two terms really synonyms? Based on their conceptual roots, do they express different ideas and principles that should prevent us from using the right to decide as a mere aggiornamento of the right to self-determination? To find an answer to these questions, we will first analyze what they mean and what they are based on, and then take a more in-depth look at the nature of the context in which they have been used.

In my view, the right to decide represents a Copernican turn. To begin with, we face a new *frame in communication*, as well as *in thought* (Druckman, 2011) that explains a good part of the growth of the Catalan sovereignty movement. As a *frame in communication*, it sends the message that the Catalan people's main desire is to express their will towards a political future, and above all, the right to vote. As a *frame in thought*, it focuses towards a democratic idea, not towards an historical right attached to the nation. It

---

1 "Vol que Catalunya esdevingui un Estat? En cas afirmatiu, vol que aquest Estat sigui independent?"

connects with the present and the future, not with the past. Consequently, it has turned into a socially inclusive demand, allowing the confluence of those who see Catalonia as a nation (more linked to the traditional demand for the right to self-determination) and those who do not, as well as those who consider this matter irrelevant.

Its importance within the Catalan process is thus fundamental. However, beyond that, what I am about to defend is that, although some might use it strategically as a way to embellish the right to self-determination, according to the main arguments used by its defenders, and given the current international context, it could become a true new political principle, a new paradigm for the twenty-first century.

2. *Right to self-determination: a legal right with a century of history*

Although the right to self-determination is well known both in meaning and significance, it would be appropriate to remember the main aspects before comparing it to the right to decide. It will soon be a century since US President Woodrow Wilson made his 'Fourteen Points' speech, laying out his proposals to end World War I and prevent future conflicts to the US Congress (1918). This text mentioned the right of peoples to self-determination in the context of the empires, with or without colonies, often made up of diverse peoples or nations that had participated in the first global conflict. President Wilson advocated taking the aspirations of those peoples into account when redefining political borders in the future, to ensure the maximum degree of stability.

In other words, this perspective presupposed an internationally recognised prior situation of conflict or conflicting interests (unresolved historical disputes within the empires or the result of colonisation) and the existence of certain peoples or national communities that were, in some sense, internationally recognised and therefore had certain historical rights to a territory. It is important to underline these two elements that at the same time are both interpretive (they explain how the right was conceived in the first place) and regulatory (they allow us to recognize their scope of application).

What seemed at first a political principle ended up enjoying a degree of universal recognition when it was included in the founding Charter of the United Nations, approved in 1945 after World War II. It is mentioned at the beginning (Art. 1.2) where the Charter lays out the principles that the United Nations seeks to promote: 'To develop friendly relations among nations based on respect for the principle of equal rights and self-determination of peoples'. Beyond such general considerations, the right to self-determination has since been mentioned in several other UN documents, always in relation to the decolonization processes that took place in the wake of World War II.

When we examine the two core elements of the initial definition of the right to self-determination (on one hand, *de facto* internationally recognised nations; on the other, a recognised international conflict, or "a context of non-self-governing territories and peoples subject to alien subjugation, domination and exploitation"[2]), it is easy to find difficulty in its application outside colonial and imperialistic contexts. It is not surprising that the legal development of this right has focused on the processes of decolonization, and that anything that might be considered a 'domestic' or 'internal' affair within a democratic state is beyond its scope.

This is the view taken by the subsequent Declaration on the Granting of Independence to Colonial Peoples and Countries (1960), and the Declaration on Principles of International Law concerning Friendly Relations and Co-operation among States in Accordance with the Charter of the United Nations (1970). The first one explicitly states that 'All peoples have the right to self-determination', understanding the scope of application to include all territories subject to colonial rule. For the rest of the world, the Declaration clearly establishes that 'Any attempt aimed at the partial or total disruption of the national unity and the territorial integrity of a country is incompatible with the purposes and principles of the Charter of the United Nations' (sixth provision).

This view of one of the few rights – perhaps the only one – to have been given an international legal definition before achieving a national or state-based one was reaffirmed in the second document 10 years later, which likewise defended this right, but also established a necessary link between equal rights (individuals), democratic government (representative of all groups) and the legitimate defense of the principle of territorial integrity.

Thus, any demand by a territorial minority that neither belongs to an empire nor has been a colony is conceived of as a conflict between certain citizens and their state and therefore falls beyond the scope of the standard legal international definition of the right to self-determination. This right is

---

2 In the words of the International Court of Justice; see paragraph 82 of the Advisory Opinion on Kosovo.

thus understood to have served to legitimise the decolonisation processes that followed the World War II, but to have had no bearing at all on the "third wave" of state formation that followed the collapse of the communist regimes, even though the lack of democracy in those countries and other restrictions on rights might have justified an indirect invocation of the principle, given the link established in the 1970 Declaration between equal treatment, democracy and territorial integrity.

According to United Nations, after 2012 there are only 17 cases of decolonization still pending (in inhabited territories). These are: in Africa, Western Sahara; in America, Anguilla, Bermuda, Cayman Islands, Malvinas Islands, the Turks and Caicos Islands, British Virgin Islands, U.S. Virgin Islands, Monserrat, Santa Helena; in Europe, Gibraltar; in Oceania, Guam, New Caledonia, Pitcairn, American Samoa, and Tokelau. In all these cases, the right and need to establish the ultimate sovereignty through self-determination referendums is defended.

From a legal point of view, therefore, the sovereignty demands found in representative western liberal democracies are left out of the narrow margins of definition of the right to self-determination.

In Catalonia, for instance, the criteria for application of the standard legal version of the right to self-determination was fulfilled only briefly, namely, in the wake of World War I when the Estat Català (Catalan State) party founded by Francesc Macià demanded this right on the grounds that Spain could still be considered an empire in the process of decolonisation. In September 1918, the Catalan independentist movement sent a letter to President Wilson explaining the "case of Catalonia" in these terms, but the position of the United States and the rest of victorious countries of World War I was to consider it an internal affair.[3] Similarly, for example, when US Secretary of State Hillary Clinton was asked during a visit to the European Union headquarters about the US position on the demands for independence in Scotland, Wales or Catalonia, she answered that she 'was not going to interfere in the internal affairs of any European country' (06/03/2009)[4].

To face these limitations, two arguments have historically been developed, and have been both used by Catalan independentists. The first is to propose a broad definition for colony and colonial relationship, which includes territories that have suffered an unfair treatment and conflictive re-

---

3 Balcells (2010).
4 "Clinton on European charm offensive", *Financial Times*, 06/03/2009.

lationship with their state. From this point of view, the concept of an 'internal colony'[5] is sometimes used. This strategy has been traditionally used by Catalan independentism, arguing a 'colonial treatment' that the Spanish state has inflicted upon Catalonia.

The other strategy focuses on broadening the scope of the right to self-determination, distancing it from strict international legality. This view connects with some regulatory theories of secession that use the same concept of self-determination, either linking it to the process of definition in a framework of autonomy within a decentralized state (internal self-determination), or to allude to the possibility of secession (external self-determination). However, politically speaking, the right to self-determination remains reserved for processes defining a new sovereign state. On this level, it is difficult to interpret it in any way that diverges from the standard (legal) definition.

3. Right to decide: a political principle for the twenty-first century?

We clearly cannot use the same method to define the right to decide. We cannot look to history or to an international way of understanding it because it is a new concept, a neologism. However, we can endow it with content from different sources, such as the rationales with which it is associated, the contexts in which it is declared, and finally link it to a legal document of exceptional importance in the establishment of the rights associated with secessionist processes, namely the advisory opinion of the International Court of Justice in The Hague on the unilateral declaration of independence of Kosovo.

Due to limited space, I will focus on the theoretical and legal reasons, which are connected. Concerning the empirical reasons, I will simply highlight that the democratic principle more than a simple appeal to the classic right to self-determination has been at the core of most of the demands for independence of new European states.

---

5 The term 'internal colony' (Salvi, 1973; Hechter, 1975) – referring first to situations of economic inequality within a state and, by extension, to unfair cultural treatment – has had very limited academic acceptance.

3.1. Theoretical reasons: democracy as a universal principle to be developed

First, it is clear that advocates of the "right to decide" are invoking and linking their demands to a democratic principle, i.e. to participate in a decision. In democratic societies, the demand can naturally be considered anodyne, since the citizens already decide by voting in the elections. Therefore, this cannot be the sense of this demand, but a much deeper one. They claim the right to vote for everything or, at least, for those matters that are traditionally left out of the people's reach. It is a position founded in democratic radicalism that would confirm that anything that does not go against fundamental rights can be subject to democratic decision, without prior restriction. It would also include the delimitation of state borders, this being the most paradigmatic choice within the right to decide.

The principle of democracy is the axis around which this demand revolves, by trying to delve into democracy as the best way of improving the collective situation and avoid violence. Within this principle's framework, and without looking for support in any other extra-democratic elements, the subjects that we may consider to have the right to decide are extant demos -not peoples or nations, but demos. They are groups that make decisions by applying the rule of the majority. The Catalan people, for instance, is such a demos, as is clear every time it votes in elections for the Catalan Parliament.

The right to decide can be linked to a cosmopolitan vision, but it goes beyond the theoretical perspectives that, under this conception, only see citizens of the world, not state borders. In other words, these positions take the states for granted without casting doubt over them. The right to decide does, and it does it by placing from the very grassroots of cosmopolitalism the citizens of the world as the final protagonists in any political decision, affirming that the maintenance of a particular state is neither a priority nor a moral end in itself. The citizens should be able to intervene in its definition, also meaning the delimitation of its borders. The cosmopolitalism of the right to decide includes a fluent conception of the borders. To put it differently in terms that have been all the rage in modern sociology, we can call it a "liquid conception of the borders". The political and administrative borders – all of them – are at the people's service, not the reverse. All this comes with the final calling of offering exclusively democratic answers for any demand to the citizens. In the twenty-first century, a political principle that offers a way for the redefinition of state borders, if the citizens so choose it, without using force or violence as the last resort, is found to be missing.

The political principle of the right to decide, understood as expressing the possibility of secession, also has a connection with the plebiscitary right version of the primary right theories of secession[6]. Indeed, according to these theories, the subject to the right is not the nation, nor is the nation its supporting basis. However, in the case of the right to decide, association of individuals is not enough. Unlike these theories, its regulatory basis does not hold itself upon the recognition of any individual's right to freedom of association (Beiner, 1998; Beran 1998; Norman, 1998), but upon existing demos already recognized institutionally, which exercises democracy and should be able to include the possibility of any institutional change that will satisfy the democratic will.

Why is the demos considered the political subject of the right to decide? Electing the demos as subject of application of the right to decide cannot only be defended as a principle of political realism. In addition, it overlaps in some way with the question of national recognition, seeing that, although the limits may not coincide exactly with certain definitions of "nation" (cultural, for instance), a demos with will to decide about a future independence (with everything this implies, from national sports teams to passports) very probably has national attributes. Finally, the fact that the right to decide is to be exercised by already-existing demos involves some recognition on the government's part that could allow previous negotiations, one of the possible requirements for its legal concretization, as we will see.

Naturally, the right to decide also brings up problems in its implementation. But the proof that we are facing a new paradigm is that their nature is completely different from those that originate from the problems caused by applying the right to self-determination according to international law. What are these problems? The first would be to determine which is the relevant demos and to what decision it applies. The problem with the relevant demos has not been resolved in theories of democracy. The universal consensus about democracy as the best form of government does not tell us about it. It is evident that a democratic majority in Catalonia might be a minority in Spain, and a democratic majority in Spain is a minority in Europe. In each of these cases, the resulting decision, while equally democratic, would be very different. Indeed, there is a need to generate a systematic theory about the relevant demos, but I would highlight that, at the least, two issues should

---

6 The focus on the demos instead of the nation moves away the right to decide principle from the adscriptive version of the primary right theories of secession.

be considered: who wants to change the status quo (or who has the will to change it)?; and who has the real capacity to exercise this decision, for instance, in becoming a viable state?

It seems evident, at least in a non-political and ideological context, that the final say in a decision should be from the one who proposed the change and can also implement it. For example, we can decide to expel someone (we have the will of change), but we cannot decide for him if he wants to leave. For instance, a European referendum to decide if the UK wants to continue being part of the European Union is inconceivable. On the other hand, it would be acceptable, at least conceptually, that the European demos decided about removing or maintaining a Member State.

It seems to me that there are other theoretical problems of a more minor nature in the development of the right to decide. Basically, there are four that I would like to mention here: the problem of instability, the permanent veto, viability, and recursive secessions. The problem of instability is more generally one of the usual critiques of the democratic or plebiscitary theories of secession (Buchanan, 1998), and we could link it partially to the theoretical basis of the right to decide. In my opinion, these critiques obviate the instability already present in many parts of the world, often due to the fact that borders were drawn without asking the will of the people.

The possibility of a permanent veto (the constant threat of seceding if the central government does not offer the desired response) is another critique launched by the defenders of the theory of just-cause secession (Buchanan, 1998) against theories based on democratic principles; by extension, it could be directed towards the right to decide. However, the permanent capacity of exercising the veto does not empirically look plausible. On the contrary, the real possibility of exercising this veto until its last consequences, and of suggesting the constitution of a new state at an international level, eliminates the continuous menace from some sub-state parties that, although unreliable, are part of the political life of many countries.

On the other hand there is the question of conditioning the exercise of the right to decide to the viability of a new state. It is neither easy to agree upon the meaning of 'viable', nor who should 'certify' this condition, in the same way the right to self-determination did not include in its original definition how to confirm its conditions. At the level of the general principles, which is where we are still placing the right to decide, we can connect 'viability' with the possibility of meeting three types of requirements (Beran, 1984), i.e. protection of liberal rights, guarantees of democratic development, and economic self-sufficiency. These criteria should suffice to address the problem of the potential generation of settlements or neo-colonial microstates in need of a metropolis. They would probably not meet the requirements for viability without the external support of a parent state. We might also ask whether exercising the right to decide could imply creating new middle-sized states that would be smaller than the current ones. This is an empirical rather than a theoretical matter. But we have to assume that this could be so, given the current context of political stability, supra-state organization development, and global markets.

3.2. Legal reasons: The right to decide in the advisory opinion of the International Court of Justice in respect of Kosovo

The right to decide, defined as such, is a political principle, as was the right to self-determination before its progressive legal concretization since 1945. It transformed into a positive right of universal scope, but with limited application. As a *frame of thought*, the right to decide can lead opinion and even political action, but in order to become a right with legal ground it must go through a process of concretization that, forcefully, also has to go along with its limitation.

The advisory opinion of the International Court of Justice on the unilateral declaration of independence in respect of Kosovo issued in July 2010 is a key component in the legal development and recognition of the right to decide defined in the previous section[7]. Although it does not make any literal reference to it, several parts of the argument clearly agree with what has been said with regard to the right to decide. The Court makes it clear by explicitly stating that the legal grounds for its argument are not the right to self-determination that applies in processes of decolonization, but rather a different type of legitimacy (paragraphs 79, 82 & 83).

With regard to the conceptual clarification entailed by this opinion, attention should also be drawn to what the Court says regarding the principle of territorial integrity contained in the Charter of the United Nations and

---

7 Although the well-known opinion of the Supreme Court of Canada regarding the legality, under both Canadian and international law, of a unilateral secession of Quebec from Canada might share some similarities in its principle of legitimacy, from a legal point of view it can be considered as a document that strictly affects the Canadian framework. In the case of the ICJ's opinion, the scope of application is international.

subsequent international texts. The Court emphasizes that this principle only applies between states, not *within* them: "the scope of the principle of territorial integrity is confined to the sphere of relations between States" (paragraph 80). A state cannot take over part of another state without violating the Charter, the judges write, but the Charter is silent on the issue of the possibility of a secession. There is no international jurisprudence to refer to on this point. Thus, the court recalls that, when the UN has come out against some unilateral declarations of independence in the past (Southern Rhodesia, Northern Cyprus, the Republika Srpska), it has done so not because any internationally recognised law was violated, but because of the accompanying unlawful use of force (paragraph 81).

The opinion concludes that if: (i) all other avenues of reaching an understanding have been exhausted, (ii) independence is declared by legitimate political actors, i.e. democratically representative ones, and (iii) it is done by non-violent means, then there is no international legal obstacle to the unilateral declaration of independence, nor violation of any international law that the United Nations Security Council or General Assembly must defend. It can likewise be inferred that, as the right to self-determination recognised by the Charter of the United Nations is not invoked, the United Nations (whose Charter does not mention the right to decide) cannot be expected to actively defend these processes. There can be no United Nations mandate that authorises or favours a unilateral declaration of independence (even though, in the case of Kosovo, the proposed rapporteur's report recommended such a solution).

Some have interpreted this opinion as a 'step forward in the recognition of the right to self-determination' (Cortada & Torra, 2011). However, for the aforementioned reasons, such a defense denies precisely the core and the value of the Court's decision, which skips over the right to self-determination in its argument in order to focus on the democratically exercised will of the demos (it says nothing about whether it is a nation or a people) in peaceful conditions, when no other possible means of accommodation within the pre-existing state are possible, as the international mediator Martti Ahtisaari (former President of Finland and Nobel Peace Laureate) stated in his report[8]. There is no international principle or law that opposes the exercise of a democratic principle in this way. On the other hand, it must be underlined

---

8 See paragraphs 68 & 69 of the advisory opinion. Paragraph 69 quotes the report of the Special Envoy of the UN Secretary-General for the future status process for Kosovo, Mr. Martti Ahtisaari.

that there is no international law (at least to date) that explicitly includes the right to decide in the terms outlined here.

However, let's examine the legitimatory principles of the Advisory Opinion in the light of what has been said about the theoretical definition of this right. i) Rather than the existence, or lack, of an *de facto* internationally recognised people (or nation), there is a demos. ii) Rather than the existence, or lack, of a colonial relationship, there is an unambiguously democratic decision. This will supersedes the constitutional law of the state. On this point, the court states that the legitimacy of a unilateral declaration of independence, from the point of view of international law, has nothing to do with its adhesion to the constitutional law of the state to which the secessionist society belongs (paragraph 120 & 121). Indeed, in the vast majority of cases, if not all, this right will violate the state's constitutional law. The court takes no position on this issue, as the scope of its analysis and concern is international law. However, it does underscore the unlawful use of force, or other serious violations of general international law, as grounds for considering certain declarations to be illegitimate, which could also be interpreted - although the court does not do so - in the opposite sense. The use of force by a state to maintain its unity could make this unity unlawful in its eyes. A fortiori, one could say that some constitutional systems, such as the Spanish one, which assign the armed forces the mission of defending state unity, might from the very outset pose a conflict of laws (constitution vs. public international law) (Abat, 2011).

How can we call this ensemble of legitimizing principles for which the Court does not have a name? From my point of view, it is leading us towards a new paradigm in international law that fits like a glove in the theoretical definition of the right to decide. In other words, should this principle settle in order to become positive law with a legal basis, there is no doubt that it will have to take into account the three conditions mentioned by the Court: no violence, democracy, and the failure of negotiations to accommodate the decisions of the demos within the current borders of the parent state.

4. Conclusion: the right to decide and Catalonia

As a result of the advisory opinion on Kosovo, we have had an international law document since 2010 that gives us some hints about the possible practical application of the right to decide, and allows us to distinguish more clearly which cases could meet the internationally-standardized requirements. For example, we can say that the referendum on the secession of Crimea (2014), organized in a context of violence and military presence of a third state, without prior negotiations to try accommodating the democratic will of the Crimea demos in the state of which they were part, cannot be considered as exercising the right to decide. In opposition to this, the case of Catalonia, without violence, with the development of a democratic process (of popular mobilization and in its parliament), and with prior negotiations between the Spanish and the Catalan governments that have never come to terms[9], places this case within the paradigm of the right to decide.

References

Abat, A. 2011. "Epíleg", in Cortada i Torra (eds.).

Balcells, A. 2010. *El projecte d'autonomia de la Mancomunitat de Catalunya del 1919 i el seu context històric*. Barcelona: Parlament de Catalunya.

Beiner, R. 1998. "National self-determination: some cautionary remarks concerning the rhetoric of rights", in Moore.

Beran, H. 1998. "A democratic theory of political self-determination for a new world order", in Lehning.

Buchanan, A. 1998 "Democracy and Secession" in Moore.

Cortada, J.; Torra, Q. (eds.) 2011. *La porta de la gàbia. La decisió del Tribunal Internacional de Justícia sobre Kosovo*. Barcelona: A Contravent.

Druckman, J.N. 2001. "Theimplications of framing effects for citizen competence". *Political Behaviour*. Vol. 23 (3): 225–256.

Hechter, M. 1975. *Internal Colonialism. The Celtic Fringe in British National Development, 1536–1966* . London: Routledge & Kegan Paul.

Lehning, P. 1998. *Theories of Secession*. London: Routledge.

Moore, M. (ed.) 1998. *National Self-determination and Secession*, New York: Oxford University Press.

---

9 The current sovereignist process started after the failure of the revision process of the current political situation of Catalonia within the Spanish state. It drove the Catalan Parliament to draw up a new statute (2005). It was amended in the Spanish Parliament, and finally, after its approval in a referendum by the Catalans (2006), it was declared in some of its key parts unconstitutional (2010). The later demand for a new fiscal treatment (2012) has not been considered by the Spanish government. In April 2014, the Catalan Parliament asked the Spanish Parliament to transfer jurisdiction to organize a referendum, but this petition was also denied.

Muñoz, J. and M Guinjoan 2013. "Accounting for internal variation in nationalist mobilization: unofficial referendums for independence in Catalonia (2009–11)". *Nations and Nationalism.*Volume 19, Issue 1, pages 44–67.

Norman, W. 1998. "The ethics of secession as the regulation of secessionist politics", in Moore.

Salvi, Sergio (1973). *Le nazioni proibite: Guida a dieci colonie interne dell'Europa occidentale.* Firenze: Vallecchi.

The Spanish constitution, the Constitutional Court, and the Catalan referendum

Antoni Abat i Ninet

1. Introduction

This chapter deals with a core topic in constitutional law, that of the conflict between constitutions and will of the *demos*. Aristotle in Book IV of the Politics had already anticipated possible conflict between these two forms of *Politeia* (constitutions), when defining the types of democracy.[1] He also distinguished the role that the *Nomophylakes* (guardians of the laws) should play in this sort of anticipated conflict after Madison v. Marbury had globally referred to it as "judicial review". But the concept of a constitution as a form of government; a document that organised the offices of a state changed through history. The Magna Carta, the French and American revolutionaries gave the concept a new meaning. After these historical episodes, constitutions were not simply political or legal norms showing how to play politics in a concrete state, but represented the conquest of fundamental rights, liberties and the juridification of each new independent state. This epic and romantic aura helped the universal triumph of constitutionalism. But the conflict between *demos* and *politeia* that Aristotle defined now clashes between two powerful symbolic and romantic phenomena.

In the Spanish-Catalan binomial scenario, there are some elements that need to be analysed to obtain a complete picture of the constitutional possibilities of accommodating a Catalan self-determination referendum. These issues demonstrate that the conceptual antagonism are not new, but come from afar, at least from the diverse constitutional interpretations and understandings of the nature of a state. This chapter deals with the current constitutional text, but some of the differences have direct antecedents in the events of 14 April 1931 in Catalonia, the path of the Catalan statute of autonomy of 1931, and the events of 6 October of 1934. What has changed is that Catalans now are simply demanding to be consulted, and they expect

---

1 Aristotle, 1996, 99.

that the European Union and other international players will be involved if there is any escalation of violence.

1.1 The people of Catalonia

The first issue to be analysed to obtain a full picture of the conceptual antagonism between Catalans and Spaniards is that the government of Spain neither recognises the Catalans as a people nor a nation. This lack of recognition contravenes not only the feeling of the vast majority of the Catalan population, but the definition contained in the preamble of the current statute of autonomy of Catalonia. In this sense, the "legalist" argument adopted by the Spanish government, as also the first party in opposition (*Partido Socialista Obrero Español*), seems to be contradictory. The political antagonism has a constitutional translation. Article 2 of the Spanish Constitution (SC) defines the unity of the nation and recognises the right of autonomy to regions and nationalities. The term "nationality" used in this article has been interpreted as "nation" by the public institutions of Catalonia, but also by the drafters of the constitution of 1978.[2] The rivalry among regions and the constitutional development dubbed "*café para todos*" (coffee for everybody) that enabled a path to symmetrise the form of state; the definition of nationality was first emptied of contents and therefore simply denied. The decision of the Constitutional Court in 28 June 2010 on the statute of autonomy of Catalonia broadened the dissent on the constitutional accommodation of Catalonia by refusing to admit the use of the term *nation* in the statute. The Court accepted that the term may relate to a cultural, historical or linguistic reality, but when talking in a legal-constitutional sense, the SC recognised only the Spanish nation.[3]

This concrete interpretation of the term "nationality" also avoids a possible bilateral relationship between the Spanish state and Catalonia affecting the possibility of negotiating a political solution to the present conflict. The Spanish state simply does not recognise the other party on this potential

---

2   See in Spanish: Diario del Congreso de Diputados of 5 May 1978, available at http://www.congreso.es/public_oficiales/L0/CONG/DS/C_1978_059.PDF, last accessed on 18 August 2014.

3   See: Constitutional Court Judgment, no. 31/2010 of 28 June 2010, unofficial translation available at http://www.tribunalconstitucional.es/es/jurisprudencia/restrad/Paginas/JCC2862010en.aspx accessed on 18 August 18, 2014.

negotiation. This is a big difference between the Scottish and the Catalan situations because the United Kingdom has recognised not only the singularity of Scotland, but also its national character and its validity as political interlocutor, whereas the government of Catalonia in Spain is just one of seventeen autonomous communities.

1.2 Different understanding of the state's territorial nature

The SC defines the autonomous state as an eclectic state, something between a federal state and a regional or centralised state. In this sense, the definition of "autonomous" advanced in terms of the decentralising the concept of the "integral" state, as defined by the Spanish Republican constitution of 1931. But the current SC regresses in terms of asymmetry, because only three subnational governments in 1931 were previewed (Catalonia, the Basque Country and Galicia). A deliberative vagueness in the constitutional text with respect to the organisation of sub-state units within the state was a vehicle of consensus among the different political forces represented in the Spanish constituent power. The consensus was necessary in 1978 – and remained so in 1981 due to a particular political incidence, the military action of Lieutenant Colonel Tejero in Congress and the military takeover of Valencia by General Milans del Bosch. But the constitutional vagueness became a source of political and constitutional conflict.The proposal of a Catalan non-legal binding referendum is the last expression of this conflict.

The SC has been understood by the government and public institutions in Madrid as a final destination on decentralisation, whereas in Catalonia and the Basque Country it was considered a starting point. This antagonist understanding of the meaning of the constitutional text and its spirit produced a constitutional development proposed by Catalans who were considered disloyal to the constitution and the state institutional structure. The answer given by Madrid to the Catalan legal and political claims was seen as threatening the self-government recognised by the Spanish constitution. The last example of this contradictory position of both governments is the demand for a referendum by Catalonia, the claim of better fiscal treatment, requests for greater respect for the Catalan language or the claim to allow Catalan sports teams to participate in international competitions being other examples. The response of Madrid to all these demands can be summarised by "how can a part play against the whole?"

The public authorities in Catalonia seem unaware that the constitutional arguments exposed to approve, or at least tolerate, the public consultation in Catalonia are affecting the essence of the Spanish territorial structure, according to the state view. At this point, it must be stressed that both understandings (Catalan and Spanish) of the constitutional structure of the state are based in political and constitutional interpretations. However, in a concentrate constitutional system like in Spain, the only (constitutional) interpretation that counts is the one of the constitutional court. The Spanish Constitutional Court, as the supreme interpreter of the text, has always had the last and unique valid word. Knowing this, the Spanish legislator never thought of encouraging judicial responsiveness to sub-state interests, such as the Canadian Supreme Court model, which, by a case law dealing with Quebec, must include at least three judges from that sub-state body. The Magistrates of the Spanish Constitutional Court are appointees as individuals favoured by state political actors, from whose ranks they may well be drawn. Nothing in such an arrangement guarantees that constitutional court judges will be more responsive to national than sub-state interests, actors in the national government, and notably with actors in the national legislative and executive branches.[4] This may in turn cause a national court to react with hostility to deals negotiated between national and sub-state governments if the court perceives such deals as encroaching in particular on its own power, the court's exclusive power to interpret the national constitution, which is its sole power of any significant consequence.[5] The referendum is naturally among these "disloyal" claims, and the reaction of the court as a political actor is not only going to be partial, but clearly hostile to the Catalan claim.

In conclusion, all the constitutional arguments that can be brought forward to justify the Catalan referendum of independence are routed from this outset. The decision of the Constitutional Court on the constitutionality of the Catalan law to develop popular consultations (a competence transferred with the current statute of autonomy to Catalonia) seems to be predictable, and thus denies any possibility of consulting the Catalan population on its political future.

---

4 Abat Ninet, Antoni and Gardner, James A, 2014, 23.
5 Ibid.

2. *Constitutional arguments in favour of a constitutional referendum*

There are several constitutional arguments that would authorise a referendum in Catalonia. The first Catalonia can argue to ground constitutionally a referendum is Article 1.1 SC, which defines the establishment of Spain as a social and *democratic* state, subject to the rule of law, advocating the highest values of its legal order – *viz.* liberty, justice, equality and political pluralism. Both the SC and the statute of autonomy of Catalonia provide the democratic principle as a core value of the political and legal framework. The appearance of the principle in the first article of the constitutional text converts this principle as foundational of the state. A claim to vote, to know the opinion of a part of the citizens, appears to be covered by this defining element of Spain. This interpretation follows the Canadian court decision of 1998 on Quebec secession, which stated: "*a clear majority vote in Quebec on a clear question in favour of secession would confer democratic legitimacy on the secession initiative which all of the other participants in Confederation would have to recognise*".[6] The constitution in Canada was not used as a tool against the will of a state of the confederation, but the Supreme Court found a way to conciliate both elements of constitution and democracy. The "legalist" position of the Spanish institutions has not favoured a better acceptance of the constitution in Catalonia; on the contrary, this imposition of a biased political view has ended in mistrust of the text by the supreme interpreters from the viewpoint of the Catalan citizens.

A second constitutional argument but related with the principle of democracy is Article 9.2 SC that creates public authorities constitutional obligation to promote conditions, which ensure the participation of all citizens in political, economic, cultural and social life. This article had no precedent in Spanish constitutional history, but establishes a generic constitutional mandate to the public administration to promote the citizen's participation in political life. Article 9.2 SC must be complemented with article 23.1 SC on the right of citizens to participate directly or through representatives elected freely in public affairs. The public consultation can be labelled among these conditions that public institutions are constitutionally obliged to promote according to these articles, but also with the constitutional foundation that appears in the Organic Law 5/1995 of May 1995, which reads as follows:

---

6   Secession of Quebec, (1998) 2 S.C.R. 217), point 150.

"The origin is found in the conception that a democratic state is characterized by the participation of citizens in public affairs"

A third constitutional argument in favour of a constitutional referendum was that initiated by the Parliament of Catalonia in Resolution 479/X, proposing the submission to the Spanish Parliament of an organic law proposal to delegate in favour of the Catalan Government the competence to hold a referendum on the political future of Catalonia. This resolution followed another of the Catalan chamber in 13 March 2013 on the initiation of a dialogue with the Spanish Government to make possible a consultation on the future of Catalonia. In the proposal submitted to the Spanish Parliament, the Catalan legislator remarked that article 149.1.32 SC reserves to the Spanish state the authorisation of the call for popular consultations through referendum. But article 150.2 SC would also allow the state to transfer or delegate to the autonomous communities competences of the state through organic law. The Catalan proposal asked for this sort of delegation to hold a sole referendum and not the transfer of the competence. The bid was rejected by 299 legislators of the 350 of the national assembly. The refusal ended with Catalan trying to hold the referendum within the Spanish constitutional framework. The President of Catalonia has accepted several times his willingness to agree a referendum with the Spanish Government, as was in the United Kingdom. He also admitted his willingness to negotiate the date and question of the consultation with the Spanish government if a referendum was accepted.

The next move to achieve the public consultation under a legal framework is the reference to article 122 of the statute of autonomy of Catalonia. According to this norm, the government of Catalonia has exclusive power over the establishment of the legal system, the modalities, the procedure, the implementation and the calling of public opinion polls, public hearings, participation forums and any other instruments of popular consultation, with the exception of those provided for by Article 149.1.32 SC (mainly the legal binding referendum). This article is now consolidated and the Catalan legislator has develop two legal instruments, Law 4/2010 of 17 March 2010 on popular consultations throughout referendum and a new law on no-referendum consultations to exercise this competence. For both legal instruments, the constitution must be acknowledges as a material limit and therefore the consultation cannot be issued against the text or the competences of the state. A non-legal binding consultation on the political future of Catalonia can be always interpreted by the Spanish Constitutional Court as unconstitutional. But in this case, the Spanish court will follow the Yugoslavian example of

January 1990 rather than the Canadian or UK models. This tendency does not seem to bother the Spanish government, which in its international recognition of Kosovo, sided with Russia and Serbia, and not with Germany, UK, France and the United States of America.

The last constitutional argument that the representatives of Catalonia can use is related to the binding of international treaties ratified by Spain. The Preamble of the SC reads: *"Protect all Spaniards and peoples of Spain in the exercise of human rights, of their cultures and traditions, and of their languages and institutions"*. The legal binding character of the preambles is disputed; some authors (QuocDinh, Daillier, Pellet et al.)[7] deny any sort of binding force. Others (Kelsen) consider that the binding force depends not only on its being part of statute or a treaty, but on having a normative character. To be precise, this is the case if its meaning is to establish by itself or in connection with other contents of the statute or treaty an obligation.[8] This seems to be a sterile debate in Spain after the decision of the Constitutional Court on the statute of autonomy of Catalonia, in which it states that the term "nation" in the preamble of the Catalan norm has no legal interpretative effects. It seems to be less sterile to argue that Article 10.2 SC states that the principles relating to the fundamental rights and liberties recognised by the Constitution shall be interpreted in conformity with the Universal Declaration of Human Rights, and the international treaties and agreements thereon ratified by Spain. Also, Article 96 SC on the reception of the international treaties in Spanish domestic law states that validly concluded international treaties, once officially published in Spain, shall be part of the internal legal system. Naturally, the question here is that, according to Spain, Catalonia is not a nation, but does this really matter? According to France, Algeria was not a nation in 1957.

From a theoretical perspective, a nation exists because it wishes to be so, which Derrida calls *ipseity*.[9] It is the people themselves who define this matter. Constitutional texts around the world state: *"we the people of the United States of America"*; "We the representatives of the united provinces of South America, the people of Ecuador", "we the people of South Africa", "whereas the people of New South Wales, Victoria, South Australia, Queensland, and Tasmania", etc. They do not need another people, entity or authority to define them as a people. Therefore, the main characteristic of

---

7 Quoc Dinh, Daillier, Pellet, 2002, 131.
8 Kelsen, 2000, 9.
9 Derrida, 2005, 22.

the people's definition is its *volitive* nature, built on the will to be considered as such. In other words, a people's conscious desire for recognition constitutes its legal-formal aspiration, with its own distinct personality and identity from other peoples.[10] The first element of the conceptual answer to the question: who are the people? would be, to which the answer is the people who want to be 'the people. The locution "the people" enhances a constitutional text, not the opposite. No constitution determines who "the people" is, but the opposite, ie a people defines and creates a constitution. This statement only appears once the act of national self-definition has been invoked in a constitutional text. This strengthens the concept of "the people" as being unitary, as a single entity without divisions in which the institutions should not be assigned to groups or sectors of the whole, but individuals acting on behalf of the ideal "people".[11]

But, there is another argument that can deny the right of self-determination to Catalonia, which limits the applicability of this human right exclusively to colonies. This is false. There is no mention to this scope's limitation in any of the treaties that Spain has ratified. It is simply a biased interpretation of international law to protect the integrity of the states. Besides this, the advisory opinion of the International Court of Justice in 22 July 2010 on the independence of Kosovo refers to the defence of the peaceful and democratic principles instead of other connotations, such as domestic legality, or the principle of unity or state sovereignty. The principle of self-determination was created and is acknowledged as a tool to peacefully regulate situations like the one that is now facing Spain. The goal is to avoid a Balkanisation of the country, military intervention and terrorism.

To sum up, the Catalan-Spanish issue is not a conflict between law (constitution) and democracy as some intellectuals are defining it, but a concrete and biased interpretation of Spanish constitutional law, international treaties and communitarian acquis ratified by Spain against a different constitutional interpretation, democracy and a universal human right.

---

10 Abat i Ninet, 2013, 47.
11 Pocock, 2006, 623

3. Conclusion

Is a non-legal binding consultation on the future of Catalonia unconstitutional? The only one that can answer this question in Spain is the supreme interpreter of the Constitution, the constitutional court. Therefore, the answer seems to me to be *no*. The antecedents are clear in a country where the *Nomophilakes* (Guardians of the Laws) have become *Homoniaphilakes* (Guardians of the Unity), who have understood unity not only as political, but also as identity.

The decision of the Constitutional Court in the Resolution 5/X of the Catalan Parliament approving the declaration of sovereignty and the right to decide of the People of Catalonia opened, according to some authors, a constitutional path to declare as constitutionally legitimate all the activities of preparation and defence of the right to decide the political future of Catalonia. According to this interpretation of the decision, if the result of this consultation is against the constitution, the constitution may be reformed through dialogue and negotiation.[12]

A different interpretation of the same decision has been made by the Spanish public actors and national media. In this case, they remark that the Constitutional Court outlawed the Catalan resolution because it breached Articles 1.2 and 2 SC, as also Articles 1 and 2.4 of the statute of autonomy. The so-called "right to decide" can be interpreted according to the SC only because this right does not mean self-determination. These interpreters also remarked that, according to the Constitutional Court decision, Catalonia cannot be defined as "sovereign" even though this definition appears in a political resolution approved by the Catalan Parliament. According to the Spanish Constitutional Court, there is only one sovereign, the Spanish people as a whole. The reference regarding the secession of Quebec (1998) in point 155 reads: "*The ultimate success of such a secession would be dependent on recognition by the international community, which is likely to consider the legality and legitimacy of secession having regard to, amongst other facts, the conduct of Quebec and Canada*". In the Catalan-Spanish scenario, the

---

12 See in Spanish: Informe sobre la Sentencia del Tribunal Constitucional, de 25 de marzo de 2014, relativa a la Resolución 5/X del Parlament de Catalunya, por la que se aprueba la Declaración de soberanía y del derecho a decidir del pueblo de Catalunya, http://www20.gencat.cat/docs/governacio/IEA/documents/Dret%20a%20-decidir/Arxius/Informe%20sentencia%20TC%20Sobirania%20Parlament %20vESP.pdf (last accessed on 18 August 2014).

same can be argued; the conduct of Catalonia is going to be observed, but also the one of Spain.

References

Abat i Ninet, Antoni and Gardner, James A.; *"Distinctive Identity Claims in Federal Systems: Judicial Policing of Subnational Variance"* 2014, *SUNY* Buffalo Legal Studies Research Papers No. 2014-018, available at: http://dx.doi.org/10.2139/ssrn. 2417407.

Abat i Ninet, Antoni, *Constitutional Violence, Legitimacy Democracy and Human Rights,* Edinburgh University Press, 2013.

Aristotle, *The Politics and the Constitution of Athens*, Cambridge University Press, 1996.

Kelsen, Hans, *The Law of the United Nations: A Critical Analysis of Its Fundamental Problems*, The Lawbook exchange LTI Union, 2000.

Pocock, J. G. A., *El momento maquiavélico. El pensamiento político florentino y la tradición republicana atlántica*, Tecnos, Madrid 2006.

QuocDinh, N., Daillier, P. Pellet, A., *Droit International Public* (7th edition), Paris: L.G.D.J. 2002.

Catalonia's independence – is there a way in international and European Union law?

Hermann-Josef Blanke / Yasser Abdelrehim

1. Secession movements during the transition from the 20th century to the 21st Century – the beginning of a new age?

Following the fall of the Berlin Wall in 1989, the reunification of Germany in 1990 and the end of the Cold War, Eastern Europe witnessed a wave of dissolution and emergence of new states that had not seen since the end of World War I. This disintegration process was not always peaceful, sometimes being very violent, as in the former Yugoslavia. At this time, Western Europe was celebrating the ratification of the Maastricht Treaty of 1992 (Treaty on European Union), which endeavors to strengthen the political integration between its Member States and the peoples of Europe towards an ever-closer Union.[1] In opposition to integration at the European level, there is an increasing desire for independence within many European states. Along with Eastern Europe, Western Europe is presently seeing a growing aspiration among several nationality and ethnic groups to seek independence from their mother states. These groups invoke the right to self-determination as the legal basis for their action, but instead of uniting or liberating peoples as it did in the past, self-determination in these instances might serve as "a divisive force".[2]

International law is governed by fundamental principles and values aimed at establishing and maintaining peace, order, and stability between states. Since the treaties of Westphalia in 1648, the principle of sovereignty developed in parallel with international law itself as its main pillar.[3] In the seventeenth century, this principle had become the backbone of the argument against the re-establishment of papal and imperial orders, and thus offered a guarantee of minimum peace and stability in those European states ruled

---

1 See Danspeckgruber (2002), p. 165; see also the preamble of 1949 in the German Basic Law. http://www.digitale-schule-bayern.de/dsdaten/118/74.pdf.
2 Cf. Tomuschat (1993), p. 4.
3 Steinberger (2000), p. 501.

by a monarchy. In contemporary international law, this principle is considered an attribute of statehood and the foundation of a number of basic principles.

The principle of sovereignty protects the territorial integrity of states and prohibits interference in their domestic jurisdiction and the threat or use of force.[4] It is also intertwined with the principle of self-determination[5] such that there is no fundamental contradiction between the principles of sovereignty and self-determination. The establishment of a sovereign state and the adoption of a constitution are fundamental modes of implementing the right to self-determination of a people. Defensive self-determination protects the territorial status of existing states. This means that the people of a state (the people in the constitutional sense) have the right to maintain the integrity of its territory.[6] Although the concept of state sovereignty is becoming more permeable because of the increasing importance of international organisations, transnational co-operation and human rights, the international community still recognises that ignoring the epicenter of international law – the principle of sovereignty – could lead to chaos and ultimately be a deathblow to the framework that preserves international law as a system.[7] It is for this reason that the international community emphasises the importance of respecting the sovereignty of states and their territorial integrity in the face of contemporary secessionist movements.[8]

Others argue that in order to overcome problems associated with the rise of secessionist movements, there is a need to abandon the traditional understanding of sovereignty and establish a new political order in which nationalities are recognised and sovereignty is shared. This means the end of state monopoly on ultimate legitimate authority. According to this conception of sovereignty, authority is not derived from a higher source and it can come from several sources.[9] Therefore, "an entity, whether it be a people or a territorial unit, may be sovereign where it has the right to determine its own

---

4 See Art. 2 of the UN Charter of 1945; Hannum (1996), p. 15.

5 See also Bleckmann (1985), p. 453; Henkin (1995), p. 8 and 100; Steinberger (2000), p. 503 and 513.

6 See in this respect Vosgerau (2015 forthcoming; manuscript, p. 129 et seqq.).

7 Cf. Tomuschat (2006), p. 40; Mangas Martín (2014), p. 31, with regard to the classics of the Spanish School of International Law: "…la organización de la Humanidad".

8 UNGA Res 68/262 'Territorial integrity of Ukraine' (27 March 2014). This resolution is a recent example in this regard.

9 Keating (2012), p. 11.

future".[10] Accordingly, under this theory of sovereignty, the national aspirations of those who would otherwise see no choice but to secede from the mother state can still be satisfied without resorting to secession. The result would be the establishment of a "plurinational" state in which individuals would have multiple national identities.[11]

1.1 The rise of the desire for independence in Western Europe

In contrast to the violent dissolution of the former Yugoslavia, the separation of Slovakia from the former Czechoslovakia in 1993 was swift and smooth. This was the result of negotiations between officials of the two states; the distribution of its assets and liabilities was provided for in the Czechoslovakian Constitution and its laws.[12] The peaceful dissolution of the former Republic of Czechoslovakia encouraged separatist movements in Quebec, Scotland and Catalonia, being considered as a model for swift secession when popular support was behind it.[13] Although many European states with different nationalities and ethnic groups have made concessions to satisfy their national ambitions, the desire for political independence has not entirely disappeared in these states. Notwithstanding the fact that Scotland has benefited from its union with England, demands for more autonomy and even independence emerge periodically.

This has led to the Scottish devolution referendum of 1997 and the Scotland Act 1998 as an alternative to independence, in order to meet the increasing nationalist demands in Scotland.[14] The Scots' aspiration for independence from Great Britain, however, has not vanished. 2014 became an important turning point in the history of both countries as the Scottish government agreed with the British government to hold a referendum on the independence of Scotland on September 18, 2014.[15] The result of the referendum showed that nearly 55% of the voters preferred unity with the United

---

10 Keating (2001), p. 15 and 27.
11 Keating (2001), p. 2, 19 and 166; Bourne (2004), p. 3.
12 See in this respect Hosková (1993), p. 693 et seqq. and p. 734; Saxer (2010), p. 810.
13 See Scottish Independence: Lessons from the Czech/Slovak Split, BBC News of 20 January 2013. http://www.bbc.com/news/uk-scotland-scotland-politics-21110521.
14 See Kellas (1989), p. 144 et seqq.; Stein and Rosecrance (2006), p. 235.
15 See Béland and Lecours (2008), p. 128 et seqq; Scottish Government, Scotland Future (Scottish Government, Edinburgh, November 2013). http://www.scotland.gov.uk/Resource/0043/00439021.pdf.

Kingdom. Since this majority is no guarantee of political stability or maintaining unity of the British state, the result will, as expected, constitute a starting point for wide-ranging constitutional reform in the United Kingdom in granting more powers, not only to Scotland, but also to Wales, Northern Ireland and England itself. The expected reform could generate a kind of "federalisation" of Great Britain.[16] Since the adoption of the devolution system in 1998, the central structures of the state have already been fragmented by the establishment of parliaments in Scotland, Wales and Northern Ireland. These parliaments were given competences in the fields of health, education, housing, and agriculture, also including fishing, environmental protection, tourism, sport, cultural goods and economic development.[17] This practice of giving greater autonomy to Scotland could serve as a model to satisfy nationalistic aspirations of other separatist movement in Europe.

Starting in 2009 a series of non-binding and unofficial referendums ("popular votes" – *consultes populars*) were held in municipalities around Catalonia. Ostensibly, it was the positive experiences in Catalonia that encouraged separatists in South Tyrol to follow suit and hold their own referendum in 2013. The region had been part of the Habsburg Empire before being annexed by Italy in 1919. To satisfy both the demands of South Tyrol separatists and resolve the conflict, which had once turned violent in the early 1960 s, an autonomy statute was issued in 1972 that provided the *Regione Trentino-Alto Adige* with legislative and administrative competences.[18] Nevertheless, strong voices continue to call for the right to self-determination in the region.[19] The separatist movement in South Tyrol is not the only one in Italy; the region of Venice also voted for secession in an online ref-

---

16 See "David Cameron Statement on the UK's Future" of 19 September 2014 (http://www.bbc.com/news/uk-politics-29271765); cf. also the analysis of Anderson, Devolution in the United Kingdom: From Creeping Federalism to a Federal Union? p. 18. Anderson assumes that "(f)ederalism ... may address some of the fundamental flaws in the British system, making for a more wholly democratic settlement, improving accountability, accommodating all nations at an equal level and reinvigorating a positive case for the union." http://www.academia.edu/7046643/Devolution_in_the_United_Kingdom_from_creeping_federalism_to_a_federal_union.

17 See Scotland Act of 1998 and Website of the United Kingdom, Devolution Settlement: Scotland. https://www.gov.uk/devolution-settlement-scotland.

18 See the *Statuto Speciale di Autonomia per il Trentino Alto Adige* as of 31.8.1972; Blanke (1991), p. 123; Wolff (2005), p. 124.

19 See also "Heute die Krim und demnächst Südtirol?", Südtirol News (17 March 2014). http://www.suedtirolnews.it/d/artikel/2014/03/16/venetien-stimmt-ueber-abspaltung-italiens-ab.html.

erendum held by local parties in March 2014, with 89% voting in favour of secession. Although the vote was not legally binding, it provided the momentum to those calling for an official referendum on Venetian self-determination. Supporters of independence have been inspired by the history of the Republic of Venice (*La Serenissima Repubblica di Venezia*), which had been an important commercial and cultural center from the 7th century until the 18th century (7th/8th century to 1797).[20]

1.2 Catalonia's struggle for independence

Over the centuries, the Catalans have considered themselves a special entity distinct from the other regions of Spain, and the emergence of Catalonia as a "nationality" within the Spanish Nation (Art. 2 Spanish Constitution) is due to several historical, linguistic and cultural reasons. The roots of Catalonia as a people with a united territory and government date back to the Middle Ages.[21] Unlike other parts of Spain, the Catalans found expression in institutions like the *Generalitat*, which was first established in 1359.[22] As a consequence of the *Nueva Planta* decrees issued by the French Bourbon, *Philip V (Philip of Anjou)*, the *Generalitat* was abolished.[23] These decrees removed the ancient privileges of all of Spain's medieval kingdoms, with the exception of the loyal Basque Country, but including the Crown of Aragon and Valencia (1707/11), the Principality of Catalonia and the Kingdom of Mallorca (in 1715/16). There were periodic attempts over the centuries to restore political status and re-establish the institutions of self-government in 1914 and 1932, but these were suppressed several times through

---

20 Veneto stimmt für Sezession, Taz.de (22 March 2014). http://www.taz.de/!135367/.
21 Rejsek (1996), p. 21 et seqq. For more details in this respect, see also McRoberts (2001), p. 6 et seqq.
22 In 1358/59 twelve permanent deputies with executive powers in terms of tax collection as well as several auditors for the control of the Administration were employed for the period between the convening of the *Corts*. This period is considered to be the beginning of the *Generalitat*. Its first president was *Berenguer de Cruïlles*, the bishop of Girona. See also the Preamble of Catalonia's Statute of Autonomy of 2006. http://www.parlament.cat/porteso/estatut/estatut_angles_100506.pdf.
23 The *Nueva Planta* decrees (1707-1716) by Philip V banned all the main traditional Catalan political institutions and rights and merged its administration into that of the Crown of Castile as a province. However, the Bourbon monarchy allowed for Catalonia's civil law code to be maintained.

the use of violence.[24] Under the dictatorship of General *Franco*, the political, cultural and linguistic identity of Catalonia was fiercely repressed by the central government in Madrid.[25] However, as the dictatorship came to an end, a new period of self-government in the region of Catalonia emerged.

1.2.1 Catalonia's statute of autonomy

In an attempt to reconcile the aspirations of self-determination of both the Basques and the Catalans with the principle of the indissoluble unity of the Spanish State provided for in Art. 2 of the Spanish Constitution (1978), Art. 2 also recognises and "guarantees the right to autonomy of the nationalities and regions of which it is composed".[26] Unlike the French Constitution of 1958 which recognises in its preamble the right of the overseas territories to internal and external self-determination, the Spanish Constitution guarantees only the right of the nationalities to internal self-determination within Spain.[27] Part VIII, Chapter 3 of the constitution includes provisions regarding the conditions and procedures of the establishment of self-governing communities (*Comunidades Autónomas*), as well as the distribution of competences between the self-governing communities and the central government in Madrid.[28] This was the historic compromise negotiated after *Franco*'s death in 1975 under severe conditions as a cornerstone of the Spanish Constitution. In response to this positive development, the region issued the Statute of Autonomy of Catalonia in 1979,[29] which was later reformed by Organic Law 6/2006.[30] The statute reform bill tried to reach a higher

---

24 See Coll (2009). https://repositori.upf.edu/bitstream/handle/10230/5182/GRTPw-p4.pdf?sequence=1.
25 Dowling (2013), p. 38.
26 See Art. 2 of the Spanish Constitution of 1978 (English translation). http://www.congreso.es/portal/page/portal/Congreso/Congreso/Hist_Normas/Norm/const_espa_texto_ingles_0.pdf.
27 Paragraph 2 of the preamble of the French Constitution of 1958 states: "En vertu de ces principes et de celui de la libre détermination des peuples, la République offre aux territoires d'outre-mer qui manifestent la volonté d'y adhérer des institutions nouvelles fondées sur l'idéal commun de liberté, d'égalité et de fraternité et conçues en vue de leur évolution démocratique".
28 See Art. 143 et seqq. of the Spanish Constitution of 1978.
29 Catalonia's Statute of Autonomy of 1979. http://www.gencat.cat/generalitat/eng/estatut1979/.
30 Catalonia's Statute of Autonomy of 2006.

degree of self-government for Catalonia. In addition, the reform statute sought, *inter alia*, to promote the political status as well as the national and cultural identity of Catalonia as a distinct nation within the Spanish state.[31] Hence, the preamble of the statute defines Catalonia as a "nation" (*nació*), referring to the "ample majority … [of] the Parliament of Catalonia in respect thereof"[32] and concurrently alluding to the wording of Art. 2 of the Spanish Constitution interpreting the constitutional notion of "nationalities" (*nacionalidades*) in the sense of its recognition of the "national reality of Catalonia".[33]

Furthermore, the preamble of the statute states that Catalonia's "inalienable right to self-government … is founded on the [Spanish] Constitution and also on the historical rights of the Catalan people, [who] have maintained a constant will to self-government over the course of the centuries". The Preamble also assumes that "Catalonia, by means of state, participates in the construction of the political project of the European Union". With regard to the exercise of governmental authority, the Statute establishes self-government with wide competences. The *Generalitat* is the core institutional system around which Catalonia's self-government is politically organised;[34] "its powers … emanate from the people of Catalonia". This not only reveals the democratic legitimation of the legislative and executive branch, i.e. of the parliament and the presidency of the *Generalitat* in Catalonia,[35] but also the self-conception of the Catalans as a national population within a nation-state. Moreover, the statute includes several provisions that try to protect and promot the national, linguistic, and cultural identity of Catalonia.[36] But the constitutionality of the Statute was challenged by one of the Spanish parties. In 2006, ninty-nine Members of the People's Party Parliamentary Group in the Congress brought an action of unconstitutionality against a number of pro-

---

31 See Coll (2009), p. 15 et seqq. https://repositori.upf.edu/bitstream/handle/10230/5182/GRTPwp4.pdf?sequence=1.
32 See Resolutions 98/III and 679/V and Resolution 631/VIII of the Catalan Parliament.
33 Closely related to this recital of the preamble is Art. 8 of the Statute which laid down the flag, the holiday, and the anthem as "the national symbols of Catalonia, established by Article 1".
34 See Art. 2.1 of Catalonia's Statute of Autonomy of 2006.
35 See Art, 2.2 of Catalonia's Statute of Autonomy of 2006.
36 See Art. 6, Art. 35, Art. 44, Art. 50 and Art. 54 of Catalonia's Statute of Autonomy of 2006.

visions of the Statute of Autonomy.[37] After four years of delibrations, the Spanish Constituitonal Court rendered its judgment, which was considered a turning point for many Catalans.

1.2.2 Compatibility of Catalonia's statute of autonomy with the Spanish constitution

To remove any contradiction between the Spanish Constitution and the Organic Law 6/2006 of July 19th (on the Reform of the Statute of Autonomy of Catalonia), the Spanish Constitutional Court determined in its judgment of June 28, 2010, that, with regards to the scope of self-government in Catalonia within the Spanish State, 14 articles of the statute are not compatible with the constitution and must therefore be deleted, and that another 27 articles of the statute should be reinterpreted to bring them into conformity with the Spanish Constitution. In the view of the Court, the term "nation" in the preamble and the phrase "national symbols" in Art. 8 of the Statute should be understood and interpreted in a way that does not contradict the Spanish Constitution of 1978, which is hierarchically superior to Catalonia's statute.[38]

Catalans can continue to claim that they are a nation in respect of cultural and social reality, but this has no merit in the constitutional and legal sense.[39] For example, the Court also held that the stipulation in Art. 6.1 of the Statute that "Catalan is the language of normal and preferential use in public administration and bodies and in the public media of Catalonia" is unconstitutional, and thereby null and void because it implies that the Catalan language has precedence over the Spanish language.[40] It is noteworthy that the Court did not object to declaring the Catalan an official language in Catalonia, but only objected to the preferential status that the Catalan language enjoys at the cost of Spanish, which is the official language in the whole of Spain. Therefore, this position could not be compared with other

---

37 See Spanish Constitutional Court, Judgment of 28 June 2010 (English translation). http://www.tribunalconstitucional.es/en/jurisprudencia/restrad/Pages/JC-C2862010en.aspx.

38 Spanish Constitutional Court, Judgment of 28 June 2010, para 12.

39 See also Nationality, Not a Nation, The Economist (3 July 2010). http://www.economist.com/node/16490065.

40 Spanish Constitutional Court, Judgment of 28 June 2010, para 14.

areas in the world where governments impose restrictions on the use of a minority language through, for example, banning families giving their children ethnic names, or changing the names of towns and villages written in the minority language. Such policies deprive the minority group the opportunity of protecting its cultural identity.[41]

The curtailment of Catalan self-government was met with indignation and anger from Catalan political parties and the populace, who accused the Constitutional Court of being politicised and not respecting the Catalan voters who had approved the Statute in an official referendum.[42] For many Catalans, the ruling closed the door on Catalonia's integration into the Spanish State and would therefore actually encourage the separatist movement. Others expressed this simply by saying: "Spain - game is over".[43] Notwithstanding the fact that the Spanish Constitutional Court held that several provisions in Catalonia's Statute of 2006 are incompatible with the Spanish Constitution of 1978, the Statute includes uncontroversial provisions that guarantee a high degree of self-government and protection of the national and cultural identity of the Catalan people.

1.2.3. The Spanish government's reluctance to consent to the referendum on the political future of Catalonia

On the basis of Law 10/2014, which the *Generalitat* of Catalonia passed on 26 September 2014 on "consultas populares no referendarias" and other forms of citizen participation,[44] on September 27, 2014, the *Generalitat* issued Decree 129/2014 on the political future of Catalonia. The "consulta popular no referendaria" is defined by Art. 3.1 Law 10/2014 as a call for the persons who are eligible to participate in the vote "to manifest their opinion

---

41 Cf. Blanke (2014), p. 13 et seq.; Coşkun (2014), p. 92.
42 See Nationality, Not a Nation, The Economist (3 July 2010).
43 See Garcia-Ruiz, The Spanish Constitutional Court ruling on the Catalan Statute and its Political Implications (1 July 2010). http://emma-col-cat.blogspot.de/2010/07/spanish-constitutional-court-ruling-on.html.
44 "Ley 10/2014, de 26 de septiembre, de consultas populares no referendarias y otras formas de participación ciudadana", Diari Oficial de la Generalitat de Catalunya Núm. 6715 - 27.9.2014, p. 1 et seqq.
See also an English translation of Law 10/2014 (http://www20.gencat.cat/docs/consulta/Documents/Arxius/Llei_angles.pdf).

on a specific action, decision or public policy, by means of a vote".[45] The aim is thus to circumvent the clear decision of the Spanish Constitution, which stipulates that in cases of political "decisions of special importance", the king reserves the right to call all citizens in a consultative referendum (*referéndum consultivo*) "on the President of the Government's proposal after previous authorization by the Congress" (Art. 92.1 and 92.2 Spanish Constitution). In the Decree, the *Generalitat* set November 9, 2014, as the date for the popular consultation (Art. 1 of the Decree). It also formulated the questions that the persons entitled to participate in the consultation would have to answer. The first question was supposed to be: "Do you want Catalonia to become a State?" If the answer was in the affirmative, the second question was supposed to be: "Do you want this State to be independent?" (Art. 3 of the Decree). People who were supposed to be eligible to participate were Catalan citizens, EU citizens who could prove a year of continuous residence in Catalonia immediately before the announcement of the consultation, and nationals of other countries who could prove legal residence in Catalonia for a continuous period of 3 years immediately preceding the announcement of the Consultation. The Decree also provided that persons entitled to participate must be over 16 years of age on the day the popular consultation is held (Art. 4 of the Decree).

The reaction of the Spanish government to these plans and calls for separation was, and remains, complete rejection of the idea of holding such a referendum considered unconstitutional. The Spanish Prime Minister, *Mariano Rajoy*, opined that Catalonia should remain in Spain, a Catalonia outside Spain being unimaginable.[46] The Spanish Government's positions aims to prevent the balance between national unity and a partial political decentralisation from failing. On September 28, 2014, the *Conjejo de Estado* issued its Opinion 965/2014, in which the Council held that the planned popular consultation is a violation of unity of the Spanish nation (Art. 2 Spanish

---

45 Art. 3.1 Law 10/2014: „1. Se entiende por *consulta popular no referendaria* la convocatoria efectuada por las autoridades competentes, de acuerdo con lo que establece esta ley, a las personas legitimadas en cada caso para que manifiesten su opinión sobre una determinada actuación, decisión o política pública, mediante votación." See also an English translation of Decree 129/2014 (http://www20.gencat.cat/docs/consulta/Documents/Arxius/DECRET%20129_ENG.pdf).

46 Ministerpräsident Rajoy: Katalonien außerhalb Spanien ist „unvorstellbar", Handelsblatt (8 April 2014). http://www.handelsblatt.com/politik/international/ministerpraesident-rajoy-katalonien-ausserhalb-spaniens-ist-unvorstellbar/9736156.html.

Constitution); only the Spanish people as the holders of sovereignty are entitled to decide on this matter (Art. 1.2 Spanish Constitution). On September 29, 2014, on the basis of Opinion 964/2014, the Spanish Government, represented by the *Abogado del Estado,* appealed to the Spanish Constitutional Court to declare Decree 129/2014 unconstitutional, null and void, and to repeal the norms of this statute and suspend its execution (Art. 161.2 Spanish Constitution). That same day, and in accordance with Art. 161.2 of the Spanish Constitution, the Spanish Constitutional Court suspended the contested Decree until a final decision could be made on its legality within 5 months (Art. 161.2 Sentence 1 and 2 Spanish Constitution).[47] With an estimated turnout of 36% of voters in an *unofficial* survey on November 9, 2014 ("9N") that was declared part of a "participatory process" and tolerated by the Spanish Government, 81% of the participants (in the sense of Art. 4 of Decree 129/2014) answered these questions affirmatively.

A unilateral separation of Catalonia from Spain is inconsistent with the principles of international and European law, linked since the time of *Jean Bodin* to the principle of state sovereignty (discussed below, see sub B and C). However, it would be increasingly difficult for Spain as a state to maintain Catalonia within its borders if the vast majority of Catalans consistently push for political independence from Spain. In view of the unresolved issues concerning Catalonia and the skilled tactics of its political elite, there is the notion that an independent Catalonia would have to undergo a serious constitutional and political evaluation. This is crucial when we consider that as in federal systems like Germany, and its institute of federal obligation (Art. 37 of the Basic Law) that regards the use of coercive measures of the federation against the individual states as possible in the event of an attempted seccession. In a situation of clear political opting-out, there would be no other rational choice for Spain than an agreed exit of the Autonomous Community of Catalonia, which would then have to struggle for recognition as an independent state in the international community.

2. The right to self-determination in international law

Through its autonomy statute, the Catalans are striving for "self-government", which is the key issue in this paper. The Catalans are once again

---

47 Spanish Constitutional Court, Case 5830-2014 (Decision of 29 September 2014).

asserting their right, which over the past few years has turned into a claim for self-determination following the perpetual historical and always mainly subliminal aspiration of the Catalans to revisit the status of independence that it enjoyed before the reign of the *Reyes Católicos*. Catalonia is one of the more prosperous regions of Spain, and it is likely that Catalans want to relish this wealth for themselves. Given the exploding debt of the Spanish regions following the economic crisis in Spain since 2011, this point is important in the expected negotiations on the financial relations between the state and the Autonomous Communities. Those who want the right to secession are not claiming a right to the usual democratic state, but rather are striving for a new type of democracy, namely a smaller, more manageable community whose members are presumably more similar to another than those of the former larger state. Therefore, a referendum on the statehood of Catalonia would not be a democratic, but rather a meta-democratic process, that would determine afresh who is allowed to have a say in the democratic society, thus making the unreasonable demands of a mass society a little more bearable.[48] This process could be endless; however, a right to opt out with a few like-minded people does not exist.[49]

The principle of territorial integrity enshrined in Art. 2.4 of the UN Charter, viewed as a limit to the right of self-determination, protects state borders and permits territorial changes only under exceptional circumstances. International documents that support the people's right to self-determination include parallel statements that call for the preservation of the political unity and territorial integrity of states. Thus, "[the] principle of self-determination has evolved within a framework of respect for the territorial integrity of existing states".[50] The right to self-determination first emerged during the Age of Enlightenment, when it was considered a democratic expression of the will and the sovereignty of peoples.[51] Until the 1960 s, the nature of the principle of self-determination was still a subject of debate among states because they were at that time far from agreeing on the existence of this right. The end of colonialism was linked to the principle of self-determination. The resolution of the UN General Assembly No. 1514 (XV) on the

---

48 Cf. the analysis of Dahms, Kein Grund für ein unabhängiges Katalonien, Frankfurter Rundschau (7 April 2014).
49 Dahms, Kein Grund für ein unabhängiges Katalonien, Frankfurter Rundschau (7 April 2014).
50 Supreme Court of Canada, Case Quebec (Decision of 20 August 1998), para 127.
51 See in this respect Ambruster (1962), p. 251; Thürer (1996), p. 37.

Granting of Independence to Colonial Peoples of 4 December, 1960 was a landmark in the history of the United Nations.[52] Thanks to this resolution and other similar UN resolutions in the 1960 s, the right of colonial peoples to exercise their right to self-determination is now undisputed.[53] Resolution No. 1514 refers explicitly in paragraph 2 to this right as a right of "all peoples". Thus, the right to self-determination could never be seen as "an exclusive right of colonial peoples". In its advisory opinion of 1971 on Nambia as well as in its opinion of 1975 on Western Sahara, the International Court of Justice (ICJ) refered to the increasing importance of the principle of self-determination which has become with the development of international law a legal right and not just a guiding principle.[54] With the passage of time, the right to self-determination has been so widely accepted and promoted by the international community that it has become a part of customary international law and even *ius cogens* rule.[55] However, its content and scope remain as controversial as when the principle was proclaimed by President *Woodrow Wilson* and others at Versailles.[56]

Catalans supporting future statehood of Catalonia argue that they have a right to secession according to Art. 1 of the UN Human Rights Pacts of 1966, and that the Spanish Constitution doesnot contradict this Article.[57] In outlining the basic aspects of the right to self-determination, let us first refer briefly to its doctrinal basis as defined in the UN Human Rights Pacts of 1966 and the UN Declaration of Friendly Relations of 1970, both of which are often invoked by separatist movements, not only in Catalonia, but in other parts in the world as a legal basis for the right to secession.

---

52 See UNGA Res 1514 (XV) 'Declaration on the Granting of Independence to Colonial Countries and Peoples' (14 December 1960).
53 Supreme Court of Canada, Case 25506, Reference re Secession Quebec (Decision of 20 August 1998), para 132.
54 International Court of Justice, Legal Consequences for States of the Contitiued Presence of South Africa in Namibia (South West Africa) notwithstanding Security Council Resolution 276 (Advisory Opinion of 21 June 1971), I.C.J. Reports 1971, para 52; International Court of Justice, Western Sahara (Advisory Opinion of 16 October 1975), I.C.J. Reports 1975, para 54 et seqq.
55 See also Thürer (1984), p. 113; Kadelbach (1992), p. 257 et seqq.
56 See Thürer (1984), p. 113; Kadelbach (1992), p. 257 et seqq.; Brühl-Moser (1994), p. 23; Manela (2007), p. 15. et seqq.
57 Edward (2013/14), p. 10.

2.1 Right of self-determination and Art. 1 of the UN pacts of 1966

With the establishment of the United Nations, the principle of self-determination turned from a philosophical and political principle into one of the main legal principles of international law.

Art. 1.2 and Art. 55 of the UN Charter take into account that respect for the principle of equal rights and self-determination of peoples is the basis for the development of friendly relations among nations. With the ratification of the UN Human Rights Pacts of 1966, the principle became a collective right of peoples. Common Art. 1.1 of both the UN Human Rights Pacts stipulates that "[a]ll peoples have the right of self-determination. By virtue of that right they freely determine their political status and freely pursue their economic, social and cultural development". The UN Pacts make the right to self-determination a basic human right, or rather a condition for the enjoyment of human rights. In contrast, the UN Charter considers that the enjoyment of human rights is also a condition for the enjoyment of the right to self-determination. This illustrates clearly the interdependence and indivisibility of human rights as recognised at the Vienna Conference of 1993 on Human Rights.[58] Applying the principle of self-determination requires full observance of human rights and vice versa.

The right to self-determination includes political, economic, social, and cultural aspects. The right to decide freely on political aspects or status includes not only the free determination of the internal status (the right to choose the constitutional status and government form), but the external status, which necessarily includes the right of secession.[59] The latter is one of the most controversial issues in international law, because the majority of the international community is not ready to accept secessionist interpretations, or calls for secession, that encourage state disintegration as this could lead to the spread of secessionist tendencies and increase of factionalism in the world.[60] The danger of chaos and fragmentation led former UN Secretary-General Boutros Boutros-Ghali to warn in his report entitled "An Agenda for Peace" submitted to the UN Security Council on June 17, 1992, of the misuse of self-determination. He wrote that "[i]f every ethnic, religious or

---

58 Maertens, EU Presidency Statement in the United Nations about the right to self-determination, EU Delegations to the United Nations (31 October 2001); see also Thürer (1984), p. 113; Kadelbach (1992), p. 257 et seqq.

59 Murswiek (1993), p. 21; Tomuschat (1993), p. 22.

60 Cárdenas and Cañás (2002), p. 102.

linguistic group claimed statehood, there would be no limit to fragmentation, and peace, security and economic well-being for all would become even more difficult to achieve".[61] The right to self-determination of people provided for in Art. 1.1 of the UN Human Rights Pacts is the right of a "people" to freely decide. Therefore, the question is: Who is entitled to decide and are the Catalans a subject of this right?

2.2 Are the Catalans a subject of the right to self-determination?

This question relates to another about whether the Catalans are considered a people in the sense of Art. 1 of the UN Human Rights Pacts, because only a people, in the sense of international law can be entitled to exercise the right to self-determination. No doubt the Catalans share characteristics, e.g. a common history, language, and culture, and these characteristics make them culturally and linguistically distinct from the rest of Spain. Moreover, Art. 2 of the Spanish Constitution of 1978 recognises the existence of different nationalities like the Catalans and the Basques. In this sense, they are peoples, but at the same time, they remain a part of the Spanish People. Therefore, the question now is: Does the term "people" in the sense of common Art. 1 of the UN Human Rights Pacts mean only the entire population of a state or does it also cover part of a state population, as in the case of the Catalans and the Basques?

In international law there is no agreement on the meaning of the term "people".[62] In his commentary on the UN Charter, Hans Kelsen argues that the term "people" means states.[63] According to a minority view, the principle of territorial integrity is directed against other states and not against a state's own people. The right to self-determination implies a right to secession that can be exercised by a part of the population of a state under all circumstances and not just as an exception or a last resort. The exercise of this right depends on the will and desire of that part of the population wanting secession, and not on the will of the whole population, who may when in majority, frustrate

---

61 Boutros-Ghali, An Agenda for Peace (1989–1992 11th Supplement) Repertoire of the Practice of the Security Council, para 17.
62 See Rumpf (1984), p. 47; Doehring (1995), p. 63; Vosgerau (2013), p. 96.
63 Kelsen (1951), p. 51 et seqq.

the separatist aspirations of the minority.[64] In the view of a number of legal writers, the term "people" mentioned in Art. 1 of the UN Pacts covers only the colonial peoples and the entire population of a state, and not groups or parts of the population.[65] Such a restrictive definition of the term people corresponds to the prevailing trend in practice and literature, which denies minorities and ethnic groups the right to secession except in cases in which it is considered a last resort.[66] But this restrictive definition is hard to accept in light of the cultural or linguistic realities which make a minority or an ethnic group distinct from the rest of the state where it lives. In line with the prevailing trend, it could be therefore more suitable to adopt a wide interpretation of the term "people" which recognises a people in the cultural sense also as a people in the legal sense, and to work parallel to avoid the dangerous legal consequences which may result from such recognition.[67] If we follow this opinion that adopts a wide interpretation of the term "people" and takes the view that this term does not necessarily mean the entirety of a state's population, the Catalans are considered a subject of the right to self-determination.[68] But this does not mean that the Catalans have a right to secession from Spain according to Art. 1 of the UN Human Rights Pacts. The right to secessionis recognised only as a last resort and under exceptional circumstances, as will be shown below (B.V.1).

2.3 The right to self-determination and the UN Declaration of Friendly
     Relations of 1970

The Declaration of Friendly Relations of 1970 has been characterised as "the most authoritative statement of the principles of international law relevant

---

64 Dumberry (2006), p. 432; Ott (2010), p. 425 et seqq.; Quaritsch (2013), p. 131 and 132.
65 See Tomuschat (1993), p. 16. Another view is represented by Murswiek who defines the term "people" not restrictively but he differentiates between the term "people" and the term "minority". In his view, only peoples and not minorities are subjects of the right of self-determination, Murswiek (1993), p. 37; Cassese (1995), 141 et seqq.
66 Kadelbach (1992), p. 262.
67 See Tomuschat (1993), p. 16; Supreme Court of Canada, Case 25506, Reference re Secession Quebec (Decision of 20 August 1998), para 124.
68 Supreme Court of Canada, Case 25506, Reference re Secession Quebec (Decision of 20 August 1998), para 124.

to the questions of self-determination and territorial integrity".[69] The Declaration provides that "[t]he establishment of a sovereign and independent State, the free association or integration with an independent State or the emergence into any other political status freely determined by a people constitute modes of implementing the right to self-determination by that people". The Declaration refers explicitly to the people's right to establish an independent and sovereign state, which means necessarily the right to secession.[70] However, it warns against interpreting the Declaration as authorising or encouraging actions that would imperil the territorial integrity or political unity of sovereign states as long as these states have a government "representing the whole people belonging to the territory without distinction as to race, creed, or colour".[71] Although the formulation of this paragraph seems to imply that it would give legal justification for secession in case of the underrepresentation of a national minority in the state government or of discriminatory policies against this minority as to race, creed, or colour, the practice of the United Nations before and after issuing the Declaration of Friendly Relations does not support this interpretation.[72] Also in state practice there is a point of view which considers that this paragraph serves as a guarantee of territorial integrity of states. This provision may authorize secession under certain circumstances that should be confined to extreme circumstances as in the case of an armed attack by the mother state against the people in question and which threatens the very existence of this people.[73]

Under all circumstances, it could be concluded from this formula that the right to self-determination – more precisely, the right to secession – could not be exercised against states whose governments conduct themselves in

---

69 UNGA Res. 2625 (XXV) 'Declaration on Principles of International Law concerning Friendly Relations and Co-operation among States in accordance with the Charter of the United Nations' (24 October 1970); International Commission of Jurists, East Pakistan Staff Study, International Commission of Jurists Review (1972), 8, p. 44; see also Raic (2002), p. 317.
70 See also UNGA Res. 1514 (XV) 'Declaration on the Granting of Independence to Colonial Countries and Peoples' (14 December 1960).
71 See also the Vienna Declaration and Programme of Action adopted by the UN World Conference on Human Rights (25 June 1993), A/CONF.157/24; UNGA Res 50/6 'Declaration on the Occasion of the Fiftieth Anniversary of the United Nations' (9 November 1995).
72 Thürer (1984), p. 129; Perea Unceta, El derecho internacional de secesión (Universidad Complutense de Madrid. Facultad de Derecho, 2008).
73 See the written statement by the Russian Federation of 16 April 2009 during the proceedings before the ICJ in the case of Kosovo, para 88.

compliance with the right to self-determination, because the people of such a state, including all different nationalities or minorities, already exercise the right to self-determination through their participation in the government on the basis of equality. Such a state is entitled to the preservation of its territorial integrity according to international law, and no claim of self-determination can legitimately be made. Hence, the Declaration of Friendly Relations made a link between internal self-determination and external self-determination. Implicitly it calls on states to respect human rights and to refrain especially from committing grave violations of human rights against minorities. It also includes a safeguard clause against secession for those states that comply with the right of internal self-determination.[74] The Declaration seeks thereby to strike a balance between the principle of territorial integrity of states and the principle of self-determination of peoples.[75] Applying the foregoing to the case of Catalonia, the conclusion can be drawn that, as long as Spain respects the collective and individual rights of the Catalans as a nationality or an ethnic group, they can enjoy their protection within the Spanish state and cannot invoke the right to secession (B.V. 1).[76] Accordingly, the Friendly Relations Declaration as Annex of the Resolution 2625 (XXV) does not constitute a legal basis for the independence of Catalonia as long as Spain conducts itself in compliance with the right of internal self-determination.

2.4 Autonomy statutes as a form of self-determination

The external right to self-determination, i.e. to secession, is required and justified under certain circumstances. The right to self-determination (external and internal) aims essentially at creating the conditions under which peoples can freely, and without foreign influence, determine their political, economic, social and cultural status, and living conditions in line with their aspirations and desires. However, if a people have the possibility to determine their own affairs and protect their own cultural identity, there will be

---

74 Rozakis (2000), p. 818; Raic (2002), p. 321; Crawford (2006), p. 119; Hilpold (2012), p. 64; Quaritsch (2013), p. 120; see also Mangas Martín, Humanización, Democracia y Estado de Derecho en el Ordenamiento Internacional (Real Academia dDe Ciencias Morales y Políticas, 2014), p. 102 et seq.
75 Quaritsch (2013), p. 120.
76 Cf. Kimminich (1993), p. 92.

no strong need to secede from the mother country. Many states that experience ethnic problems refuse to recognise an ethnic group as a people or give it the right to actual self-government for fear that such a step may lead to the separation of the group from the mother state. However, many cases show that giving minorities or different nationalities the right to self-government in the form of a federal state, or through autonomy statutes, satisfies the national demands of minorities and ethnic groups, thereby preventing the disintegration of the state.[77] This is also viewed as a suitable alternative to independence, especially when the disintegration of the state is likely to create new conflicts. The creation of a (new) state should lead to the improvement and not to the worsening of the situation of human rights. To this end, the new state should prove that it will respect and protect the rights of the minority or minorties living on its territories.[78] In contrast to Serbia, which abolished Kosovo's autonomy, Catalonia's Autonomy Statute of 2006 guarantees the *Generalitat* those strong competences mentioned above (1.2.1). But if the Catalans insist on declaring their independence from Spain, although they enjoy autonomy within the Spanish state, the question may arise as to what extent this position would be compatible with the principles of international law and state practice. The international community's responses to attempts at secession can provide more insight on the question of whether Catalonia has a right to statehood and sovereignty.

2.5 Secession in international law

2.5.1. State practice and the position of the United Nations on cases of secession

The international community is composed of states whose main interest is to maintain their statehood and protect their territorial integrity. A close look at state practice in previous decades shows that states generally favour the principle of sovereignty and territorial integrity of states when it conflicts with the right to self-determination.[79] There are also concerns that the dis-

---

77 See Tomuschat (1993), p. 14; Kimminich (1993), p. 97; Carley (1996), p. 2; Gutiérrez Espada (2000), p. 93 et seqq.; Cárdenas and Cañás (2002), p. 108; Pazartzis (2006), p. 360.
78 Hilpold (2013), p. 1083.
79 Murswiek (1993), p. 36.

integration of a state may lead to violence or further disintegrations inside the new entity that has declared itself an independent state. These concerns compelled some to call for restricting the right to self-determination in favour of the right of individuals and minorities to be treated equally within the borders of the existing state.[80] For these reasons, states usually ignore cases in which the national ambitions of groups striving for independence could be fulfilled by other means, even if those ambitions could not be completely satisfied. This solution would at least maintain stability and avoid risks that could arise from opening the door to attempts at secession that could go on indefinitely.

The UN has adopted a similar position regarding the right to secession. Although it was strongly involved in defending the right to self-determination in the 1960 s, during this period it began taking a very different view towards attempts at secession by entities outside the colonial context. This view finds expression in the statement of the then UN General-Secretary *Sithu U Thant* who said, "as far as the question of secession of a particular section of a Member State is concerned, the United Nation's attitude is unequivocal... [It] has never accepted and does not accept and I do not believe it will ever accept the principle of secession of a part of its Member State".[81]

However, in several cases serious violations directed against a definable group within the state as to race, language or religion present a major challenge for the international community and require its intervention. The state is not an objective in itself, but has functions and duties that it must fulfill in order to serve the interests of its citizens. Therefore, when a state fails to fulfill its duties, it puts the legitimacy of its existence into question. One of these basic functions is the protection of the right to life and the physical integrity of its citizens. When a state turns itself into a band of assassins who targets and persecutes a specific group of the state population, in this case it becomes difficult to demand that the targeted group remains loyal to the state. The state that commits, for instance, the crime of genocide against an ethnic group within the state, forfeits its right to territorial integrity.[82] Resorting to secession is also justified in cases of intolerable discrimination that may lead to the destruction of the identity of a people, e.g. where these

---

80 Falk (2002), p. 38.
81 U. Thant, Secretary-General's Press Conference, UN Monthly Chronicle (1970) 7, p. 36 and 39; Ott (2008), p. 232.
82 See Tomuschat (1993), p. 9.

people are not allowed to use their own language.[83] In contrast, there are authors who opine that a general right to secession outside the colonial context and cases of occupied territories could not be proved or not easily be proved. In his view, the existence of a right to self-determination as a right to self-defence (right to remedial secession) in cases of severe violations of human rights is not evident.[84]

State practice includes several examples of unsuccessful attempts at secession. Katanga, Biafra, Republika Srpska, Somaliland, Quebec and other secessionist attempts in republics of the former Soviet Union such as in the case of Transnistria which declared with the support of Russia in 1991 its independence from the Republic of Moldova, are just a few examples.[85] In all these cases, the international community's response was the rejection of the secession, and the emphasis on the sovereignty and territorial integrity of the states concerned.[86] For our discussion, the case of Quebec enjoys a special place of importance. Quebec and Catalonia are similar in many respects, both perceiving themselves as stateless nations, and both enjoying a high degree of autonomy. The decision of the Canadian Supreme Court in 1998 sheds much light on the interpretation and application of the principle of self-determination. Therefore, the Court's opinion contains much interest for multinational states suffering from secessionist movements.[87] The Court held that a people has a right to internal self-determination, and when a people is blocked from a meaningful exercise of this right, it is entitled as a last resort to exercise it by secession.[88] The Court noted that:

> [International law] only generates, at best, a right to external self-determination in situations of former colonies; where a people is oppressed, as for example under foreign military occupation; or where a definable group is denied meaningful access to government to pursue their political, economic, social and cultural development. In all three situations, the people in question are entitled to

---

83 See Art. 27 UN Pact on Civil and Political Rights of 1966. According to this article, states are obliged not to deny persons belonging to ethnic, religious or linguistic minorities the right to enjoy their own culture, to practice their religion and to use their own language. See also Murswiek (1993), p. 27.
84 See e.g. Hilpold (2012), p. 56; Hilpold (2013), p. 1062.
85 See also Ott (2008), p. 294.
86 Cf. Pazartzis (2006), p. 368.
87 Walters (1999), p. 372 et seqq.
88 Supreme Court of Canada, Case 25506, Reference re Secession Quebec (Decision of 20 August 1998), para 134.

a right to external self-determination because they have been denied the ability to exert internally their right to self-determination.[89]

If we adopt this view, then secession of a region from the mother state is justified from the perspective of international law only under exceptional circumstances, which seemingly does not apply either in the case of Quebec or Catalonia.[90]

In contrast to cases in which the international community may favour the maintenance of the territorial integrity of the state concerned, there are situations in which the international community has no issue in accepting and recognising secession when it occurred as the result of an agreement between the parties concerned, the dissolution of Czechoslovakia being a good example. This occurred in 1992 upon the agreement and consent of the governments of Czech and Slovakia. Through this peaceful dissolution, the former Republic of Czechoslovakia as a subject of international law ceased to exist as a state as of December 31, 1992. According to Art. 1.2 of the Constitutional Act on the Dissolution of the Czech and Slovak Federal Republic of November 25, 1992, the Czech and Slovak Republics would be the successor states of Czechoslovakia. Therefore, other states had no quandary concerning the recognition of the new state because in such cases its independence reflected an undisputed right to self-determination.

Nevertheless, there are other cases in which restoring and maintaining peace can only be reached by territorial alterations and the acceptance of new entities as new states, as in Kosovo. According to the Yugoslav Constitution of 1974, Kosovo was one of the eight political entities of which the former Federal Republic of Yugoslavia comprised.[91] Abolition of the autonomous status at the hands of former President Milosevic spurred the Kosovars to declare their independence from Serbia in 1991, which was met with force by the Serbs in an attempt to prevent the Kosovars from gaining their independence.[92] At the same time, the states did not respond positively to the independence declaration of Kosovo. In the first years of the conflict in Kosovo, states (with the exception of Albania) did not recognise Kosovo's independence. There was a desire by the international community to respect

---

89 Supreme Court of Canada, Case 25506, Reference re Secession Quebec (Decision of 20 August 1998), para 138.
90 Cf. Supreme Court of Canada, Case 25506, Reference re Secession Quebec (Decision of 20 August 1998), para 138.
91 Hasani (1996), p. 232 and 235 et seqq.
92 Ott (2008), p. 332 et seqq.

the territorial integrity of the Federal Republic of Yugoslavia. This desire found expression in the UN Security Council Resolution No. 1244 of 1999, which affirmed the commitment to the sovereignty and territorial integrity of the Federal Republic of Yugoslavia.[93] At that time, these states believed that peaceful coexistence between Albanian Kosovars and Serbs within the borders of the Serbian state remained possible. But this position changed as a result of the severe violations of human rights committed by the Serbian government, as well as the continuation of the conflict for many years without reaching a peaceful solution acceptable to both sides of the crisis. After a year of negotiations with the Serbian government and the Albanian Kosovars, UN Special Envoy *Martti Ahtisaari* submitted his report in 2007, in which he recommended that Kosovo should be an independent state. *Ahtisaari* justified his recommendation by saying that "[re]integration [of Kosovo] into Serbia is not a viable option". The conflict between the two sides created a history of enmity and mistrust that makes peaceful coexistence between Kosovo's Albanians and Serbs unlikely. For this reason, he concluded that "[i]ndependence is the only option for a politically stable and economically viable Kosovo".[94]

Hence, in light of the above, the special case of Kosovo cannot serve as a precedent for Catalonia or other separatist movements in Europe.[95] Whereas states were reluctant in the beginning of the crisis in Kosovo to recognise it as an independent state, they immediately recognised Slovakia and Czech Republic because the dissolution was a product of a negotiated agreement between both countries. Only in certain cases does the people's right to self-determination take precedence over the state's right to territorial integrity. Thus, the right of secession is not applicable to all situations where a people

---

93 On 10 June 1999, the UN Security Council issued the Resolution No. 1244 which established an interim administration in Kosovo under the supervision of the United Nations for the purpose of maintaining order in Kosovo until political settlement on the final status of Kosovo is reached. See Website of the United Nations. http://www.un.org/en/ga/search/view_doc.asp?symbol=S/RES/1244(1999).

94 Report of the Special Envoy of the Secretary-General on Kosovo's future status of March 2007. http://www.unosek.org/docref/report-english.pdf.

95 This meaning was also expressed by former US Secretary of State Condoleeza Rice on 18 February 2008 on the occasion of the recognition of Kosovo by the United States. See statement of former US Secretary of State Condoleeza Rice on 18 February 2008. http://tirana.usembassy.gov/08pr_0219.html.

or a group aspires for political independence, but rather functions only as a last resort.[96]

There are exceptions – or at best 3 situations – where a people have the right to exercise external self-determination and secede.[97] These exceptions do not apply to Catalonia, as mentioned above; it is an autonomous community within the Spanish state and is recognised as a nationality according to Art. 2 of the Spanish Constitution (which concurrently prohibits secession of any of the regions belonging to the Spanish territories.) Thus, it could not be claimed that the Catalans have been denied the ability to internally exert their right to self-determination. Not even the positive outcome of a referendum on the question of the desire for sovereignty, unilaterally held in that part of a state whose population strives for independence, can compensate the lack of the above-mentioned exceptional circumstances of last resort.[98] As the UN General Assembly has put it in Resolution No. 68/262 with regard to the "Territorial integrity of Ukraine" such a referendum "(has) no validity" if it is "not authorized" by the responsible institutions on the national level.[99] Accordingly, the Spanish state is entitled to preserve its territorial integrity and political unity according to international law, and the Catalans do not have the right to secede from Spain without having an agreement with the general government in Madrid.[100]

---

96 Rosas (1993), p. 238.
97 Supreme Court of Canada, Case 25506, Reference re Secession Quebec (Decision of 20 August 1998), para 138.
98 For an apparently differing view on this key issue see Pons Rafols (2013) who refers to the reference jurisdiction of the Supreme Court of Canada, Case 25506, Reference re Secession Quebec (Decision of 20 August 1998), to underline the principle of democracy, the fundamental rights of the citizens and the rule of law as the decisive aspects for a political solution of the conflict due to the Catalans search for independence.
99 UNGA Res. 68/262 'Territorial integrity of Ukraine' (27 March 2014), 7th indent of the preamble and para 5.
100 Cf. Supreme Court of Canada, Case 25506, Reference re Secession Quebec (Decision of 20 August 1998), para 136.

2.5.2 Advisory Opinion of the ICJ in the Case of Kosovo as an Encouraging Factor for Catalonia's Independence?

In its advisory opinion regarding the legality of Kosovo's unilateral declaration of independence of 2008, the International Court of Justice determined that the declaration did not violate the rules of international law. The ICJ's advisory opinion on the declaration of independence was rejected not only by Serbia, but by other states, such as Spain, concerned that the ICJ's advisory opinion may encourage separatist movements to follow suit and unilaterally declare independence in the regions that they represent, as long as such an act does not violate international law. At first glance, it would appear that the ICJ's advisory opinion encourages separatist movements, which in fact it does not. The Court reached this conclusion because international law does not contain any guarantee against the disintegration of states. The ICJ noted that "general international law contains no applicable prohibition of declaration of independence".[101] Although the ICJ referred to the importance of the principle of territorial integrity of states, it rejected the claim that a prohibition of unilateral declarations of independence could be derived from this principle. The Court also rejected the invoking of the UN Security Council resolutions that condemned declarations of independence in Southern Rhodesia, Northern Cyprus and the Republika Srpska as evidence for the prohibition of unilateral declarations of independence. The Court justified the Security Council's condemnation of these declarations by saying that they were connected with the unlawful use of force or egregious violations of *ius cogens*.[102]

The ICJ's holding is not unique. In its decision in the case of Quebec on August 20, 1998, the Canadian Supreme Court noted that "[i]nternational law contains neither a right of unilateral secession nor the explicit denial of such a right".[103] The ICJ's Advisory Opinion also could not be interpreted to mean that international law prohibits a state from declaring itself in its

---

101 International Court of Justice, Accordance with International Law of the Unilateral Declaration of Independence in Respect of Kosovo (Advisory Opinion of 22 July 2010), I.C.J. Reports 2010, para 84.

102 International Court of Justice, Accordance with International Law of the Unilateral Declaration of Independence in Respect of Kosovo (Advisory Opinion of 22 July 2010), I.C.J. Reports 2010, para 80 and 81.

103 Supreme Court of Canada, Case 25506, Reference re Secession Quebec (Decision of 20 August 1998), para 112; Bothe (2010), p. 837.

constitution to be indissoluble, as Spain does in Art. 2 of the Spanish Constitution.[104] The constitutional status of a state, including the form of the state and the government, is left to the free determination of the people of the state. Spain is not the only state whose constitution includes a provision on the indissolubility of the nation. Notably, the French Constitution of 1958 stipulates in Art. 1 that "La France est une République indivisible". The ICJ's advisory opinion could still be criticised, however, because the ICJ missed the opportunity to interpret several disputed questions relating to the principle of self-determination.[105] The ICJ did not answer the question regarding the extent of the right to self-determination and the existence of "remedial secession", but rather recognised that there are different views on this issue. The ICJ also left open the question of whether the mother state is entitled to prevent a secession or not. It also left open the question of whether states are required to recognise the newly-born state (in the Kosovo case) because independence is an expression of the right of self-determination.[106] Moreover, the Court did not take a position on the effectiveness of declarations of independence proclaimed by non-state actors.[107]

2.6 Recognising Catalonia as a state against the will of Spain

The question arises: How would matters be if the Catalans insisted on independence and the Spanish government maintained its opposition to Catalonia's independence, insisting by legal means of preserving the territorial integrity and political unity of the Spanish state (A.II.3)? As mentioned above, the Catalans have no right under the Spanish Constitution or international law to secede unilaterally, although a unilateral declaration of independence cannot be ruled out from the perspective of international law. Yet from the perspective of Spanish law, a unilateral declaration of independence would be unconstitutional because it expressly violates Art. 2 of the Spanish Constitution of 1978. According to some opinions, a declaration of secession without this right violates international law by infringing the principle of territorial integrity of states and even the principle of self-de-

---

104 Another opinion is represented by Jamar (2010), p. 923.
105 Cf. López-Jurado Romero de la Cruz (2011), p. 17 et seqq.; Perea Unceta (2011), p. 134 et seqq.
106 See also Muharremi (2010), p. 867.
107 See Libarona (2012), p. 123.

termination (which includes the right to secession only as a last resort.)[108] But this opinion was refuted by the ICJ in the case Kosovo as already discussed (B.V.2).[109] Secession of a region from the mother state in violation of the constitution does not necessarily mean that this non-constitutional act also violates international law, because the latter as a law of coexistence between states constitutes an autonomy norms order vis-à-vis national constitutions.[110] Accordingly, a unilateral declaration of secession by Catalonia without the consent of the general government of Spain would not constitute a violation of international law. Nevertheless, irrespective of the constitutional legality or illegality of a unilateral declaration of independence by a political entity, it would be difficult to justify such a declaration before international law, which considers secession a last resort. Sovereignty, being the cornerstone in international law, protects the territorial integrity of states in order to maintain peace and stability,[111] which could be endangered if the principle of self-determination is given priority at the expense of the principle of territorial integrity of states. A unilateral secession as a last resort is an expression of the rule of proportionality, which is considered one of the principles of international law. It creates a balance between the principles of sovereignty and territorial integrity of states on the one hand, and the principle of self-determination of peoples on the other hand, as basic principles of international law. In essence, it prevents misuse of the right of self-determination.[112]

In the case of secession, it is also not enough that the new entity declares its independence to become a state. The entity must also show that it has sufficient and real independence from the mother state, which means that it is not subject to the authority of any other state.[113] In the case of declaring independence, therefore, Catalonia must show sufficient independence from Spain. The state practice since the secession of the American colonies from Great Britain indicates that the condition of sufficient independence is ful-

---

108 Raic (2002), p. 419; Ott (2008), p. 464.
109 See International Court of Justice, Accordance with International Law of the Unilateral Declaration of Independence in Respect of Kosovo (Advisory Opinion of 22 July 2010), I.C.J. Reports 2010, para 84.
110 Saxer (2010), p. 169. Galán Galán (2013) concludes that international public law refers this issue to the law of the European Union, p. 106; see also Medina Ortega (2014), chapter VI.
111 Steinberger (2000), p. 513.
112 Ott (2008), 462.
113 Crawford (2006), p. 63 et seqq.

filled when the government of the new entity controls its territory effectively and with sufficient stability. Unlike national law, international law lacks a central authority for enforcing rights and duties. Therefore, individual factual situations are important. The existence of an *effective government* in the entity striving for independence is crucial for proper assessment of its legal position and the extent of third-party states' willingness to recognise it as a new state.[114] However, the extent of the new regime's effectiveness does not play a decisive role in cases where the secession took place with the consent of the previous sovereign, and the required degree of effectiveness could be reduced in secession movements that are based on the right of self-determination.[115] In general, in order to become an internationally recognised state, the government of the new entity must exercise an effective control over a particular population within a particular territory. Without an effective government, the new state will be incapable of enforcing individual rights and duties at the internal level, and of guaranteeing the observance of international duties. Therefore, the establishment of a new state and its recognition by the international community is contingent on this prerequisite. The recognition by states of an entity that lacks an effective government may constitute a wrongful act.[116] However, there is no duty under international law to recognise a new entity just because its government sufficiently controls its territory. Recognition of states is an optional and political act; when it occurs, it resolves uncertainties regarding the status of the new state.[117] Nonetheless, non-recognition of an entity as a state does not mean that other states should neglect having any relation with it. In some cases, states may find that it is necessary to distinguish between the external and internal consequences of non-recognition and recognise the de facto status in order to achieve hu-

---

114 Verdross (1959), p. 80; Doehring (1995), p. 44.
115 Haverland (2000), p. 356 et seqq.
116 Doehring (1995), p. 45.
117 Crawford (2006), p. 25.

manitarian goals or avoid causing damage to individuals.[118] As to the question of the membership in the United Nations, it is noteworthy that, since its establishment in 1945 and except for situations relating to former colonies, the United Nations have been reluctant to admit a seceding entity to membership without the consent of the mother state.[119] As a result, it is very probable that most, if not all, states would be reluctant to recognise Catalonia as an independent state, not only because state practice favours the preservation of the territorial integrity of the existing states, but because the recognising states might through an early recognition of Catalonia violate the principle of non-intervention in the internal affairs of states, according to Art. 2.7 of the UN Charter.[120]

The Catalans recognise that they would face obstacles if Catalonia unilaterally declared its independence from Spain; e.g. the Catalan government would have to decide whether to replace Spanish documents with ones in the Catalan language. However, to avoid causing damage to individuals in the event that independence is declared without a previous agreement with the central government in Madrid, states may recognise the status quo in Catalonia and recognise acts issued by Catalonian authorities, including marriage, employment contracts or even passports. Foreign courts may recognise the laws of Catalonia, even if the state where the court is located

---

118 After the collapse of the government of President Mohammad Said Barre in 1991 and the spread of chaos in Somalia, the north of Somalia declared its independence following an assembly of clans in the region and established the "Republic" of Somaliland. Although Somaliland has a government that exercises its functions in the territories and maintains public services in the region and although its government has managed to maintain its de facto independence for decades, and has contacts and visits with the foreign world, no state has recognised Somaliland as an independent state. The Port of Berbera, which lies in Somaliland, was used frequently to send international aid to Ethiopia; see Crawford (2006), p. 18 and 414. In 2003, a German court ruled that the Republic of Somaliland is a "state" for purposes of asylum law; see Hesse Administrative Court, Kassel, 4 UE 4952/96 (Judgment of 30 October 2003).

119 See in this respect Crawford (2006), p. 417.

120 Cf. the positions taken by states in the case of Katanga which declared in 1960 its independence from the Congo, in the case of Biafra which declared its independence in 1967 from Nigeria, in the case of Chechnya which declared its independence from the Russian Federation in November 1991 and in the case of Republika Srpska during the war in the former Yugoslavia in the 1990 s. See in this regard Crawford (2006), p. 406 – 408; Ott (2008), p. 222. See also Art. 1 of the General Framework Agreement for Peace in Bosnia and Herzegovina initialed in Dayton on 21 November 1995 and signed in Paris on 14 December 1995.

has not recognised Catalonia as an independent state. Yet, there will be states which might refuse to recognise acts issued by Catalonian authorities after a secession. This would cause damage to individuals, if some states refused to recognise, for example, Catalonian passports or qualifications and documents about periods of study and training. In the end, this would still equate with a high degree of legal uncertainty for the people of Catalonia.

3. Catalonia's independence as a challenge for the European Union

3.1 Catalonia as a constituent of a "Europe of the regions"

The regional blindness that existed in the Treaties of Rome (1957/58) has been replaced by the Treaty of Maastricht (1992/93) through the federal dimension of a "Europe of the Regions".[121] At the institutional level, the Committee of the Regions, which consists of representatives of regional and local bodies, participates in reaching the goal of a united Europe. The Committee should guarantee the regional features, diversity, and competition in the institutional framework of the treaties in accordance with the principles of the European Union (hereafter the Union or EU), such as the principles of proximity to citizens, subsidiarity, and respect for the national identity of the Member States. In the sense of the vertical distribution of competences, the Committee should represent an effective counterbalance against tendencies of centralization at the level of the Union. The underlying idea is that national states are too small to solve big problems and too big to solve small problems.[122] In the Spanish Delegation, Catalonia is represented by two members in the Committee of the Regions.

The Treaty of Lisbon (2007/09) stipulates in Art. 4.2 TEU that the Union has to "respect the national identities [of the Member States]." This provision both reflects and strengthens the notion that "[fundamental structures] of the Member States, both political and constitutional, inclusive of regional and local self-government" should be seen as inherent elements of national identity. This was the first instance in which the Union had been expressly defined as a multi-level governance system comprised of regions and munic-

---

121 Cf. Blanke, in Grabitz et al. (2011), Art. 300 AEUV para 57 et seqq. ("Das Europa der drei Ebenen").
122 Cf. D. Bell, cited by Teufel (1992), p. 2.

ipalities, the Member States, and the Union.[123] However, specific regional or local identities comparable with what the Treaty recognises as national identities are not protected.[124] The integration of the third level can also be seen in other parts in the treaties. In the context of the exercise of competences under the principle of subsidiarity, not only are possibilities for achievement at the central national level taken into account, but at the regional or local level (Art. 5.3 [1] TEU). The Committee of the Regions is also invested with the right to instigate proceedings in case of alleged infringements of the principle of subsidiarity (Art. 263.3 TFEU; Art. 8.2 of Protocol No. 2 TEU). Moreover, regional ministers are allowed to participate in the Member States delegations (Art. 16.2 TEU). This provision, introduced in 1992 in the Maastricht Treaty at the request of the German Government to enable ministers from the German *Länder* to participate in Council meetings, empowers members of state governments in federal or semi-federal states to be the representatives of the Member State, providing that the minister in question is competent to bind the Member State as a whole.[125]

Spain as a regional and not a federal state is represented by the national government in the Council of the European Union according to its constitution, which accords the central government the competence in the field of international relations (Art. 149.1 [3] Spanish Constitution). Since 2004 a representative of the autonomous regions can join as a member the Spanish delegation when the Council is dealing with matters that affect regional interests. This question is regulated by an agreement between the central government and the regional bodies.[126] Giving Catalonia, like all the other Spanish regions, the opportunity to participate effectively in the Spanish delegation and in the decision-making process in the EU may contribute to satisfying the Catalans' national aspirations and prevent conflicts between

---

123 Also Schink (2005), p. 865, says that (with regard to the equivalent provision of the Constitutional Treaty) "local self-government will become a building block of the European multi-level governance system and will form part of the fundamental political and (especially!) constitutional structure" of the Union (our translation). Cf. Pernice (2009), p. 372 et seqq.
124 Cf. Blanquet, in Burgorgue-Larsen et al. (2007), Art. I-5 para 4, 14.
125 Edjaharian, in Blanke and Mangiameli (2013), Art. 16 para 33.
126 Cf. the agreement of the "Conference for EC-Related Affairs of 9.12.2004 (now called "Conference for EU-Related Affairs" - CARUE - http://www.seap.min-hap.gob.es/en/areas/politica_autonomica/participacion-ccaa-eu/ccaa_y_ue/CARUE.html).

the *Generalitat* and the central government in Madrid. The initial refusal of the Spanish government to involve a representative of the *Comunidades Autónomas* (*un consejero autonómico*) in the Spanish delegation to the EU Council was one of the reasons for Catalans' dissatisfaction.[127] Indeed, European integration contributed to creating a process in which power is shared across multiple levels of government in Spain.[128]

3.2 EU's core values and the right to self-determination of Catalonia (Art. 2 TEU)

As Spain's representation in the Council of the Union shows, Catalonia's status as an autonomous region within the Spanish regional state remains low in its relations with the EU. This is undeniable in comparison with the status of the regional entities in federal states, such as Germany, Belgium and Austria. But does this justify a region's right to secession within the EU? This would be the case if Spain does not comply with the fundamental rights of minorities as set out also in relevant European conventions, and thereby violates the core values of the Union (Art. 2 TEU).[129] These catalogues provide for the right to internal self-determination for national and ethnic minorities *within* the national state. This right is recognised explicitly by the Union, which confirms in Art. 2 TEU to have "respect for human rights, including the rights of persons belonging to minorities". Beyond this article, the Union's dedication to human rights is apparent not only from legal texts, but from the positions it has taken on several occasions, and from statements made by the officials on behalf of the Union in international forums.[130]

The Framework Convention for the Protection of National Minorities, which was signed by Member States of the Council of Europe in 1995, stipulates in its preamble that "the protection of national minorities is essential for stability, democratic security and peace" in Europe. It also emphasises that "a pluralist and genuinely democratic society should not only respect the ethnic, cultural, linguistic and religious identity of each person belonging to a national minority, but create appropriate conditions enabling them to

---

127 Bourne (2004), p. 12.
128 Roller (2004), p. 88.
129 Medina Ortega (2014), chapter IV.
130 Maertens, EU Presidency Statement in the United Nations about the Right to Self-determination, EU Delegations to the United Nations (31 October 2001).

express, preserve and develop this identity". These principles emphasising protection of minorities may be considered structural principles of the EU.[131] The Convention transfers the principles mentioned in various documents of the Organisation for Security and Cooperation in Europe (Helsinki Final Act of 1975, as well as Final Act of the Copenhagen Meeting of the Conference on the Human Dimension and "Charter of Paris for a New Europe" both of 1990) into legally binding provisions. It requires states to guarantee every person belonging to a minority group fundamental human rights, such as freedom of thought, belief, association and expression, violation of which would be based on race, religion or language. According to Art. 4 of the Convention, states are required to "guarantee to persons belonging to national minorities the right of equality before the law" and to prohibit "any discrimination based on belonging to a national minority". Art. 5 of the Convention requires States "to promote the conditions necessary for persons belonging to national minorities to maintain and develop their culture and to preserve the essential elements of their identity, namely their religion, language, traditions and cultural heritage". However, the provisions enshrined in the Convention constitute only programme-similar principles that could be considered minimum standards that states have to guarantee to persons belonging to minority groups.[132] Therefore, states are required to ensure greater protection for minorities according to their national laws.

If we examine the extent to which Spain respects these standards in Catalonia as an autonomous region, we shall come to the following conclusion: Ten million Catalans living in the northeast of Spain have, according to the Spanish Constitution of 1978 (Art. 3.2 and 3.3), everything that numerous linguistic minorities in other states could only dream of. The Catalans have their own schools, media, literature and public institutions. The Spanish Constitution provides that Catalan as "[another] language of Spain … is recognised as official in the respective Self-governing Communities in accordance with their Statutes". This constitutional guarantee became a political reality in Catalonia. This compliance with the Union's values and principles should help reduce tensions and promote integration between "the peoples of Spain" (Preamble, 4th indent of the Spanish Constitution), including their nationalities. However, Catalans aspirations for "autonomy" go far beyond the right to self-government within a nation-state. Like other

---

131 See also Mangiameli, in Blanke and Mangiameli (2013), Art. 2 para 34.
132 See Article 22 of the Framework Convention for the Protection of National Minorities.

separatist movements in Europe, the Catalans may argue that the will of the majority should be respected if it voted for independence, which is considered in this case a collective reflection of the aspiration of the Catalans for self-government within a national state. This aspiration for independence is consistent with the Union core values, which include respect for human dignity, freedom and democracy.[133] In any event, Art. 2 TEU cannot be interpreted in isolation from other principles of the Union, which also include respect for the territorial integrity of the Member States (Art. 4 TEU).

3.3 Would an independent Catalonia have membership in the EU?

3.3.1. The principle of territorial integrity as a legal condition of European integration

According to Art. 4.2 TEU, the Union respects not only the national identity of the Member States, but "essential State functions, including ensuring the territorial integrity of the State, maintaining law and order and safeguarding national security". These elements constitute the "essential conditions for the enjoyment of national sovereignty".[134] The legal order of the Union is based on international law, and obligates the Union in its relation with the Member States (as well as the Member States in their relation with each other) to behave in a manner consistent with international law (Art. 4.3 TEU).[135] Observance by Member States of territorial integrity in their relations with each other and within their national borders is an essential condition to achieve peaceful integration and establish an area of peace, security and justice. This is politically characterised by ensuring the absence of internal border control and framing a common policy on asylum, immigration and external border control (Art. 67.2 TFEU). Therefore, the principle of territorial integrity of a state as one of the basic principles of international law provides Spain with an inherent right that enables it to make the required decisions to preserve its territorial integrity and political unity without any

---

133   Cf. Scottish Government (2013), Scotland in the European Union, p. 2 and 81. http://www.scotland.gov.uk/Resource/0043/00439166.pdf.

134   French Constitutional Council, Decision No. 2004-505 DC, The Treaty Establishing a Constitution for Europe (Decision of 19 November 2004), para 24.

135   Medina Ortega (2014), chapters II and V.

alien interference from any source, including the EU. Thus, the principle of sovereignty and territorial integrity of the Spanish state would serve as a safeguard against possible Union pressures on Spain to compel acceptance of the secession of Catalonia. The Union would also be required to respect the Spanish state's right to maintain law and order, and ensure internal security in Catalonia.[136]

3.3.2 Accession of Catalonia to the European Union after its secession from Spain

In an effort to quell some of the Catalans' fears, the government of the region voiced its opinion that Catalonia would remain in the EU if it ever seceded from Spain. In its view, independence of part of an EU Member State is unprecedented; it holds therefore that it is "untrue to declare that Catalonia would cease to be an EU member." In its opinion, such suggestions are "designed to scare Catalan voters away from supporting independence".[137] This point of view is similar to the one adopted by the Scottish government during its campaign supporting independence from Great Britain before the referendum of September 18, 2014.[138] In contrast, the position of both the Spanish and British governments is that secession from the mother state portends an exit from the Union.[139] Since EU treaties contain no provision on the legal consequences of independence of parts of a Member State, and due to the absence of a legal precedent in this regard, every party has asserted the correctness of its position. However, the point of view of the central governments is supported by statements of EU officials.

According to the former vice-president of the European Commission, *Joaquin Almunia*, "[i]f one part of a territory of a Member State decides to

---

136 Blanke, in Blanke and Mangiameli (2013), Art. 4 para 75.
137 See Website of the Government of Catalonia, President Artur Mas explains the process of how to decide the future of Catalonia (2 January 2014). http://prem-sa.gencat.cat/pres_fsvp/AppJava/notapremsavw/detall.do?id=239550&idioma=0.
138 Scottish Government (2013), Scotland in the European Union. http://www.scotland.gov.uk/Resource/0043/00439166.pdf.
139 HM Government (2014), Scotland Analysis: EU and International Issues. https://www.gov.uk/government/uploads/system/uploads/attachment_data/file/271794/2901475_HMG_Scotland_EUandInternational_acc2.pdf; see website of BBC News Europe, Scottish or Catalan Vote 'Torpedoes EU', Says Spain's Rajoy (17 September 2014). http://www.bbc.com/news/world-europe-29234242.

separate, the separated part isn't a member of the European Union".[140] The former President of the European Commission, *José Manuel Barroso*, and the former President of the European Council, *Herman Van Rompuy*, both expressed this same view. At the European level, there are obviously fears that secessionist movements would feel emboldened if seceding parts of Member States were allowed to remain in the Union.

Almunia's statement is supported by international law and state practice. At first glance, one may think that the opposite is true. Art. 34.1 (a) of the Vienna Convention on Succession of States in respect of Treaties of 1978 stipulates that "any treaty in force at the date of the succession of States in respect of the entire territory of the predecessor State continues in force in respect of each successor State so formed". This means that the newly-born state also takes on some of the obligations (and privileges) of the predecessor state.[141] However, Art. 4 of this Convention includes a restriction regarding the continuation of a treaty, which is the constituent instrument of an international organisation. Art. 4 stipulates that:

> The present Convention applies to the effects of a succession of States in respect of:
> (a) any treaty which is the constituent instrument of an international organisation without prejudice to the rules concerning acquisition of membership and without prejudice to any other relevant rules of the organisation.

In its commentary on Art. 4 of the Convention, the International Law Commission justified this restriction in Art. 4 by saying that "[i]nternational organisations take various forms and differ considerably in their treatment of membership".[142] Admission to membership of an international organisation is subject to specific conditions that should be fulfilled before the applicant

---

140 Nielsen, EU Commission: Catalonia must leave EU if it leaves Spain (17 September 2013). http://euobserver.com/enlargement/121466. In a reply to a parliamentarian question in 2004, the EU Commission stated that when a part of the territory of a Member State ceases to be a part of that state, e.g. because that territory becomes an independent state, the treaties will no longer apply to that territory. In other words, a newly independent region would, by the fact of its independence, become a third country with respect to the Union and the treaties would, from the day of its independence, not apply anymore on its territory. Parliamentary Questions of 1 March 2004. http://www.europarl.europa.eu/sides/getAllAnswers.do?reference=P-2004-0524&language=EN.

141 See Chamon (2013), p. 613 et seqq.

142 International Law Commission, Yearbook of the International Law Commission (1974), II (Part One), p. 177.

state becomes a member of the organisation. The practice of the United Nations shows that new states have been regarded as entitled to membership in the UN by *admission* and not by succession. The leading precedent in this regard was the case of Pakistan after it had separated from India and established an independent State in 1947. As Pakistan wanted to be a member, the UN Security Council, acting upon advice from the UN General Assembly, treated India as a continuing member and recommended that Pakistan applied for UN membership as a new state.[143]

Ultimately, the EU is also an association of like-minded and sovereign states, and there are certain conditions that every applicant state has to fulfill before it becomes a member. The EU is conceived as "a new legal order", creating rights and obligations not only for its Member States, but for its citizens. Therefore, in case of a conflict, EU law, and not the rules of international law related to succession regarding membership of international organisations, would apply to the case of an independent Catalonia.[144]

However, like the UN Charter, the EU treaties are silent as to what should happen when a part of a Member State decides to secede and establish a new state. The silence of the EU treaties in this regard is also similar to the situation that existed in the Union before the ratification in 2009 of the Lisbon Treaty, which provides the Member States in Art. 50 TEU the possibility of withdrawal. Before this treaty, the EC/EU treaties did not include an explicit provision on this case. This led at the time to different interpretations about the permissibility of withdrawal from the EC/EU. The absence of a provision explicitly permitting the withdrawal from the EC/EU did not prevent the emergence of attempts at withdrawal, as happened with the United Kingdom when it conducted a referendum in 1975 on remaining in the European Community. The attempt was not opposed by other Member States as being a violation of the European Community (EC) Treaty. However, some authors considered that Member States might not withdraw because they no longer had this right. According to this view, "individuals became the new subjects of the Community".[145]

Using a literal interpretation of Art. 50 TEU, only Member States would be entitled to withdraw from the Union. However, it could be argued that

---

143 International Law Commission, Yearbook of the International Law Commission (1974), II (Part One), p. 178.

144 See European Court of Justice, Case 26/62, Van Gend en Loos (1963), ECR, p. 12; see also Blanke, in Blanke and Mangiameli (2013), Art. 1 para 31.

145 See Wyrozumska, in Blanke and Mangiameli (2013), Art. 50 para 1, 2 and 3.

Art. 50 TEU might be interpreted in light of its purpose as permitting the withdrawal of parts of states. However, the view that, if Catalonia decided to separate from Spain, it would have to leave the EU is supported by Art. 52 TEU on the territorial scope of the treaties. This article mentions the official names of the Member States. EU law applies to Catalonia because it is constitutionally a part of Spain as one of the Member States mentioned in the list provided in Art. 52 TEU. In the event that Catalonia became an independent state, it would cease to be part of Spain. Consequently, Catalonia would also exit automatically from the Union if it were to become independent.[146]

The fact that the EU Treaties are silent as to the legal consequences related to the independence of a part of a Member State applies also to the question of the allocation of seats at the EU Parliament. However, and in spite of the principle of degressive proportionality (14.2 TEU), the number of seats allocated to Spain in the EU Parliament would need to be adapted in the event that Catalonia became an independent state.

Regardless of the legal reasons that may speak for or against Catalonia's retaining Union membership, the Union would be reluctant to give separatist movements in Europe an encouraging signal through the permissive continuation of an independent Catalonia as an EU Member State without going through the admission process provided for in Art. 49 TEU. Therefore, it is probable that the EU would follow an approach similar to that of the UN concerning the membership of a new-born state after a separation from the mother state. This conclusion is consistent with Art. 52 TEU, and with statements on this matter by Union officials. Hence, it is expected that an independent Catalonia would be required to apply for EU membership as new states have done if it wishes to become a Member State. But this does not mean necessarily that Catalonia would exit automatically after independence. An automatic exit would have several implications not only at institutional level, but for individuals. The Catalans have already become Union citizens, and Catalonia has already applied the law of the EU and uses its

---

146 See in this respect Quesada, in Blanke and Mangiameli (2013), Art. 52 para 4; see also Galán Galán (2013) who thus excludes the applicability of Art. 50 TEU, p. 110 et seqq. and p. 115.

currency.[147] The admission process can take years. The accession application of Catalonia must also be approved unanimously by the European Council, which consists of governments of the Member States. Spain or any other Member State can effectively veto the Council's consent.

3.3.3 Preference for a smooth transition

In the event that Catalonia were to declare its independence, it would therefore be very probable that the Union's institutions would enter into negotiations with Catalonia and Spain to avoid problems and complications that would result. An example of these problems includes issues such as Erasmus students studying in Catalan universities being reclassified as foreign students. Catalans working in other Member States such as Germany or France would lose their rights under EU law. Therefore, it is not out of the question that the Court of Justice of the European Union might be involved in this matter and not allow the Council to expel Catalonia after a secession automatically from the European Union since this would violate the individual rights of current Union citizens. This scenario is possible if, for example, an individual argued before a Spanish court that some measure by the Spanish government connected with Catalonia's independence violated EU laws, and as a result the court made a preliminary referral to the Court of Justice of the EU.[148]

In any event, if Catalonia were to declare its independence, negotiations between the Union institutions, Member States, Spain and Catalonia would be necessary. Negotiations based on good faith and sincere cooperation would be required under EU law to find a solution consistent with the core values, spirit and objectives of the Union.[149] Such negotiations might aim at helping relevant parties reach a political solution concerning Catalonia's status in its relations with Spain or the EU. They might also seek to agree on a transition period and transitional arrangements. During this period, EU

---

147 See Catalan Government's Advisory Council: an independent Catalonia would not be excluded from the EU. http://www.catalannewsagency.com/politics/item/catalan-government-s-advisory-council-suggests-that-an-independent-catalonia-would-not-be-excluded-from-the-eu.

148 See O'Neill (2011), A Quarrel in a Faraway Country?: Scotland, Independence and the EU. Eutopialaw. http://eutopialaw.com/2011/11/14/685/.; Crawford and Boyle (2012), p. 104 et seq; cf. Tierney (2013), p. 4.

149 Cf. Edward (2013/14), p. 20.

laws would apply to Catalonia until negotiations had been concluded.[150] The reason for determining this transition period is, as in the case of the withdrawal of a Member State according to Art. 50 TEU, to overcome the complications and problems arising out of Catalonia's exit from the Union.[151] Hence, the negotiations and proposed transition period would be in the interest of Catalonia, all Member States, EU citizens and the Union in general.[152]

Thus, it could be argued that – contrary to the opinions of *Almunia*, *Barroso* and *Van Rompuy* – Catalonia's exit from the Union would not be automatic if it declared its independence from Spain. Indeed, the legal situation is far from clear, and the solution would be political rather than legal. This state of uncertainty demonstrates that there is a lacuna in EU law regarding the legal consequences related to the independence of part of a Member State. This also explains why the Union welcomed the result of the Scottish referendum.[153] Like European governments, the Union also thinks that the rise of secessionist movements in various European states not only constitutes a threat to the territorial integrity of Member States, but also goes against the spirit of European integration.

4. Conclusion

International law, as it currently stands, does not spell out all the implications of the right to self-determination. However, it is well established that international law permits – whatever the circumstances – secession only in certain situations, none of which are applicable in the case of Catalonia. Neither international law nor EU law guarantees an overall right to secession. The Catalans as a people and nationality are entitled to exercise internally the

---

150 Cf. Murkens (2001), p. 10; Scottish Government (2013), Scotland in the European Union, p. 81. http://www.scotland.gov.uk/Resource/0043/00439166.pdf; Enlightening the Constitutional Debate (2014), Scotland and the EU (Walker's opinion), The Royal Society of Edinburgh, p. 30. http://www.royalsoced.org.uk/series-book.

151 Edward (2013/14), p. 19.

152 Cf. Scottish Government (2013), Scotland in the European Union, p. 81. http://www.scotland.gov.uk/Resource/0043/00439166.pdf.

153 See: No! Schotten stimmen gegen Unabhängigkeit, Frankfurter Allgemeine (19 September 2014). http://www.faz.net/aktuell/politik/referendum-in-schottland/ergebnis-des-referendums-no-schotten-stimmen-gegen-unabhaengig-keit-13161748.html.

right to self-determination. Accordingly, the Catalans are entitled to all the rights accorded to minority and ethnic groups under international law and EU law.

Moreover, integration at the level of the EU provides Catalonia and other stateless nations and minorities with different opportunities to have their voices heard. Giving regions stronger competences will not only promote the political idea of subsidiarity, helping decision-making in the Union to become more democratic, more transparent, more efficient and closer to citizens. It may also contribute to satisfying the national demands of regions aspiring for greater autonomy, as the case of Scotland. Accordingly, Spain is entitled to protect its territorial integrity and political unity. Other states and the Union are required to respect the sovereignty, and in particular the territorial integrity of the Spanish state, as long as the Spanish government conducts itself in compliance with the right of self-determination. The Union is, as the German Federal Constitutional Court described it, "an association of sovereign states".[154] Despite the conferral of some sovereign powers by the Member States upon the Union, the vast majority of sovereign rights, including those related to the essential functions of the state, remain with the Member States. Since an independent Catalonia after secession from Spain would be outside the EU in the medium-term, it would be required to apply for Union membership as new states do and to go through the admission process as provided in Art. 49 TEU.

However, this does not necessarily mean that Catalonia would automatically exit from the Union if it declared its independence from Spain. There would have to be negotiations between the EU, Member States, Spain and Catalonia. Therefore, the relevant parties might agree on a transition period to overcome the complications that would arise from Catalonia's exit. The fact that EU law contains no provision on the legal consequences related to the independence of part of a Member State leaves a state of uncertainty, revealing a legal lacuna in this respect.

Since Catalonia has only a right to internal self-determination and no right to secession, conducting a referendum on independence against the will of the Spanish government would not be justifiable from the perspective of international and Union law, not to mention the Spanish Constitution of

---

154 Federal Constitutional Court of Germany, 2 BvE 2/08, Lisbon Case (Judgment of 30 June 2009), para 249; French Constitutional Council, decision No. 2004-505 DC, The Treaty Establishing a Constitution for Europe, (Decision of 19 November 2004), para 5.

1978, which stipulates in Art. 2 that the unity of the Spanish nation is indissoluble. Therefore, if the Catalans insist on independence, there would be no way fully compatible with international law and Union law to achieve it, other than reaching a negotiated agreement with the Spanish government. The consent of the Spanish government is indispensable not only to avoid troubles that may arise if the Catalans unilaterally declared their independence, but for recognition by the international community and membership of international organisations. Without the consent of Spain, most, if not all states, would be reluctant to recognise Catalonia as an independent state. With respect to membership in the UN and the EU, it would be difficult if not impossible for an independent Catalonia to be a member state of these organisations against the will of Spain. Therefore, the way to Catalonia's independence, if constitutionally admissible and politically unavoidable, would necessarily be through Madrid.

References

Alcock, A. (2001). *The South Tyrol Autonomy*. Bozen/Bolzano.

Ambruster, H. (1962). Selbstbestimmungsrecht, in Strupp, K. & Schlochauer, H. (Eds.), *Wörterbuch des Völkerrechts* (Vol. 3, p. 250). Berlin.

Béland, D. & Lecours, A. (2008). *Nationalism and Social Policy*. Oxford.

Beltran, S. (2010). La aplicación de los acuerdos que regulan la participación de las Comunidades Autónomas en el Consejo de la Union europea – Variaciones o desvaríos sobre un mismo tema, *Revista General de Derecho Europeo*, n° 22, p. 25.

Blanke, Herm.-J. (2014). Völker- und europarechtliche Vorgaben des Minderheitenschutzes, in Scherzberg, A. & Can, O. (Eds.), *Der Schutz der ethnischen Minderheiten in der Türkei und die Dezentralisierung der Staatsorganisation* (p. 9). Berlin.

Blanke, Herm.-J. (1991). *Föderalismus und Integrationsgewalt*. Berlin.

Blanke, Herm.-J. & Mangiameli, St. (Eds.) (2013). *The Treaty on European Union (TEU). A Commentary*. Heidelberg.

Bleckmann, A. (1985). Das Souveränitätsprinzip im Völkerrecht. *Archiv des Völkerrechts*, 23, p. 450.

Bothe, M. (2010). Kosovo – So What? The Holding of the International Court of Justice is not the Last Word on Kosovo's Independence. *German Law Journal*, 11 (8), p. 837.

Bourne, A. (2004). The Domestic Politics of Regionalism and European Integration, in Bourne, A. (Ed.), *The EU and Territorial Politics within Member States, Conflict or Co-operation?* (p. 1). Leiden.

Brühl-Moser, D. (1994). *Die Entwicklung des Selbstbestimmungsrechts der Völker unter besonderer Berücksichtigung seines innerstaatlich-demokratischen Aspekts und seiner Bedeutung für den Minderheitenschutz*. Frankfurt am Main.

Burgorgue-Larsen, L., Levade, A. & Picod, F. (Eds.) (2007). *Traité établissant une Constitution pour l'Europe. Parties I et IV. Commentaire article par article* (Vol. I). Brussels.

Cárdenas, E. & Cañás, M. (2002). The Limit of Self-Determination, in Danspeckgruber, W. (Ed.), *Self-Determination of Peoples* (p. 101). London.

Carley, P. (1996). *Self-Determination: Sovereignty, Territorial Integrity, and the Right to Secession* (online version http://www.usip.org/sites/default/files/pwks7.pdf).

Cassese, A. (1995). *Self-determination of peoples*. Cambridge.

Chamon, M. &Van der Loo, G. (2013). The Temporal Paradox of Regions in the EU Seeking Independence: Contraction and Fragmentation versus Widening and Deepening? In *European Law Journal*, 20 (5), p. 613.

Coll, F. (2009). *Revealing the dark side of traditional democracies in plurinational societies. The Case of Catalonia and the Spanish "Estado de las Autonomías"* (online version: https://repositori.upf.edu/bitstream/handle/10230/5182/GRTPwp4.pdf?sequence=1).

Connolly, C. (2013). Independence in Europe: Secession, Sovereignty, and the European Union. *Duke Journal of Comparative & International Law*, 24, p. 51.

Coşkun, V. (2014). Democracy, Participation, and Minorities, in Scherzberg, A. & Can, O. (Eds.), *Der Schutz der ethnischen Minderheiten in der Türkei und die Dezentralisierung der Staatsorganisation* (p. 89), Berlin.

Crawford, J. (2006). *The Creation of States in International Law* (Second Edition). Oxford.

Crawford, J. & Boyle, A. (2012). *Annex A Opinion: Referendum on the Independence of Scotland – International Law Aspects* (online version: https://www.gov.uk/government/uploads/system/uploads/attachment_data/file/79408/Annex_A.pdf).

Dahms, M., *Kein Grund für ein unabhängiges Katalonien*, Frankfurter Rundschau, (7 April 2014).

De Becker, A. (2012). La representación de Bélgica en el Consejo de la UE y la participación directa de las regiones, *Revista CIDOB d'afers internacionals*, n.º 99, p. 39.

Danspeckgruber, W. (2002). Self-Determination and Regionalization in Contemporary Europe, in Danspeckgruber, W. (Ed.), *Self-Determination of Peoples* (p. 165). London.

Doehring, K. (1995). Effectivness, in Berhardt, R. (Ed.), *Encyclopedia of Public International Law* (Vol. II, p. 43). Amsterdam.

Doehring, K. (1995). Self-Determination, in Simma, B. (Ed.), *The Charter of the United Nations: A Commentary* (p. 56). Oxford.

Dowling, A. (2013). *Catalonia since the Spanish Civil War: reconstructing the nation*. Chicago.

Dumberry, P. (2006). Lessons learned from the Quebec Secession Reference before the Supreme Court of Canada, in Kohen, M. (Ed.), *Secession* (p. 416). Cambridge. Edward, D. (2013). *European Union Law*. Cheltenham.

Edward, D. (2013/14). Scotland`s Position in the European Union. *Scottish Parliamentary Review*, 1 (2), p. 1.

Eide, A. (1993). In Search of Constructive Alternatives to Secession, in Tomuschat, Ch. (Ed.), *Modern Law of Self-Determination* (p. 139). London.

Falk, R. (2002). Self-Determination under International Law, in Danspeckgruber, W. (Ed.), *Self-Determination of Peoples* (p. 31). London.

Galán Galán, A. (2013). Secesión de Estados y pertenencia a la Unión Europea: Cataluña en la encrucijada. *Istituzioni del Federalismo*, 1, p. 95.

Grabitz, E., Hilf, M. & Nettesheim, M. (2011). *Das Recht der Europäischen Union. Kommentar*. Looser leaf. Munich.

Gutiérrez Espada, C. (2000). Uso de la fuerza, intervención humanitaria y libre determinación (La guerra de Kosovo). *Anuario de Derecho Internacional Público*, XVL, p. 93.

Hannum, H. (1996). *Autonomy, Sovereignty, and Self-Determination*. Philadelphia.

Hasani, S. (1996). Kosovo – an entity waiting for a solution according to the right of self-determination, in Reiter, E. (Ed.), *Grenzen des Selbstbestimmungsrechts* (p. 228). Graz.

Haverland, C. (2000). Secession, in Berhardt, R. (Ed.), *Encyclopedia of Public International Law* (Vol. IV, p. 354). Amsterdam.

Henkin, L. (1995). *International Law: Politics and Values*. Dordrecht.

Hilpold, P. (2012). Die Sezession im Völkerrecht – Erfordert das Kosovo-Gutachten des IGH eine Neubewertung dieses Instituts? In Hilpold, P. (Ed.), *Das Kosovo-Gutachten des IGH vom 22. Juli 2010* (p. 49). Leiden.

Hilpold, P. (2013). Das Selbstbestimmungsrecht der Völker. *Juristische Schulung*, 53 (12), p. 1081.

Hilpold, P. (2013). Von der Utopie zur Realität - das Selbstbestimmungsrecht der Völker im Europa der Gegenwart. *JuristenZeitung*, 68 (22), p. 1061.

Hosková, M. (1993). Die Selbstauflösung der ČSFR – Ausgewählte rechtliche Aspekte. *Zeitschrift für ausländisches öffentliches Recht und Völkerrecht*, 53, p. 689.

Jamar, H. & Vigness, M. (2010). Applying Kosovo: Looking to Russia, China, Spain and Beyond after the International Court of Justice Opinion on Unilateral Declarations of Independence. *Germal Law Journal*, 11 (8), p. 813.

Kadelbach, St. (1992). *Zwingendes Völkerrecht*. Berlin.

Keating, M. (2012). Rethinking Sovereignty. Independence-lite, Devolution-max and National Accomodation. *REAF*, 16, p. 9.

Keating, M. (2001). *Plural Democracy: Stateless Nations in a Post-Sovereignty Era*. Oxford.

Kellas, J. (1989). *The Scottish Political System* (Fourth Edition). Cambridge.

Kelsen, H. (1951). *The Law of the United Nations: A Critical Analysis of Its Fundamental Problems*. London.

Kimminich, O. (1993). A "Federal" Right of Self-Determination? In Tomuschat, Ch. (Ed.), *Modern Law of Self-Determination* (p. 83). London.

Kimminich, O. (1992). *Das Selbstbestimmungsrecht der Völker*. Cologne.

Libarona, I. (2012). Territorial Integrity and Self-Determination: The Approach of the Internation Court of Justice in the Advisory Opinion on Kosovo. *REAF*, 16, p. 107.

López-Jurado Romero de la Cruz, C. (2011). Kosovo ante la Corte Internacional de Justicia: La opinión consultiva de 22 de Julio de 2010. *Revista Electrónica de Estudios Internacionales*, 21, p. 1.

Manela, E. (2007). *The Wilsonian Moment*. Oxford.

McRoberts, K. (2001). *Catalonia: Nation Building without a State*. Oxford.

Medina Ortega, M. (2014). *El derecho de secesión en la Unión Europea*, Madrid.

Muharremi, R. (2010). A Note on the ICJ Advisory Opinion in Kosovo. *Germal Law Journal*, 11 (8), p. 867.

Murkens, J. (2001). *Scotland's Place in Europe, The Constitution Unit, UCL*. London.

Murswiek, D. (1993). The Issue of a Right of Secession – Reconsidered, in Tomuschat, Ch. (Ed.), *Modern Law of Self-Determination* (p. 21). London.

Nielsen, N. (2013), *EU Commission: Catalonia must leave EU if it leaves Spain* (http://euobserver.com/enlargement/121466).

Ott, M. (2008). *Das Recht auf Sezession als Ausfluss des Selbstbestimmungsrechts der Völker*. Berlin.

Pazartzis, P. (2006). Secession and International Law: The European Dimension, in Kohen, M. (Ed.), *Secession* (p. 355). Cambridge.

Perea Unceta, J. A. (2011). Las cuestiones sobre Kosovo que no quiso responder el Tribunal de La Haya'. Anuario Jurídico y Económico Escurialense, XLIV, p. 117.

Pernice, I. (2009). The Treaty of Lisbon: Multilevel Constitutionalism in Action. *Columbia Journal of European Law*, 15 (3), p. 349.

Pons Rafols, X. (2013). Legalidad internacional y derecho a decidir, *Revista catalana de dret public*. Online version: http://blocs.gencat.cat/blocs/AppPHP/eapc-rcdp/2013/02/18/legalidad-internacional-y-derecho-a-decidir-xavier-pons-rafols/).

Quaritsch, H. (2013). Selbstbestimmungsrecht des Volkes als Grundlage der deutschen Einheit, in Isensee, J. & Kirchhof, P. (Eds.), *Handbuch des Staatsrechts der Bundesrepublik Deutschland* (p. 111). Heidelberg.

Raic, D. (2002). *Statehood and the Right to Self-determination*. The Hague.

Rejsek, J. (1996). *Die Politische Autonomie Kataloniens* (First Edition). Catalonia.

Roller, E. (2004). Conflict and Cooperation in EU Policy-Making: the Case of Catalonia, in Bourne, A. (Ed.), *The EU and Territorial Politics within Member States, Conflict or Co-operation?* (p. 79). Leiden.

Rosas, A. (1993). Internal Self-determination, in Tomuschat, Ch. (Ed.), *Modern Law of Self-Determination* (p. 225). London.

Rozakis, Ch. (2000). Territorial Integrity and Political Independence, in Berhardt, R. (Ed.), *Encyclopedia of Public International Law* (Vol. IV, p. 812). Amsterdam.

Rumpf, H. (1984). Das Subjekt des Selbstbestimmungsrechts, in Blumenwitz, D. & Meissner, B. (Eds.), *Das Selbstbestimmungsrecht der Völker und die deutsche Frage* (p. 47). Köln. Saxer, U. (2010). *Die internationale Steuerung der Selbstbestimmung und der Staatenentstehung*. Heidelberg.

Schink, A. (2005). Kommunale Daseinsvorsorge in Europa. *Deutsches Verwaltungsblatt*, 120 (14), p. 861.

Spain, A. (1980). *The Political Theory of John C. Calhoun*. New York 1980.

Stein, A. & Rosecrance, R. (2006). The Dilemma of Devolution and Federalism: Secessionary Nationalism and the Case of Scotland, in Stein, A. & Rosecrance, R. (Eds.), *No More States?* (p. 235). New York.

Steinberger, H. (2000). Sovereignty, in Bernhardt, R. (Ed.), *Encyclopedia of Public International Law* (Vol. IV, p. 500). Amsterdam.

Streinz, R. (Ed.) (2012). *EUV/AEUV: Vertrag über die Europäische Union und Vertrag über die Arbeitsweise der Europäischen Union.* Munich.

Teufel, E. (1992). Föderalismus als Ordnungsrahmen für Europa, in Vogel, B. & Oettinger, G. (Eds.), *Föderalismus in der Bewährung* (p. 1). Cologne.

Thürer, D. (1984). Selbstbestimmungsrecht der Völker. *Archiv des Völkerrrechts*, 22, p. 113.

Thürer, D. (1996). Entwicklung, Inhalt und Träger des Selbstbestimmungsrechts, in Reiter, E. (Ed.), *Grenzen des Selbstbestimmungsrechts* (p. 34). Wien.

Tierney, S. (2013). *Accession of an Independent Scotland to the European Union: A View of the Legal Issues, ESRC Scottish Centre on Constitutional Change.* (http://www.futureukandscotland.ac.uk/sites/default/files/papers/ESRC%20Briefing%20on%20Scotland%20and%20European%20Union.pdf).

Tocci, N. (2011). The EU in Conflict Resolution, in Wolff, S. & Yakinthou, Ch. (Eds.), *Conflict Resolution: Theories and Practice* (online version: http://www.ethnopolitics.org/isa/Tocci.pdf).

Tomuschat, Ch. (2006). Secession and Self-determination, in Kohen, M. (Ed.), *Secession* (p. 23). Cambridge.

Tomuschat, Ch. (1993). Self-determination in a Post-Colonial World, in Tomuschat, Ch. (Ed.), *Modern Law of Self-Determination* (p. 1). London.

Verdross, A. (1959). *Völkerrecht* (Fourth Edition). Wien.

Vosgerau, U. (2015). *Staatliche Gemeinschaft und Staatengemeinschaft. Grundgesetz und Europäische Union im internationalen öffentlichen Recht der Gegenwart.* Tübingen.

Vosgerau, U. (2013). Das Selbstbestimmungsrecht des Volkes in der Weltgemeinschaft, in Isensee, J. & Kirchhof, P. (Eds.), *Handbuch des Staatsrechts der Bundesrepublik Deutschland* (p. 91). Heidelberg.

Walters, M. (1999). Nationalism and the Pathology of Legal Systems: Considering the Quebec Secession Reference and its lessons for the United Kingdom. *The Modern Law Review*, 62, p. 371.

Wolff, S. (2005). Complex autonomy arrangements in Western Europe, in Wolff, St. & Weller, M. (Eds.), *Autonomy, Self-government and Conflict Resolution*, London.

Catalonia: a failure of accommodation?

Ivan Serrano

1. Introduction

Contrary to expectation of a progressive federalization of the so-called 'State of Autonomies', Spain has experienced a growing tension between nationalist demands for recognition and the national project of the State. This chapter gives an overview of the institutional developments at the parliamentary level and the evolution of attitudes about self-government in Catalonia since 2003, when the proposal for a new statute of autonomy entered the political agenda. The first section focuses on the Statute of Autonomy approved in 2006 and the reaction of Catalan nationalism, which is based upon the idea of a 'right to decide' that would make legitimate Catalonia's unilateral exercise of self-determination, including a non-binding referendum scheduled for November 9th 2014. Second, empirical data from opinion studies is used to provide an overview of the social basis underpinning the evolution of preferences for self-government and independence during this period.

The interpretative framework used here departs from a discursive shift of Catalan nationalism analysed from the perspective of normative theories of secession. First, the outcome of the statutory reform is perceived as a failure of accommodation: a satisfactory – if not optimal – level of autonomy is not likely to be achieved within the existing state. Second, this perception gives rise to a remedialist discourse based on an alleged right to self-determination of Catalonia, in the form a unilateral 'right to decide'. According to this narrative, independence is the only alternative left for Catalonia to achieve a significant level of self-government.

2. The State's response to self-government claims

In 2003, after the long term of office of Jordi Pujol, a coalition of left-wing parties agreed to form a new government in Catalonia. The new government's agenda proposed a new framework of relations with Spain, by means of a new statute of autonomy. This was a change to the traditional role used by Pujol's CiU coalition that had traditionally obtained new regional competences in exchange for parliamentary support to national governments in Madrid. In the elections of 2004, the unexpected victory of Rodríguez-Zapatero after the terrorist attack in Madrid opened up the possibility of negotiating this new agreement, given that the candidate had publicly declared that he would support any new statute the Catalan parliament might approve. Catalan parties belonging to the *Catalanist* tradition, the *Partit dels Socialistes de Catalunya* (PSC), *Esquerra Republicana de Catalunya (*ERC), *Iniciativa per Catalunya-Verds* (ICV-EUiA) and *Convergència i Unió* (CiU) started negotiations for drafting a new statute in the Catalan parliament. In 2005, the Catalan parliament sent a proposal for a new Statute of Autonomy to the Spanish Congress, where the text was amended after a controversial negotiation.

One of the most illuminating controversies during the negotiations was the definition of Catalonia as a nation and the extent to which this could fit into the Spanish constitutional framework. First, the legitimation of autonomy confronted the different views of Catalan and Spanish nationalism. For nationalism, Catalonia is a nation in a pluri-national Spain, while Spanish nationalism accepts the plurality of the State under a unitary conception of the nation that is reflected in the territorial decentralization of power organized in autonomous communities (Serrano, 2008). This symbolical debate confronts not only different sources legitimating self-government, but also points to the limits of decentralization from the State perspective. The first draft approved by the Catalan parliament stated in its first article (Art. 1.1) that 'Catalonia is a nation'. This definition was the fundamental basis to legitimate a wide range of political rights in terms of recognition and competences. In accordance with this definition, the proposal was designed to provide a significant level of autonomy in areas such as fiscal autonomy and bilateral relations with the state or foreign policy. It also reinforced the idea of Catalonia as a 'subject of decision', including the possibility of organizing non-binding referendums within the existing constitutional framework. This definition and its implications challenged the national conception of the State enshrined in the Constitution and would be modified during the negotiations in the Spanish Congress. The reference to Catalonia as a nation would eventually be moved to the preamble of the final version of the Statute, recognizing the national character of Catalonia as a political statement expressed by the regional parliament within the limits of the Constitutional conception of Spanish nationalities:

In reflection of the feelings and the wishes of the citizens of Catalonia, the Parliament of Catalonia has defined Catalonia as a nation by an ample majority. The Spanish Constitution, in its second Article, recognises the national reality of Catalonia as a nationality (Llei Orgànica 6/2006, de 19 de juliol, de reforma de l'Estatut d'autonomia de Catalunya, 2006).

The preamble also entrenched the right of Catalonia to 'self-government' within the limits established by Article 2 of the Spanish Constitution recognizing the existence of 'nationalities and regions'. This article also establishes that the right to autonomy can not affect the "indissoluble unity of the Spanish nation, common and indivisible homeland *(patria)* of all Spaniards" (Spanish Constitution, 1978). The proposal would be passed by referendum in Catalonia in June 2006, with a low turnout and the rejection – from opposing perspectives – by ERC and PP. However, many aspects were challenged before the Constitutional Court by the *Partido Popular* (PP) and the Spanish Ombudsman, a former member of the *Partido Socialista Obrero Español* (PSOE), as well as some Autonomous Communities. Four years later, the Court would amend several articles of the text in a controversial decision that would prompt a strong political and social reaction in Catalonia. In this period, the social mobilization around the organization of popular, unofficial referendums in more than 800 municipalities between 2007 and 2009 was to put the question of independence at the forefront of the political agenda.

The decision of the Constitutional Court affected the *contents* of autonomy, overruling and amending several aspects on sensitive areas, such as language, education policy, and financial and fiscal policy, but it also reflected a particular *conception* of autonomy. There are three elements that characterize this conception as established by the Court's decision. First, on the question of defining Catalonia as a nation, the Court emphasized the absence of any 'interpretative legal effectiveness' of such a definition. That is, the national character of Catalonia could not become the basis for the legitimation of self-government arrangements. To the contrary, the Court defined a top-down legitimation of autonomy based on the Constitutional recognition of 'nationalities and regions'. Second, the Court reinterpreted regional statutes of autonomy – which have a special procedure of reform that include bilateral negotiations with the national congress and eventually a regional referendum of approval – as ordinary laws rather than regional constitutions. This interpretation also strengthened the *negative legislator* role of the Court and the central state, which would effectively include an extensive discretional capacity to supervise and delimit *ad hoc* the scope of regional competences. Third, the recognition of the regional *demos* and particularly the possibility for an autonomous community to organize non-binding referendums remained under the discretion of the State, following the doctrine established in the ruling against the so-called *Plan Ibarretxe* of 2008. Under this approach, the Constitutional Court in 2014 would suspend the decree calling for a non-binding referendum to be held on November 9th.

The long awaited decision of the Constitutional Court in 2010 prompted a massive demonstration with the slogan 'We are a nation. We decide', reflecting both the basis for the so-called 'right to decide' and the discursive evolution of Catalan nationalism (Vilaregut, 2011, Chapter 4). In this context, early elections were called for November 25th. The shift in the discourse can be seen as a 'remedialist' response to the perception of a 'failure of accommodation' within Spain. Later, the persistent rejection of the State to agree the terms for a referendum would eventually legitimate a unilateral scenario. This approach is based on arguments that are linked to normative theories of secession, such as the permanent minority argument, the unfair treatment of the state in economic terms or the violation of self-government agreements, which are linked to welfare and democracy rather than to ethnocultural features (Serrano, 2015). Even though the idea of a 'right to decide' was one of the key elements of the electoral campaign, political parties did not fully transform this claim into a pro-independence agenda. The main proposal of CiU for instance was an agreement to grant a specific fiscal arrangement similar to the existing one for the Basque Country and Navarre, while ICV-EUiA's coalition manifesto aimed at the federalization of Spain as a way to restore the autonomy envisaged in the Statute of 2006. The new elected parliament resulted in a relative majority of CiU. A proposal to negotiate a new fiscal arrangement with the central government was agreed by the new government, ERC and ICV-EUiA in 2012. As expected, this proposal was rejected by the Spanish government, which was presented by Catalan nationalism as a new failure for a stable accommodation within the State, and an additional legitimation for some kind of unilateral decision in Catalonia. After a massive demonstration on September 11th 2012, the Catalan Parliament embraced a clear pro-sovereignty position, passing a resolution that established the priority to hold a referendum for Catalans to decide upon 'their collective future freely and democratically', and new elections were called for November 2012. The electoral manifesto of CiU reflected this change by introducing the possibility of a unilateral referendum if the state were not to accept a bilateral agreement to hold a consultation. The coalition finally suffered a significant loss of representatives in the new parliament, but the good results of pro-independence ERC kept a strong pro-sovereignty majority in the parliament.

After the elections of 2012, the new Parliament approved a number of resolutions that included a non-binding referendum scheduled for November 9th 2014. The rhetoric used in the parliamentary resolutions at this point reflects the consolidation of a remedialist discourse. A clear example is found in the main resolution of this new period, the 'Declaration of Sovereignty' of January 25th 2013, approved by CiU, ERC, ICV and partially by the *Candidatura d'Unitat Popular* (CUP), a pro-independence radical left coalition that obtained representation in the Catalan Parliament for the first time. It tells of the failure to reach a stable accommodation within Spain, and that the electoral results and the massive demonstrations of civil society conveyed a mandate to the parliament to organize a referendum for the Catalan society to decide about Catalonia's political future. The declaration also assumed that this mandate must be fulfilled with or without the State's consent.

In December 2013, the four parties agreed on a date and a referendum question. Finally, the question was twofold; the first one asked "Do you want Catalonia to become a State?" and the second was a follow-up: "In case of an affirmative response, do you want this State to be independent?" While this kind of structure and wording does not follow standards and recommendations as established by some precedents or international bodies, it actually reflects the widest possible consensus among Catalan political parties that agree on the recognition of Catalonia as a *demos,* in spite of their ideological differences – from radical left to liberal and conservative positions – and constitutional preferences – from outright independence to the possibility of an agreement within Spain[1]. In March 2014, the Catalan Parliament presented a proposal in the Spanish Congress to agree the terms for handing down the power to hold a referendum, but it was rejected by the two main Spanish parties, PP and PSOE, among others. In September 2014, the Catalan parliament approved a new law that would serve as the regional framework on popular non-binding consultations as a reaction to the State's ar-

---

1 Regarding some international references on referendums, see for instance the well-known opinion of the Supreme Court of Canada about the necessity of a "clear question" (Supreme Court of Canada, 1998), the recommendations of the British Electoral Commission on the Scottish referendum (The Electoral Commission, 2013), or the Code of Good Practices in Referendums of the Venice Commission (Venice Commission, Council of Europe 2009).

gument that a referendum was illegal under the Spanish Constitution. Under the new law, the Catalan government issued the decree formally calling for the referendum of November 2014. However, the Spanish government immediately brought both the law and the decree to the Constitutional Court, where it was temporarily suspended until the Court's eventual ruling about its constitutionality. The Catalan government then adopted a new legal strategy by promoting a participatory process using the same question. As a preventive measure two weeks before the scheduled date of the referendum, the Constitutional Court also decided to suspend this new format. However, the consultation eventually took place with the support of voluntaries. Over 2.3 million votes were cast and, in the aftermath of the consultation, the Spanish Government planned to promote the indictment of the President of the Generalitat and some other members of the Catalan government involved in the process.

3. Social attitudes towards independence

Beside the institutional and partisan debate, one of the key questions in the current context of Catalonia is whether support for independence is simply a matter of identity, that is, to what extent other social and political factors, more or less contingent, are also relevant in shaping attitudes towards independence. Different studies have pointed out how an identity-driven approach, taken too narrowly, has difficulties in analysing the change and reflecting the dynamic character of constitutional preferences in Catalonia, which tend to be less stable than identity. However, identity is not only shaped by ethnocultural factors and secondary socialization processes. In fact, political attitudes can also influence national self-identification (Muñoz & Tormos, 2014; Serrano, 2013 a). This is of particular importance, given the socio-demographics of Catalonia, where a majority of the population has ascendancy ties with the rest of Spain, which indicates the importance of factors other than ethnocultural reproduction to understand recent changes in attitudes towards self-government.

According to the classical literature, in pluri-national states, individuals can feel attached to both their regional and state identities (Miller, 1995; Moreno, 2001). This 'traditional' approach expects that secessionist tensions appear where the ethno-territorial identity is shared by the majority of the population. Conversely, when dual identities are strong secessionist, tensions would tend to be weaker, especially if devolution arrangements are in place (Brancati, 2006).

In accordance with this view, decentralisation should have resulted in an increasing identification with both Spain and Catalonia. However, the evolution of national identity since the recovery of democracy shows interesting variations in the long and the short term. The percentage of the population identifying themselves as equally Spanish and Catalans remained quite stable until 2010, but then it fell almost ten points in the next five years. Asymmetrical and exclusive identifications follow a diverging path. Predominant identification as Catalan, either expressing a feeling of being More Catalan than Spanish or Only Catalan, show an increasing trend, more stable in the first case and more accelerated in the second case, particularly after the approval of the Statute in 2006. Identification as More Spanish than Catalan has remained stable throughout the period, while exclusive identification (Only Spanish) shows an almost linear decline to current levels below ten per cent of the population. Different factors can account for the evolution of national identification, from the ageing population that moved to Catalonia during the massive migrations of 1960 s, to the socialization of younger generations under a regional government with nation-building competences in key areas such as education and mass media. Much can be discussed as to what extent political changes and perceptions can influence national identity, and not just the other way round, as well as the extent to which this two-way interaction responds to the recent political and economic juncture. Nonetheless, the overall evidence clearly puts into question the expectations that devolution would foster dual identities as a stable scenario.

Graph 1. Evolution of national identification 1979-2104

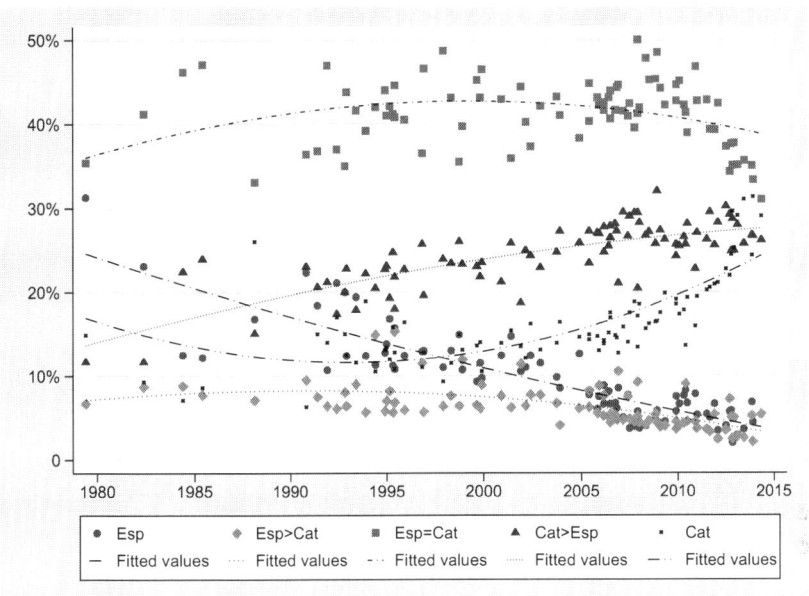

Source: Opinion Studies from Centro de Investigaciones Sociológicas (CIS), Centro de Investigaciones de la Realidad Social (CIRES), Centre d'Estudis d'Opinió (CIS) and Institut de Ciències Polítiques i Socials (ICPS).

While change in national identification can be slower than political attitudes, the analysis of territorial preferences offers a more sensitive dimension to political and institutional events. The process of statutory reform started in 2003 was seen as an opportunity to advance towards a stable accommodation of self-government demands and even towards the federalisation of the state. Since the mid-1990 s, and until the ruling of the Constitutional Court in 2010, support for independence remains stable, representing around one fifth of the population. Elements such as the economic crisis or the government of the People's Party since 2011 can play a significant role reinforcing the growing support for independence. Nonetheless, the data raises the question of whether the triggering factor of current levels of support for independence is rather a political response to the process of Statute reform (Guibernau, 2013; Serrano, 2013 b) .

Graph 2. Evolution of constitutional preferences 1991-2014

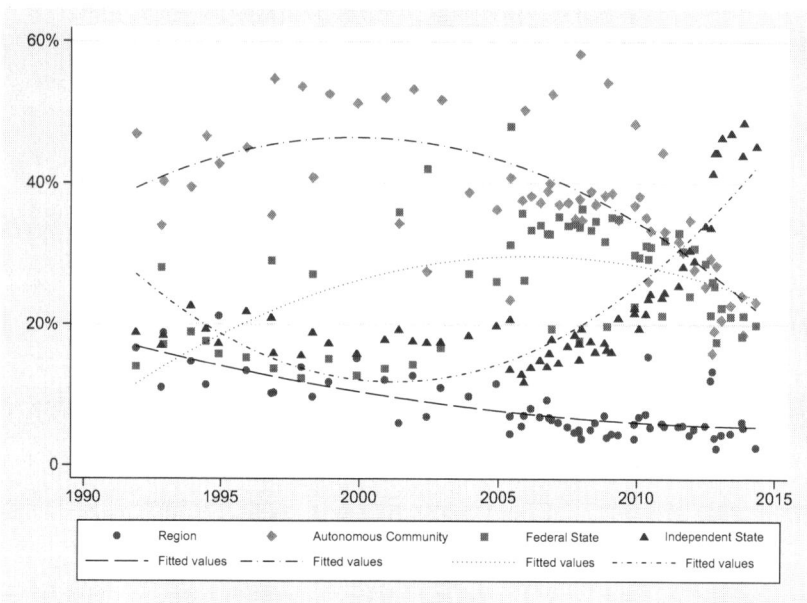

Source: Opinion Studies from CIRES, CEO, CIS and ICPS.

Analysis of the evolution of attitudes towards independence and identity suggests that the Catalan case does not clearly follow the exclusivist hypothesis, which suggests that support for independence corresponds only to those individuals with an exclusive sense of Catalan identity. Despite the growing support for independence over the last few years, the weight of exclusive Catalan identity has remained quite stable since mid- 1990 s, representing around one half of the total. There are two elements that account for this stable pattern in the distribution of support for independence by identity groups. First, exclusive Catalan identity has grown around ten points during the process to reform the Statute of Autonomy. Simultaneously, support for independence within this group has also grown, becoming the most preferred option for nine out of ten respondents. On the other hand, support for independence has also spread among groups with dual identities, particularly those declaring a feeling of being More Catalan than Spanish and, to a much lesser degree, those declaring themselves as Equally Catalan and Spanish.

Graph 3. Support for independence and exclusive identities

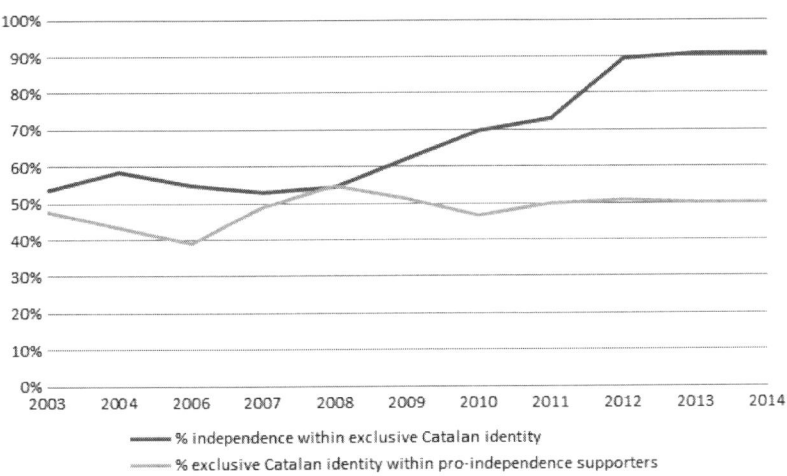

Source: CEO

This evolution raises a number of questions about the relation between identity and attitudes towards independence, and how they can change with time. Both territorial preferences and national identification have significantly changed during the last years. This suggests the possibility that not only identity shapes political attitudes, but it could be the other way around. In other words, political attitudes could also influence national identification. This would imply that the identity of individuals can also be, at least partially, a rationalisation of their political preferences (Fernández-i-Marın, Rodon & Serrano, 2013; Muñoz & Tormos, 2014). The existence of this mechanism would improve our understanding of some of the particularities of the Catalan case.

Thus, individuals may shape their identity based on ethnocultural reproduction mechanisms, but they can be also influenced by nation-building policies. Moreover, national identification and its political expressions can be the result not only of ethnocultural reproduction mechanisms, but of socialization processes linked to competing state's and sub-state's nation-building policies. This complexity is clearly seen from analysis of the attitudes towards independence with regard to national identity and origins, or to the perceptions about the existing levels of autonomy.

In the case of identity and origins, different patterns can be found when analysing support for independence. Identity seems to follow an exponential distribution, with relevant levels of support for independence mostly found among predominant and exclusive Catalan identities. While this structure shows the important effects of identity, we cannot take for granted that it is only explained by an ethnocultural factor. In fact, if we distinguish by origins, we find a linear pattern in which all groups do feature relevant levels of support for independence.

Graph 4. Vote in the referendum by national identity

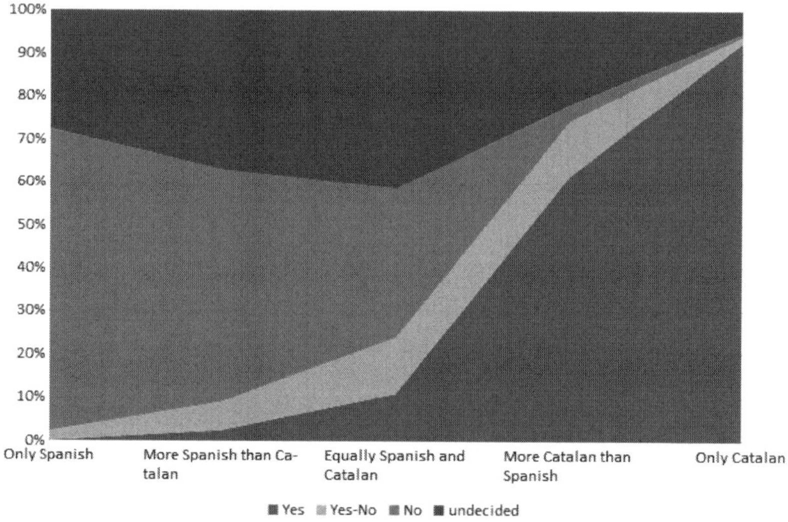

Source: CEO, April 2014.

Graph 5. Vote in the referendum by origins

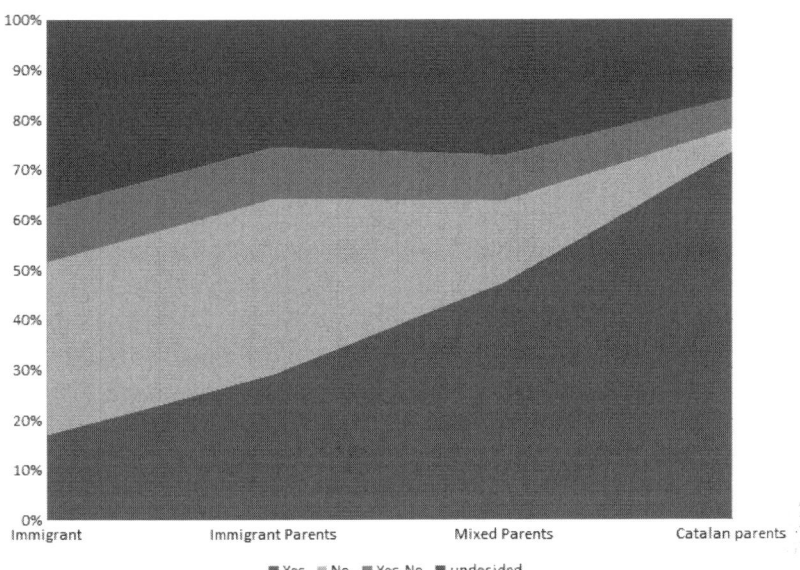

Source: CEO, April 2014. Categories of origins include 'Immigrant' for those respondents born in the rest of Spain, 'Immigrant parents' for population born in Catalonia with both parents born in the rest of Spain, 'Mixed parents' for respondents with one parent born in the rest of Spain, and 'Catalan parents' for those individuals with both parents born in Catalonia.

Together with the evolution of territorial preferences, identity and origins, along with the complex relations that emerge among them, the perception and attitudes towards self-government may have also affected attitudes towards independence. Territorial preferences reflect how individuals express their general views about the existing levels of self-government. Around two-thirds of the population consider the current autonomic arrangements insufficient. This perception has followed an increasing trend, but it is actually within a stable interval between 60 and 70% of the population. This trend is shown in Graph 6.

Graph 6. Perception of the current level of self-government

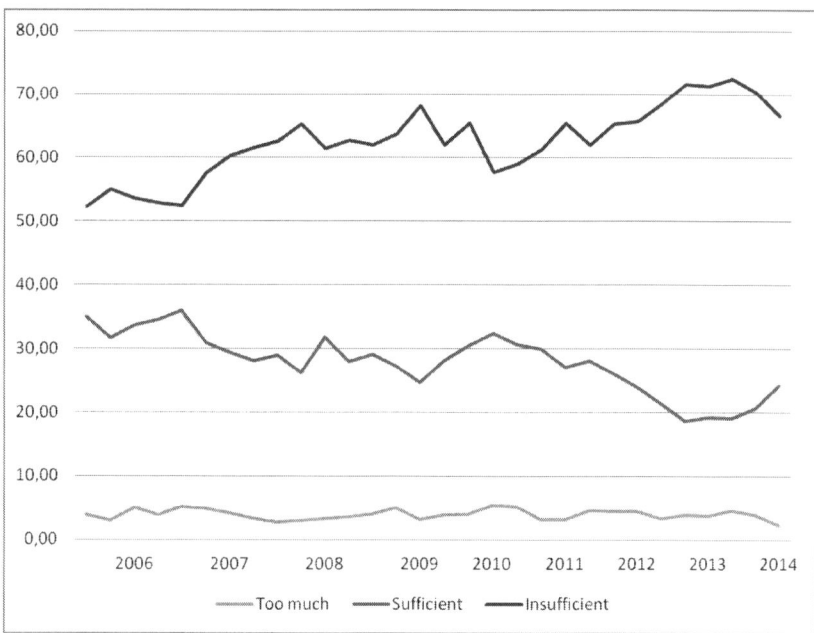

Source: CEO

After the ruling of the Constitutional Court, the perception of a failure of accommodation seems to have a relevant, though limited, effect on the evaluation of autonomy. On closer analysis, we find a relevant effect on the territorial preferences of those considering the existing autonomy as insufficient. Preferences within this group have dramatically changed during this period. At the beginning of the process of statutory reform, just one fifth of respondents considering autonomy as insufficient opted for independence. Instead, the majority preferred the existing framework to accommodate the demand for more self-government, basically in the form of a federal state. After the ruling of the Constitutional Court in 2010, self-government preferences in the form of more autonomy (as a federal State within Spain) rapidly declined. Conversely, support for independence becomes the most preferred option by more than 60% of respondents within this group.

Graph 7. Preferences for a federal or independent state among those considering self-government as insufficient.

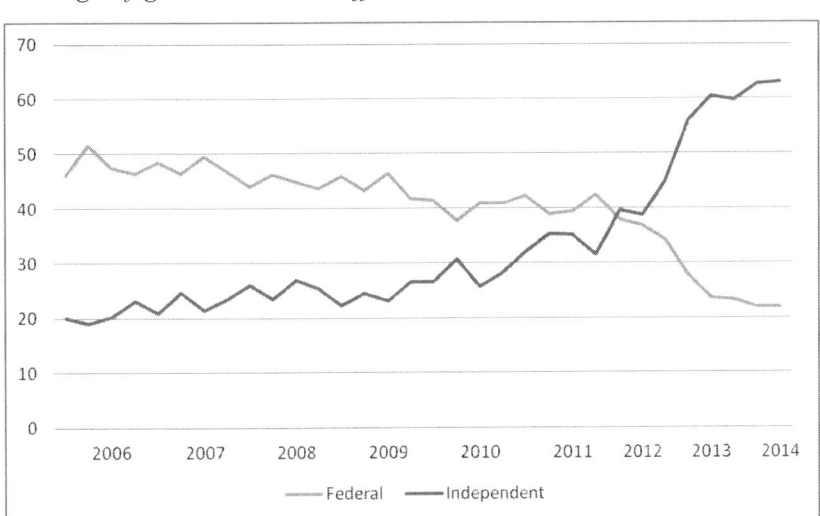

Source: CEO

A final question to address is why individuals support or reject independence, i.e. how they explicitly mention the reasons for opposing or supporting independence. The literature has discussed a number of factors to explain the probability of a given individual to support or reject independence, from identity to instrumental or material reasons. However, to establish clear causal relations between attitudes and reasons argued in support or opposition to secession raises important questions, such as to what extent individuals rationalise their preferences, or, on the contrary, to what extent do their perceptions and policy preferences shape their position towards the question. Beyond further implications in terms of causality, the reasons explicitly mentioned to support or reject independence well reflect some of the classical debates in the literature about the identity-driven factors in state and sub-state nationalism. Among the reasons for supporting independence, the most frequently mentioned refer to welfare and economic factors. Conversely, less than 15% of respondents mention ideas referring to Catalan identity or the concept of Catalonia as a nation. More interestingly, respondents rejecting independence mention their concerns about the unity of Spain or Spanish identity as the main reasons to oppose independence. The range of responses is closely related with the terms of the current debate and the nationalist discourse on independence, which emphasize welfare and democratic reasons. Nonetheless, the structure of reasons for favouring or opposing independence also raises an interesting research area because it questions the dichotomy between a civic nationalism at the state level and an ethnic one at the sub-state level (Kuzio, 2002; Máiz, 2004; Serrano, 2008).

Graph 8A. Reasons for supporting independence
Graph 8B. Reasons for rejecting independence

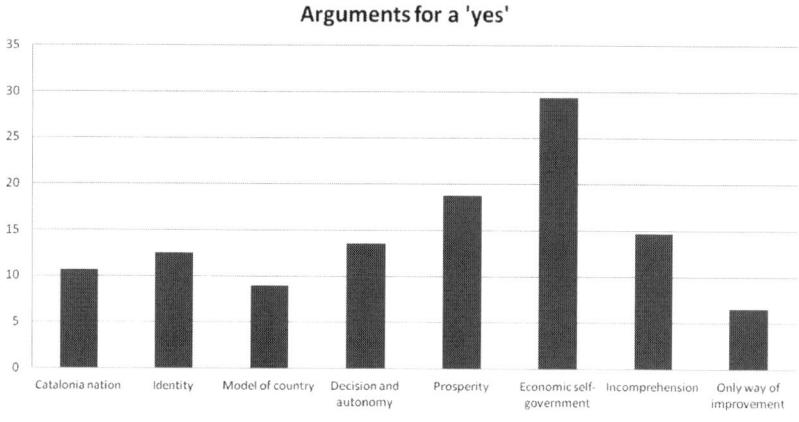

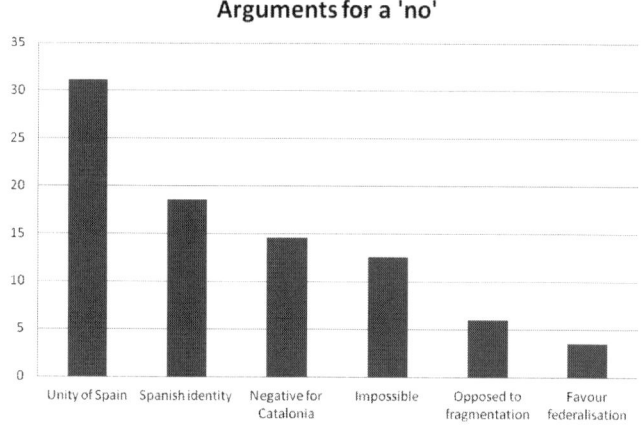

Source: CEO, November 2013

4. Conclusions

Spain can be defined as a pluri-national state with an institutional and constitutional framework that would potentially allow for a significant territorial decentralisation. On the other hand, Catalonia is a sub-state region in which approximately 70% of the population have been born or have at least one parent born in the rest of the State, with a minority nationalism that had been traditionally non-secessionist. These are some of the features that made the Catalan and Spanish case a clear candidate for a sustainable arrangement of self-government short of independence. Despite these elements, the question of self-determination and even independence has nonetheless become the fundamental issue of the political agenda in the last few years. This chapter has offered an overview of institutional and public opinion factors to better understand this trend, even though this is an ongoing process with an uncertain outcome that will surely deserve attention in the future.

References

Brancati, D. (2006). Decentralization: Fueling the Fire or Dampening the Flames of Ethnic Conflict and Secessionism. International Organization 60, Summer, 60(3), 651–685.

Commission, T. E. (2013). *Referendum on independence for Scotland Advice of the Electoral Commission on the proposed referendum question.* United Kingdom. Retrieved from http://www.electoralcommission.org.uk/find-information-by-subject/elections-and-referendums/upcoming-elections-and-referendums/scottish-referendum

Fernández-i-Marın, X., Rodon, T., & Serrano, I. (2013). Decided or undecided: An investigation of individual's (in) decision to Catalan independence. Retrieved from http://www.aecpa.es/uploads/files/modules/congress/11/papers/823.pdf

Guibernau, M. (2013). Secessionism in Catalonia: After Democracy. *Ethnopolitics*, *12*(4), 368–393.

Kuzio, T. (2002). The myth of the civic state: a critical survey of Hans Kohn's framework for understanding nationalism. *Ethnic and Racial Studies*, *25*(1), 20–39.

Llei Orgànica 6/2006, de 19 de juliol, de reforma de l'Estatut d'autonomia de Catalunya (2006). Retrieved from http://www20.gencat.cat/portal/site/portaldogc/menuitem.c973d2fc58aa0083e4492d92b0c0e1a0/?vgnextoid=485946a6e5dfe210Vgn-VCM1000000b0c1e0aRCRD&appInstanceName=default&action=fitxa&documentId=401680

Máiz, R. (2004). Per modum unius: más allá de la dicotomía nacionalismo cívico vs. nacionalismo étnico. In Ander Gurrutxaga Abad (Ed.), *El presente del Estado-Nación* (pp. 107–128). Bilbao: Universidad del País Vasco.

Miller, D. (1995). *On nationality* (p. 210 p.). Oxford: Oxford University Press.

Moreno, M. F. (2001). *The Federalization of Spain* (p. 210). London: Frank Cass.

Muñoz, J., & Tormos, R. (2014). Economic expectations and support for secession in Catalonia: between causality and rationalization. *European Political Science Review*, 1–27.

Supreme Court of Canada. (1998). "Reference on the Secession of Quebec". Retrieved from http://scc-csc.lexum.com/scc-csc/scc-csc/en/item/1643/index.do

Serrano, I. (2008). The state's response to the Catalan question: an emerging ethnic component in contemporary Spanish nationalism?. In: Nationalism, East and West: Ethnic and Civic Conceptions of Nationhood. Association for the Study of Ethnicity and Nationalism. London School of Economics. London, 15 - 17 April.

Serrano, I. (2013 a). Just a Matter of Identity? Support for Independence in Catalonia. *Regional & Federal Studies*, 23(5), 523–545.

Serrano, I. (2013 b). Secession in Catalonia: Beyond Identity? *Ethnopolitics*, *12*(4), 406–409.

Spanish Constitution (1978). Spanish Congress. Retrieved from http://www.tribunal-constitucional.es/en/constitucion/Pages/ConstitucionIngles.aspx

Venice Commission: Council of Europe. (2008). Retrieved from http://www.venice.coe.int/webforms/documents/?pdf=CDL-INF(2000)002

Vilaregut, R. (2011). *Memòria i emergència en l'independentisme català. El cas de la Plataforma pel Dret de Decidir*. Doctoral dissertation. Retrieved from http://tdx.cesca.cat/handle/10803/96812

Which people? Exploration of the role of immigration in the secessionist process of Catalonia

Núria Franco-Guillén

1. Introduction

On January 2nd 2014, the former leader of the anti-immigrant Plataforma per Catalunya (PxC), Josep Anglada, ignited the Web after commenting on a picture of a black child wearing the Catalan secessionist flag, "Estelada". His tweet said: "We are screwed. If these are the new Catalans, I leave Catalonia. Our people first!".[1] Within two days, the child's parents had already answered the politician and created an account in which hundreds of so-called "new Catalans" sent pictures of themselves saying "Mr. Anglada, I'm also a new Catalan; you can leave if you like," and many of them wore the secessionist flag. It was one of the first *mass* political expression with regards to the Process[2] by immigrants in Catalonia. We have, however, little information about how immigration relates to processes of secession, and even less when it comes to the case of Catalonia.

Catalonia, self-defined as a *terra d'acollida*[3], takes for granted that it is a land where several migration waves have contributed to the construction of the country, and therefore this question is of vital importance. Theories of secession often deal with questions such as: "what sort of group is entitled to secession?", often leaving aside the individuals entitled to join the group. Even in current debates on the Process in Catalonia, some independentists have defended the idea of using the current electoral census that excludes individuals who are not Spanish nationals (E-notícies, 2014) as the basis defining the group. In other words, immigrants are somehow ignored in this process. Among all the parties' proposals for the Declaration of Sovereignty of the Catalan People approved by the Parliament in 2013, only one (the

---

1 Own translation. Notice must be taken that this political party does not participate in the Process (see footnote 2) and in fact is opposed to it.
2 The political situation in Catalonia has received many names. For the sake of brevity I call it "the Process" as it currently appears in the media.
3 Land of reception, welcome.

Candidatura d'Unitat Popular, CUP) took this explicitly into account, mentioning 'the People of Catalonia, regardless of their citizenship status' (Candidatura d'Unitat Popular, 2013).

One may wonder whether within the Process immigration is a relevant phenomenon to be taken seriously by political elites. This chapter tries to justify the relevance of the link between secession and immigration regarding Catalonia, and provide an overview of the main positions of the elites with regard to this issue. To do so, I first try to map out the literature that links immigration to stateless nations so as to refer to the territorial cleavage and how immigration relates to it. The case of Catalonia is then addressed, starting with a contextualisation of immigration in Catalonia. Finally, the main pro-independence stakeholders' positions and strategies related to it are examined[4].

2. Immigration and secession

Normative theories on secession and the right of self-determination often seek to answer questions such as: under what conditions does a group have the right to secede, and, more concretely, under what conditions the group should be considered as entitled to that right? Buchanan (1997) made a distinction between Remedial Right Only Theories and Primary Right Only Theories, the latter revolving around the characteristics that the group must possess to have a primary right to secede. Thus, the question of "who is the People" is key in this field of research, just as it is in theories of nationalism that have often distinguished between civic and ethnic forms of nationalism[5]. This distinction has often been linked to the dichotomy liberal (plus civic) versus illiberal (plus ethnic) nationalism (Ignatieff, 1995). In this context, most stateless nations have been included in the second group, despite

---

4 This information has been gathered through interviews with the main representatives charged with immigration issues among pro-referendum elites, including political parties and civil society, between May and July 2014.

5 See Smith (1971) for a broader classification. Although broadly criticized, as Keating (1997) points out, the civic/ethnic dichotomy is the most commonly used by scholars and is based on the contraposition of subjective (willingness) versus objective (race, religion, blood or, in certain cases, language) characteristics to determine inclusion/belonging to a nation.

claims by some scholars that they are often more liberal than some State-wide nationalisms (Kymlicka, 2001; Keating & McGarry, 2001).

The arrival of immigration to stateless nations opened a branch of research that deals with the intersection of different cultural claims.[6] This research has often departed from the premise that immigrants tend to integrate into the State nation (Zapata-Barrero, 2009). Thus, immigration poses specific challenges for stateless nations as it strengthens a fear of internal minoriza-tion, which could contribute to their assimilation into the majority nation. This interaction raises several questions related to both political and policy responses on the one hand[7], and immigrant responses on the other. The pos-sibility of a referendum in Catalonia raises important questions when it comes to immigration. Immigration policy can be seen as a tool not only for the central State[8], but for the Stateless Nation, who may consider immigrants as allies (Hepburn, 2014). In this sense, immigration intersects with the cen-tre-periphery cleavage and has an influence in its three main dimensions (identity, territory and economy) with the underlying question of whether minority nationalism can incorporate newcomers to its nation-building project. In the extreme case of secession, the general question is, again, whether Stateless Nationalism can incorporate immigrants into their State-building project.

This question remains largely under-researched. However, the case of Quebec after its two referendums on sovereignty has caught the interest of researchers. In the context of the latest referendum and according to the 1993 Canadian Election Study, Anglophones (92.2%) and Allophones (94.2%) opposed sovereignty, and, as Conley (1997) argued, sovereignty cleaved Quebecers along ethno-linguistic lines. This left almost all immigrants on the "no" side. Regardless of whether immigration really was an obstacle to Quebec's independence, this experience is interesting and serves as a prece-dent for examining the Catalan case.

As already mentioned, immigration is clearly interlinked with the main dimensions of the centre-periphery cleavage - identity, territory (power) and economy. The existence of an identity distinct from the centre (and therefore loyalty) is a necessary condition for the emergence/maintenance of the

---

6 See Zapata-Barrero (2007) for an overview of the main challenges.

7 For an overview including several cases, see Hepburn and Zapata-Barrero (eds.) (2014).

8 The central State can follow a policy of encouraging immigrants to settle in the State-less Nation's territory with the purpose of undermining national diversity.

cleavage (Rokkan & Urwin, 1983). Arguably, the stronger the loyalty to the periphery, the more likely that secessionist movements might emerge. Conversely, high levels of loyalty to the centre should help to attenuate the rise of secessionist movements. In this context, subjective national identification (SNI) can help to predict certain voting decisions on an eventual referendum on independence. As Serrano (2013) shows, in Catalonia where dual identity is widespread, while individuals reporting an exclusive Catalan identity significantly express support for independence, the contrary does not hold, and feeling exclusively Spanish does not predict opposition to independence. The realm of identity is complex, not only in Stateless nations where important proportions of dual identity are reported, but in general in Western Democracies and more concretely in old immigration countries in which multiple identities are reported by individuals. It is, however, one of the key issues at stake when thinking about stateless nationalism, and more concretely, secessionism within these political regimes. Hence, elites may well wonder how newcomers feel about their reception societies. In the case of Quebec, Banting & Soroka (2012) showed how the existence of competing loyalties in Quebec prevent immigrants from developing a sense of belonging to either Quebec, Canada or both, as strongly as in the rest of the Canadian provinces.

The distribution of power in the management of immigration might, however, influence party positions towards immigration (Hepburn, 2009), and it has influenced the intensity of debates and the relationship with the centre. It even has a potential influence on the case for independence (Zapata-Barrero, 2012). In fact, the lack of these powers on immigration not only affects sub-state governments, but the immigrants themselves who are often obliged to follow long paths towards resident and/or work permit acquisition with the central administration, while using public services that are provided by other levels of administration. It has also been suggested that the opposition of some stateless nationalists to the central-state's policies might explain their positive stance towards immigration (Jeram, 2012). Indeed, they often propose more progressive policies (especially in realms where they have no power, such as citizenship) than the ones proposed by the central state.

In the realm of the economy, there is no doubt that the relative economic status of the different regions helps us to understand a part of the relationship between the centre and the periphery. For some, including Urwin and Rokkan, the economy only acts as a catalyst for political mobilisation, with identity and territory being the necessary conditions for the emergence of the cleavage, and therefore of relatively more important. The prominent role of immigration for the economic growth of developed democracies is clear, and on these grounds immigration has been a source of conflict between the centre and the periphery, as in Scotland, where it has been seen as a booster for the economy (Salmond, 2003).

3. *Immigration in Catalonia*

As a receiver of newcomers, Catalonia presents some interesting features. In Spain in general it is a so-called "new immigration country". It started receiving immigrants from other parts of the world in the 70's when the rest of Autonomous Communities were net senders of migrants, with a flow that grew in the 80's and rapidly accelerated in the 90's (Ribas, 1997). This migratory wave is characterised by its intensity and diversity of origins. Indeed, in 2000 international migration represented 2.9% of the Catalan population, increasing to 15.6% in 2012 (Brugué & González, 2013). Today, 17.6% of its residents were born outside Spain (INE, 2014).[9] 80 countries are represented by groups larger than 500 residents, 50% of them coming from African and South American countries.

Despite this seemingly intense activity, Catalonia has a long experience in receiving people from beyond its border. In fact, having one of the lowest fertility rates in the world, migration has been the main pillar of the so-called Catalan System of Reproduction, which was initially based on receiving people from the rest of Spain[10]. Catalonia's migratory experience is in fact frequently tabled in Parliamentary debates (Franco-Guillén & Zapata-Barrero, 2014), which helps to explain why the idea put forward by the socialist, Rafael Campalans, that "anyone who lives and works in Catalonia is Catalan," has been embraced by all political forces.

We still do not know how the Process will culminate; whether a referendum or plebiscitary elections will take place, let alone who will be entitled to participate in the final decision. To date, a "participative process" has been

---

9 To be clear, immigrants are considered here as those habitants born outside the country, regardless of their citizenship.

10 See Cabré (2008) for an in-depth explanation of this System. As this demographer ironized in a reference to another Catalan demographer who predicted this process at the beginning of century, technically speaking, Catalonia ceased to be "Catalan" by 1954.

held on the 9th November 2014.[11] The process was open to anyone residing in Catalonia and to Catalan expatriates. The following table gives estimates of two scenarios showing the relative importance of immigrants within the Process. (1) The distribution resulting under the application of Spanish electoral rules (which would apply in case of plebiscitary elections and includes only Spanish nationals). (2) The distribution between autochthonous voters and voters born outside Spain, used for the Participative Process (residents over 16 years old).

	Autochthonous voters	Voters with immigrant background
Scenario 1	5.004.698	252,554
	95,2%	4,8%
Scenario 2	5,082,212	1,180,783
	81.1%	18.9%

[Source: Own elaboration. INE, 2014[12]]

We can see that the Participative Process held on the 9th November 2014 called on more than one million people born outside Spain, representing almost 19% of the "census". Besides, if plebiscitary elections were to be held, 5.4% of the census would have an immigrant background, which shows that immigrants can have an important influence on the results.

We have very little information about the voting behaviour of immigrants in Catalonia. In some cases, immigrants voting behaviour has been described as a "block vote" against the "social vote" of autochthones, as it seems there is a transition period during which all immigrants tend to vote in the same way as the majority of their community members do (Lavoie & Serré, 2002). If this was to be the case in Catalonia, the main nationalities (Morocco, Romania, Ecuador and Colombia) all voting in the same way could be crucial to the outcome.

---

11 In September 2014, the Catalan government approved a consultation law and its subsequent decree, calling on a ballot. A few days later, the law was suspended by the Constitutional Court until its final decision over the constitutionality of the norm, thereby preventing the applicability of the decree. As a reaction, the Catalan government opted for maintaining the date and the question, but altering the procedures and the name of the event, now being a "participative process".

12 For scenario 1 the data has been retrieved from the election register, and for scenario 2, from the general census register (Padron Municipal). The data is approximate as it does not include Catalans living abroad..

The only indication as to how immigrants might vote that exists in Catalonia is the wave of consultations that were organised by civil society associations in over 500 municipalities between 2009 and 2011.[13] Despite not having the global disaggregated results, the results for the city of Barcelona (consultation celebrated in 2011) show overall a low interest in this issue:

Table 2. Participation in Barcelona's Consultation

	Total votes	Immigrant votes	Immigrants over 16	Population over 16
Totals	257,645	10,247	246,066	1,070,317
% of population Over 16	24.1%	1.0%	23.0%	

Source: Instituto Nacional de Estadística (INE, 2013) and Barcelona Decideix webpage: http://www.barcelonadecideix.cat/noticia/4221/vots-per-districtes

Table 2 shows that in the city of Barcelona, 23% of the population eligible to participate had an immigrant background. However, only 4.16% of immigrants entitled to vote did so. This low turnout might be explained by three factors: first, by a lack of knowledge or interest within immigrant communities; second, because those referendums had no legal basis at all and were semi-spontaneous activities; and third, because immigrants were very reluctant to show the required identity documents to vote, even more so when the electoral board had to register them[14]. Some of these aspects have or could change in the near future and therefore would change immigrants' decisions on participating.

Unlike the rest, the ICPS Opinion Survey (2012) includes people born outside Spain. The following table shows which people would vote "if a referendum on independence was held tomorrow", but bear in mind that this sample only comprises 234 individuals of this kind.

---

13 As for the Participative Process of the 9th November, residents over 16 years, regardless of their citizenship, were entitled to vote.

14 These were the main arguments observed during the referendum campaign in an immigrant neighborhood in Mataró, were the author carried out participant observation.

Table 3. Positions on an eventual referendum.

	Immigrants	Autochthones	Totals
Yes	73	485	558
	13.1%	86.9%	100 %
	31.2%	50.2%	46.5%
No	71	274	345
	20.6%	79.4%	100%
	30.3%	28.4%	28.8%
Abstention	70	126	196
	35.7%	64.3%	100%
	29.9%	13.0%	16.3%
Blank vote	3	17	20
	15.0%	85.0%	100.0%
	1.3%	1.8%	1.7%
Don't know	16	58	74
	21.6%	78.4%	100%
	6.8%	6.0%	6.2%
No Answer	1	6	7
	14.3%	85.7%	100%
	0.4%	0.6%	0.6%
Totals	234	966	1200
	19.5%	80.5%	100%

Source: Institut de Ciències Polítiques i Socials (ICPS) Sondeig d'opinió Catalunya, 2012.

While a majority of autochthones (50.2%) would vote yes, in the case of people born abroad there is no clear winning option, and immigrants are split between voting yes, no or abstaining.

4. Stateless nationalist elites and immigration

This section maps the positions of the main actors' on immigration, which are briefly described and are based on previous analysis of the author (Franco-Guillén & Zapata-Barrero, 2014); strategic actions, if any, are also explained.

4.1 Political parties[15]

Convergència i Unió (CiU):

CiU is a centre-right coalition of two parties, currently ruling the Catalan government (Generalitat): the centrist Convergència Democràtica de Catalunya (CDC) and the Christian democrats Unió Democràtica per Catalunya. Overall, CiU has expressed positive stances towards immigration at the Autonomous Community level, especially in their electoral manifestos. This positive stance can be identified in discourses highlighting positive or neutral aspects about immigration. This has been accompanied by a (re)description of the Catalan nation into overall civic terms, which is suited to the integration of immigrants into the minority nation. At the local level, however, the attitude of CiU is quite volatile, ranging from a very positive stance in the case of the Barcelona branch to a more negative one in the case of Vic and other important Catalan municipalities, such as Reus or Mataró (Garcés Mascareñas, Franco-Guillén, & Sánchez-Montijano, 2011). Strategically, the CDC has created the Fundació Nous Catalans that acts as a mobiliser for immigrants and as a think tank for the party. This foundation, as its president, Angel Colom (interview, May 2014), acknowledges, invests most of its time today disseminating information about independence among immigrants and immigrant associations. As its president explained, the Foundation has developed a briefing on the benefits of independence, which is translated and adapted to several minority languages and dialects. A series of conferences on independence for immigrant groups across the territory are also being programmed.

Esquerra Republicana de Catalunya (ERC):

Since transition to democracy, this left wing party has traditionally been smaller than CiU in electoral terms, but managed to substantially increase its success in the last elections in 2012, after which it supported CiU's minority government. ERC's discourse on immigration is clearly positive and mainly based on the principle of equal opportunities. The party's positions

---

15 Interviews with responsible on immigration of the main parties were held, with the exception of the Candidatura d'Unitat Popular (CUP), which, due to its specific organization, has no responsible as such.

are the same both at the local, autonomous and central levels of government. Despite its current success, ERC has a smaller structure and less resources, which means it is unable to invest in immigrant mobilization. As a former regional minister of welfare commented, the party struggles to recruit new members, especially women, and cannot afford to create specific campaigns or structures (Interview, April 2012). Therefore, there is no institution like the Nous Catalans. According to its representative (Oriol Amorós, interview May 2014), ERC also holds an inclusive vision of citizenship that does not look at origins. In this sense, a specific strategy aiming at immigration is hardly predictable.

According to both party representatives, in the event of a referendum or consultation, anyone residing in Catalonia for at least two years and is older than 16 should be entitled to vote. In the hypothetical case of the creation of a Catalan State, both representatives defended the approval of a "Juridical continuity law" in which all rights and status possessed under the Spanish Regime would remain in place until the approval of a Catalan Constitution. On this last issue, CiU considers that the status of foreigners should be decided in the constituent discussions, while ERC defends that anyone residing in Catalonia (for two years) at the time of independence should be considered part of the "Founding People," thus having equal rights to Catalan Citizenship.

Iniciativa per Catalunya-Verds (ICV):

This eco-socialist party has not adopted an official position on independence, and members have different individual positions ranging from federalism to independence. The party clearly defends the right to decide and the celebration of a consultation on sovereignty. In a vein similar to ERC, the party takes a positive stance towards immigration, and considers citizenship in an inclusive way. According to its representative, newcomers should have the right to participate in the consultation and be considered Catalan citizens in case of independence (Gabriela Poblet, interview May 2014). In this context, the party organized a debate with immigrants' representatives to get an overview of the main challenges that should be taken into account in the Process, and in the hypothetical scenarios after the consultation.

4.2 Civil society[16]

Assemblea Nacional Catalana (ANC):

The ANC is the main civic organization that is today driving the Process towards the use of the right to decide and independence. It was the main organizer of the main civil society's actions, as in the massive demonstration on the 11th September (Catalonia's national day), 2012, the human chain that went from the French Pyrenees to the Valencian community (the so-called Via Catalana) on the 11th September 2013, and the demonstration in 2014 that took the shape of a V, with over one million people occupying two main streets in Barcelona. The assembly is organized into territorial sub-units and sectorial assemblies. The Immigrants' Sectorial assembly of the ANC was created by Diego Arcos (Argentinian House of Barcelona, interview May 2014) and other prominent individuals of the immigrant associative world in Catalonia. Despite the interviewee's acknowledging that the sectorial has few members, during its years of existence it has organized several activities throughout the country with the purpose of inviting newcomers to participate in the process of creating a new State. The main objective is to raise awareness that all individuals who reside in Catalonia are part of its People, and therefore should be entitled not only to participate, but to vote in an eventual referendum.

4.3 Government

Generalitat de Catalunya:

The Catalan government has not taken an official stance in favour of independence, despite the governing party being so. However, it received a clear mandate from the Catalan Parliament to hold a consultation on independence. The executive has a Directorate General for Immigration within the Social Welfare and Family Department. Its Citizenship and Migration Plan (Horitzó 2016) contains five axes/cross-sectional areas of action, the last one being called "national transition". This section sets the objective of informing newcomers of and raising their awareness to the "process of national

---

16 Notice must be taken of the existence of Súmate, an organization created by Spanish-speaking independentists. However, this entity does not target immigrants.

transition" that the country is undergoing with the objective of fostering their engagement in it. The Plan, however, does not include more concrete actions or proposals, and no budget is provided for it. On this issue, the Directorate General is awaiting clearer formulations of the "Process" in order to design a concrete strategy, and the budget is to be taken from different departments as immigration is a cross-sectional issue (General Director of Immigration, interview July 2014).

5. Conclusions

This paper has explored the relationship between immigration and independence. Primary and secondary sources of information have been analyzed, including data from interviews and the exploitation of quantitative data available.

Whether immigration can be an asset for independence is a question that depends on how the Process will materialize, and whether and how immigrants will be included and involved. The more inclusive the consultation is, the higher the influence immigrants may have on the final result. The position of the pro-consultation elites is that immigration is to be taken into account in the process and immigrants should be invited to participate. The general view is inclusive, rather than exclusive, and each actor, as far as respective circumstances allow, tries to include immigrants into the Process. Awareness about the lack of information about immigrants' opinion on politics in Catalonia also needs to be raised.

References

Banting, K., & Soroka, S. (2012). Minority nationalism and immigrant integration in Canada. Nations and Nationalism, 18(1), 156–176. doi:10.1111/j. 1469-8129.2011.00535.x

Brugué, Q., & González, S. (2013). *Informe sobre la integració de les persones immigrades a Catalunya*. Barcelona.

Buchanan, A. (1997). Theories of Secession. *Philosophy & Public Affairs*, 26(1), 31–61. doi:10.1111/j.1088-4963.1997.tb00049.x

Cabré, A. (2008). Les onades migratòries en el sistema català de reproducció. *Papers de Demografia*, 328, 1–10.

Candidatura d'Unitat Popular. (2013). Declaració de sobirania del Parlament de Catalunya. Barcelona: Candidatura d'Unitat Popular. Retrieved from http://cup.cat/sites/default/files/declaricio_de_sobirania_del_poble_catala.pdf

Conley, R. S. (1997). Sovereignty or the status quo? The 1995 pre-referendum debate in Quebec. *The Journal of Commonwealth & Comparative Politics, 35*(1), 67–92. doi:10.1080/14662049708447739

E-notícies. (n.d.). Campanya perquè puguem votar. *E-Notícies*, p. online. Barcelona. Retrieved from http://noves-tecnologies.e-noticies.cat/campanya-perque-puguem-votar-85212.html

Franco-Guillén, N., & Zapata-Barrero, R. (2014). Catalunya terra d'acollida: Stateless Nationalist Parties Discourses on Immigration. In: E. Hepburn & R. Zapata-Barrero (Eds.), *The politics of immigration in multi-level states: governance and political parties* (pp. 261–284). Basingstoke: Palgrave Macmillan.

Garcés Mascareñas, B., Franco-Guillén, N., & Sánchez-Montijano, E. (2011). Entre la inclusión y la exclusión. Los discursos políticos en las elecciones municipales de 2011 en Cataluña. In: E. Aja, J. Arango, & J. Oliver Alonso (Eds.), *La hora de la integración: Anuario de la Inmigración en España (edición 2011)* (pp. 263–285). Barcelona: CIDOB Foundation.

Hepburn, E. (2009). Regionalist Party Mobilisation on Immigration. *West European Politics, 32*(3), 514–535. Retrieved from http://dx.doi.org/10.1080/01402380902779071

Hepburn, E. (2014). Multilevel Party Politics of Immigration. In: E. Hepburn & R. Zapata-Barrero (Eds.), *The Politics of Immigration in Multi-Level States* (p. 22). Basingstoke: Palgrave Macmillan. doi:10.1057/9781137358530.0010

Ignatieff, M. (1995). *Blood and belonging: journeys into the new nationalism* (p. 263). New York: Noonday Press.

INE (Instituto Nacional de Estadística). (n.d.). Estadística del padrón municipal.

Jeram, S. (2012). Immigrants and the Basque nation: diversity as a new marker of identity. *Ethnic and Racial Studies*, 1–19. doi:10.1080/01419870.2012.664281

Keating, M. (1997). Stateless Nation-Building: Quebec, Catalonia and Scotland in the Changing State System. *Nations and Nationalism, 3*(4), 689–717. doi:10.1111/j.1354-5078.1997.00689.x

Keating, M., & McGarry, J. (2001). *Minority nationalism and the changing international order*. New York: Oxford University Press. Retrieved from http://cataleg.upf.edu/record=b1245212~S11*cat

Kymlicka, W. (2001). *Politics in the vernacular*. Oxford: Oxford University Press.

Lavoie, N., & Serré, P. (2002). Du vote bloc au vote social: le cas des citoyens issus de l'immigration de Montréal, 1995-1996. *Canadian Journal of Political Science/Revue Canadienne de Science Politique, 35*(01), 49–74. doi:10.1017/S0008423902778177

Ribas, N. (1997). Immigració a Catalunya als anys noranta, quelcom de nou? *Revista Catalana de Sociologia, 6*, 33–48.

Rokkan, S., & Urwin, D. W. (1983). *Economy, territory, identity :politics of West European peripheries* (p. 218). London etc.: Sage.

Salmond, A. (2003). "Welcoming incomers can help reverse Scotland's decline" - Salmond speech at St Andrew's University. *Press Release, Scottish National Party.* Edinburgh. Retrieved from www.snp.org

Serrano, I. (2013). Just a Matter of Identity? Support for Independence in Catalonia. *Regional & Federal Studies, 23*(5), 523–545. doi:10.1080/13597566.2013.775945

Smith, A. D. (1971). *Theories of nationalism* (p. 344). London: Duckworth.

Zapata Barrero, R. (2009). *Immigration and self-government of minority nations* (p. 177). Brussels: P.I.E. Peter Lang.

Zapata-Barrero, R. (2007). Setting a Research Agenda on the Interaction Between Cultural Demands of Immigrants and Minority Nations. *Journal of Immigrant & Refugee Studies, 5*(4), 1–25. doi:10.1300/J500 v 05n04_01

Zapata-Barrero, R. (2012). La communauté politique en tant que fondement d'une théorie politique catalane de l'immigration. Enjeux clés. In: M. Labelle, J. Couture, & F. Remiggi (Eds.), *La communauté politique en question. Regards croisés sur l'immigration, la citoyenneté, la diversité et le pouvoir.* (pp. 71–94). Québec: Presses de l'Université du Québec.

Language policy and Catalan independence

Peter A. Kraus

1. Autonomy and 'normalització lingüística'

Since the formative period of the Catalan national movement in the second half of the 19th century, language has been at the core of the *fet diferencial*, thereby constituting the main marker of the socio-cultural features setting Catalonia apart from Spain. For one of the leading figures of early political Catalanism, Enric Prat de la Riba, it was unquestionable that 'language is the most genuine expression of the national spirit and the most powerful instrument of nationalization' (Prat de la Riba 1978 [1906]: 84, own translation). The emphasis on language as the key element of a distinctive nationality was a characteristic that Catalanism shared with the bulk of national movements that emerged in Europe under the influence of Herder and romanticism. The great salience of the language issue continued to be a key factor of Catalan politics after the reestablishment of autonomy in 1980. Jordi Pujol, head of the *Generalitat*, Catalonia's autonomous government, for over 20 years, made the point quite explicitly when he declared in an interview with the Spanish newspaper, *El Mundo* (published on 18 April 1994, own translation): 'Our language policy is the pillar of all our policies in Catalonia, as well as of our policies in Spain'.

The normative frame of language policy in Catalonia was set out in the Statute of Autonomy of 1979. On the basis of the regulations of Spain's new democratic constitution, the Statute assigned Catalan a co-official status, together with Castilian/Spanish. According to the Spanish Constitution (Article 3), Castilian is official throughout the whole territory of the Spanish state, and all citizens have not only the right to use it, but the duty to know it. In addition, the Statute declared in its third article that 'Catalan is Catalonia's own language', which can be interpreted as a subtle formula for giving the vernacular special attention (Kraus 2007: 208). For the vast majority of Catalonia's political forces, this special attention was, and is, sorely needed to compensate for the effects of the massive repression of the Catalan language under the Franco regime. Spanish is also well protected in Catalonia, as elsewhere on Spanish territory, both by the institutional apparatus of the Spanish state and its status as a dominant world language.

The political meaning of the concept of 'own language' – *llengua pròpia* – was fleshed out in the *Llei de Normalització Lingüística*. After long and meticulous preparation, the Law on Language Normalization was passed by the Catalan Parliament in 1983, receiving the support of all political parties represented in the chamber (Moll 1984). This overarching consensus reflects the intention, which has remained a defining trait of Catalan language policy to the present, of avoiding language becoming a matter of socio-cultural divisions, as a substantial portion of Catalonia's citizens have Spanish as their mother tongue. Thus, the Law's purpose was not to ban Spanish, but to improve knowledge of Catalan among the population of Catalonia and increase its use in both public and private settings, thereby contributing to a more balanced bilingualism. This was to be reached by focusing on four main lines of political intervention that should: 1) set up the structures of a regional and local administration functioning in Catalan; 2) successively strengthen the position of Catalan in the educational system; 3) promote Catalan in the mass media by creating the *Corporació Catalana de Radio i Televisió*; and 4) foster the use of Catalan in all domains of social life. With hindsight, one can say that two of these lines turned out to be of particular strategic relevance. On the one hand, the creation of TV 3, the first public TV station broadcasting in Catalan, played a pivotal role in the process of language normalization. On the other hand, at the level of Catalan schools, the instrument used to secure a good knowledge of Catalan among all pupils regardless of their linguistic background, was immersion. Linguistic immersion implies that Catalan is not only a compulsory subject at Catalan schools, as is Spanish, but the standard medium of instruction in most other subjects in the educational curriculum.

Since its introduction, immersion has not generally been a contested issue in Catalan society. In fact, it can be considered a relatively successful instrument, as pupils who have gone through the Catalan school system attain linguistic proficiency in both Catalan and Spanish. With very few exceptions, Spanish-speaking and allophone parents do not object that their children reach a satisfactory level of Catalan, as the language enjoys a relatively high social prestige, at least when one compares it with most other minority languages spoken in Europe. A good knowledge of Catalan is a significant asset on the regional labour market. Nonetheless, immersion has become a highly controversial matter between the Catalan and the Spanish governments, particularly in periods when the right-wing *Partido Popular* holds the Spanish executive with an absolute majority, as at present.

Thirty years of language normalization have left their imprint on Catalonia's socio-linguistic map. It is a matter of continuous disputes within the Catalanist camp if, and to what extent, Catalan has ultimately challenged the hegemony of Spanish in Catalonia which is particularly well-entrenched in the conurbation of Barcelona and in the larger cities. Yet it is out of the question that the knowledge of Catalan, and in particularly the proficiency of reading and writing in Catalan, has increased in substantial ways since the normalization process began. In 1986, 90% of the Catalan population indicated that they were able to understand Catalan, 64% could speak it, and 32% write it (Hall 1990: 32). 25 years later, in 2007, the corresponding figures read 96%, 81%, and 65% (Generalitat de Catalunya. Departament de Cultura 2011: 6). Ultimately, one can argue that it is the very success of – regional and local – Catalan authorities, as well as of Catalan civil society, in turning a formerly minoritized language into a quasi 'normal' vehicle of collective communication what has triggered current language conflict, which rather has to be conceived of as a conflict between Catalan actors and the stakeholders of Spanish nationalism at the level of the central state than as a conflict within Catalan society.

2. Conflictual multilingualism

In European media, Catalonia is typically categorized as a 'region', and this is also the status it is assigned in the institutional context of the European Union, where it is just one of the presently 344 members of the Committee of the Regions. However, the majority of Catalan citizens conceive of their country as a nation, albeit a – thus far – stateless one. Since 1980, Catalonia has the status of an Autonomous Community within Spain's semi-federal state structure. In similar ways as the Scots or the Quebecers do, many Catalans aim at higher quotas of sovereignty, which are to be conquered either by obtaining additional space for self-government from Madrid, or by means of achieving independence, an option that, for reasons explained in other chapters of this book, seems to have become the order of the day for an increasing number of Catalans since 2010 (Requejo 2010). As an Autonomous Community, Catalonia holds significant competences in the field of language policy. The main constraint to these competences lies in the fact that the Spanish constitution defines Castilian as the official language in the whole of Spain's territory. Other languages – i.e. Basque, Catalan and Galician – are given the option of sharing a co-official status with Spanish in the Autonomous Communities where they are spoken. Reflecting this logic, Catalonia has two official languages, Catalan and Castilian/Spanish. It has to be noted that, due to the institutional architecture of the autonomy system, the powers of the *Generalitat* in the field of language policy are devolved powers, and thereby remain ultimately subject to Spanish prerogatives.

Since the re-establishment of Catalonia's autonomy after the end of the Franco dictatorship, the co-official status of Catalan has recurrently been a matter of political disputes. As the Catalan language was publicly banned and prosecuted by Spanish authorities for much of the 20th century, and underwent a long period of intense repression after the end of the Civil War and the conquest of Catalonia by Franco's troops, the institutions of the *Generalitat* have put major efforts into improving its sociolinguistic standing. That Catalan is defined as Catalonia's 'own' language in the autonomy provisions, reflects the attempt to symbolically emphasize the weight of the vernacular vis-à-vis Spanish. Whereas broadly accepted in Catalonia itself, this approach to language policy has generated considerable animosity on the Spanish side, especially (but not exclusively) on the right wing of the political spectrum, where there is concern about the questioning of the hegemonic status which the Castilian language has enjoyed for centuries all over Spain by mobilized peripheries with distinct linguistic features, in particular the Basque Country and Catalonia (Linz 1975).

One of the major practical consequences of politically implementing the 'own language'-formula has been immersion. As pointed out above, instruction in most subject areas at Catalan schools is given in Catalan. At the same time, the schools have to make sure that all students achieve the same levels of competence in Castilian as they do in the Catalan language. In view of the long record Spanish has as a dominant language, the philosophy of Catalan language immersion programmes has been grounded on the premise that establishing a more balanced bilingualism in Catalonia requires special institutional support for Catalan (Balcells 1996: 189–190), a support that follows the logic of 'positive discrimination'. In this respect, one can summarize that the forces of Catalanism – a term which is used here for denominating those actors, who are not necessarily all nationalists, supportive of the Catalan cause – aim at overcoming a linguistic situation that they consider unfair, as it entails an inequality of status between Spanish and Catalan.

Throughout the last decades, the language issue in Catalonia has been characterized by a high level of politicization. The parameters of language conflict are quite intricate, as 'internal' interact with 'external' factors. On the internal side, there is a remarkably strong consensus, shared by the bulk of the political parties represented in the Parliament of the Autonomous Community, on the priority of giving Catalan special protection, not the least because of its politically enforced structural subordination to Spanish. By and large, this consensus seems to reflect linguistic attitudes that one will also find at the level of civil society: Although the first language of the majority of Catalan citizens is Spanish, the cultural hegemony attained by Catalanist forces in the struggle for democracy and self-government has come to mean that there is a stable social basis for granting the Catalan language special institutional protection.

On the external side, this view collides with the approach generally adopted by Spanish decision-makers in Madrid, who are not prepared to accept what they perceive to be a relegation of Spanish to a secondary role (Kraus 2007: 211–214). Spain's political elites tend to reject the Catalan strive for achieving linguistic status equality. In particular, Spanish governments led by the conservative *Partido Popular* have rejected to abandon monolingualism in major state institutions, be it the Senate (supposedly the chamber of territorial representation) or state-run corporations. Political campaigns against immersion have recurrently been orchestrated from Madrid, often in combination with the adoption of legal measures against the backbone of Catalan language policy. While in Catalonia such measures meet the stubborn resistance of regional institutions, the forces of Spanish nationalism have had some success in cutting down the public presence of Catalan in Valencia, the Balearic Islands and Aragon (Buch 2013). The concern about the standing of the Spanish language in Spain apparently lacks a socio-linguistic basis. Nowhere in the country is there is a graspable decrease in the relative number of Spanish speakers or in the levels of proficiency in the state language. What drives policies designed to 'defend' the status of Spanish rather is an uneasiness of state elites with a situation where what was primarily meant to be 'symbolic' (yet not substantial) recognition may become actually consequential and alter linguistic power relations. Such uneasiness might well be related to a robust tradition of Spanish linguistic imperialism that can be traced back to the 16th century (Moreno Cabrera 2014). The very continuity of this tradition fuels the resentment of many Catalans who are bilingual, yet who experience that the (relative) socio-linguistic and socio-political strength of their 'own' language does not translate into a status of equal recognition.

Ultimately, what explains the salience of linguistic issues in the Catalan context is that language occupies an important space on the battleground of two competing – and, as it seems, increasingly incompatible – nation-building projects: the objective of reframing Spain as *one* nation after the Franco dictatorship is challenged by Catalan aspirations for higher quotas of sovereignty. In consequence, language policies in Catalonia are policies designed and implemented in a context of *conflictual multilingualism*.

3. Complex linguistic diversity in the Catalan context

Present-day Catalonia has turned into a particularly interesting laboratory for the study of the political challenges connected with multilingualism, as it combines a well-entrenched *endogenous* patrimony of linguistic diversity, together with the conflicts that this patrimony has entailed, with new layers of *exogenous* linguistic differentiation introduced by recent, and quite massive, waves of immigration.[1] In addition, through the last three decades Catalans have been increasingly exposed to the impact of Europeanization, an impact that on the communicative side entails the continuous spread of English as a trans-European lingua franca, which is being more and more frequently used not only at the level of high business, research and academic networks, but also in the service sector and in commerce. Thus, the linguistic cleavages of the past have become intermingled in intricate ways with the imprint of new and complex forms of diversity.

To assess how this dynamic in connection with the politics of conflictual multilingualism, we have to cast a second, and a bit more thorough, glance on Catalonia's linguistic scenery. There is no proper census data on the linguistic identity of citizens in Catalonia, as the political regulation of language issues is based on the assumption that bilingualism applies evenly over the Catalan territory. Still, language use and levels of linguistic competence have been scrutinized in numerous studies. As a comprehensive survey from 2008 shows, Catalan is the first language – the term used in the survey is *llengua inicial* – of 31.6% of the population of Catalonia *older than 15 years*; for Castilian, the corresponding figure is 55.0%. 3.8% indicate both Catalan and Castilian, 2.6% Arabic, 6.7% other languages (Generalitat de Catalunya 2009: 43). When looking at these percentages, we have to take into account

---

1 This section draws on Kraus 2011 (31–33).

that from 2001 to 2008, the Catalan population increased by 16.75%, basically as a consequence of immigration. In 2008, the number of residents in Catalonia born abroad (i.e. outside of Spain) was 1,204,711 (16.4%). The migration cycle has come to a halt since then, so that demographic figures have only changed moderately.

When it comes to linguistic competence, according to the same survey, 94.6% understand Catalan, 78.3% speak it, and 61.8% can write it; for Castilian, the figures approach 100% for the first two competence levels, the writing competence being 95.6% (Generalitat de Catalunya 2009: 139, 142). It has to be noted that writing proficiency in Catalan increases considerably among younger age cohorts, as school instruction of Catalan was banned for most of the Franco period, but became successively normalized after 1975 (the age factor also explains why the Catalan competence levels measured in 2008 are slightly lower than those documented in the 2007 survey, reported in the first section of this chapter). Interestingly enough, there is no strict coincidence between the proportions of what people indicate as their 'first language' and their 'language of identification': 46.5% give Castilian as their language of identification, 37.2% Catalan, 8.8% both Catalan and Castilian, 2.4% Arabic, and 4.3% other languages (Generalitat de Catalunya 2009: 48). Moreover, the survey data show that the use of two languages in everyday communication is an extended practice at the individual level (Generalitat de Catalunya 2009: 57–82).

What does the interaction of different patterns of multilingualism look like in Barcelona, the capital of Catalonia, where diversity has become an all-pervasive phenomenon? One has to be aware of the sheer quantitative dimensions of recent immigration to the Mediterranean metropolis: from January 2001 to January 2010, the number of foreigners in Barcelona went up from 74,019 (4.9% of the total population) to 284,632 (17.6%). Evidently, the impact of immigration on the city's demography has been very strong by all comparative standards. If we look at the data for 2010, immigrants from Central and South America comprise 40.7% of the city's foreign population. The vast majority of these immigrants have Spanish as their first language, so that there is a significant overlap between 'old' and 'new' varieties of multilingualism in Barcelona. There is no clear-cut information on the linguistic affiliations of the city's residents. Still, the ranking of foreign nationals does offer some indirect evidence on the languages of the immigrant communities; in view of the relative strength of citizens from North Africa and from Pakistan among the foreign population, one can conclude that Arabic and Urdu carry special weight in Barcelona's changed multilingual setting (Ajuntament de Barcelona 2010: 11, 25, 116). Otherwise, the linguistic composition of the immigrant universe is as manifold as in the bulk of metropolitan areas of the West.

The *Generalitat* holds key competences in the field of education. In consequence, how multilingualism is regulated in schools depends substantially on the policies designed by the Catalonia's *Departament d'Ensenyament*. In general terms, and to a great extent independent from the political composition of the Catalan governments, the Department has embraced multiculturalism and multilingualism as the appropriate means for creating positive models of coexistence for a more and more diverse citizenry. In addition, great emphasis is placed on linking the sensitivity towards difference and the rejection of linguistic prejudice with the aim of achieving social cohesion.[2] Another specific aspect of the approach developed for tackling multilingualism in Catalan schools is the explicit support shown for minority languages: when depicting the linguistic situation in the countries of origin of immigrant children, such as Morocco or Bolivia, special and extensive mention is made of Berber (Tamazight) and Quechua. This may be taken as a statement of intent based on the Catalans' own experience as a linguistic minority. To some extent, one might venture, the context of conflictual multilingualism reverberates in the field of organizing mother tongue instruction for immigrant children.

Catalan schools are encouraged to offer extracurricular classes in foreign pupils' languages and cultures of origin both at the primary and at the compulsory secondary level. However, the institutional input, as defined in the regulations formulated by the *Departament d'Ensenyament,* does not include the supply and the remuneration of teaching staff, but is essentially limited to the facilitating of school locations. The financial funds for mother tongue instruction have to be provided by other (non-public) institutions or bodies. As a result, the scope of mother tongue instruction thus far remains modest. On an Education Department web page containing information about mother tongue instruction in the school period 2010–2011, we learn that nine languages have been on offer for extracurricular classes. For the

---

2 See Annex 2 (Protocol for extracurricular classes in foreign pupils' languages and cultures of origin) to the *Language and social cohesion plan* introduced in 2007 by the *Departament d'Ensenyament.* http://www.xtec.cat/lic/intro/documenta/annex2_extracurricularclasses.pdf [last accessed: 25.11.2014]

whole of Catalonia, the number of pupils in these classes was 2,952.[3] This is a modest figure, which allows the conclusion that the importance given to the fostering of an extensive multilingualism in official discourses is thus far not really matched by material efforts.

Somewhat paradoxically, the salience of language conflict may be a factor that explains why immigrants achieve a comparatively high level of effective proficiency in Catalonia's two official languages. A survey with data from 2010 shows that 40% within the population segment composed by those born abroad have learnt to speak Catalan (fundacc – Institut d'Estudis Catalans 2011: Gràfic 3). The figure can be considered rather impressive, if we take into account the linguistic background of the many immigrants from Latin America, and the lingua franca qualities of Spanish, which is spoken by virtually all Catalan citizens and serves as the vehicle of communication not only between Catalonia and Spain, but also between Catalonia and other parts of the world. The capacity of cultural penetration into allophone communities (including the Spanish speaking groups) exhibited by Catalan must be related to the weight this language carries as a symbol of political identification.

By combining the effects of a 'new' heterogeneity with 'old' cultural cleavages in particularly intricate ways, Catalonia and Barcelona offers almost laboratory-like conditions for studying what transnationalism represents in environments where national identities of different types are still powerful forces. The politics of multilingualism demonstrates how the national is 'transnationalized': think, for instance, of the multiple ways of relating established patterns of linguistic identification – in this case, Catalan vs. Castilian – to the new cultural and communicative practices introduced by immigrant groups. In a parallel way, however, the politics of multilingualism is a politics that nationalizes the transnational: in the referendums on independence organized in a great number of Catalan municipalities by civil society actors between autumn 2009 and spring 2011, mobilizing (in Catalan) for immigrant participation was a strategic goal shared by all convoking local entities. Although the 'hybridization' that is often associated with the dynamics of immigration may well change the parameters of iden-

---

3 Arabic leads the ranking, with 1,682 pupils. It is followed by Chinese (501), Portuguese (227) and Romanian (177). The list also includes Tamazight/Berber (98) and Bengali (57). See Generalitat de Catalunya, Departament d'Ensenyament, Servei de Llengües: Llengües d'origen. Presentació. http://blocs.xtec.cat/llenguadorigen/presentacio/[last accessed: 25.11.2014]

tity politics, the Catalan case apparently corroborates the view that processes of this kind do not entail the waning of all cultural identities in a cosmopolitan pastiche of sorts (Calhoun 2007).

What comes to the fore with the new heterogeneity in the Catalan setting is not just an exuberance of diversity, in the sense of a ubiquitous proliferation of interlocking, complementary or interchangeable cultural and linguistic attachments. As we have seen, institutional attempts at coming to grips with the challenges of multilingualism rather involve a delicate exercise in defining the proper space for acquiring and using different linguistic competences. At the individual level, the situation to tackle may be even more demanding. To give one concrete example: the children of Moroccan immigrants with a Berber background in Barcelona will have to make substantial efforts to acquire a linguistic repertoire that 'fully' corresponds to their equally multinational as transnational environment. Such a repertoire would have to include Catalan, Spanish, Tamazight, Arabic, as well as ultimately English. This type of situation takes us far away from the *one nation – one language – one state* approach that was characteristic of the high time of European modernity. We are facing a new context of multilingual politics, marked by the challenges of *complex diversity* (Kraus 2012). The concept underlines the multi-dimensionality and fluidity that diversity has attained in our societies. Its use may therefore help us to avoid essentializing simplifications when we talk about culture and identity. Yet, at the same time, the concept of complex diversity also renders tribute to the relevance culturally embedded contexts of praxis – such as languages – continue bearing for articulating a reflective identity politics.

In which ways do the more and more complex patterns of diversity observable in Catalan society relate to the politics of language? Apparently and, again, somewhat paradoxically, a loosening of the bond traditionally established between language – in the sense of *llengua pròpia* – and Catalan identity has paralleled the rise of the sovereigntist movement in the last ten years. All in all, the identity component has lost salience in the Catalanist discourse, while instrumental considerations focusing on Catalonia's negative fiscal balance and on the poor quality of the public services and infrastructures provided by the Spanish state have gained weight. The perception of what the role of Spanish in Catalonia is and should be has changed as well. To some extent, this change may be connected to the influx of immigrants from Latin America, whose commitment to the Spanish language can hardly be seen as an immediate expression of Spanish nationalism. Symptomatically, there are sectors of the independentist movement, such as

Súmate, who articulate their demands in Spanish and specifically target those citizens who do not have Catalan as their first language. This may be a tendency that responds to tactical considerations, as the Spanish newspaper *El País* (edition for Catalonia, 8.10.2012) has speculated; but it may also reflect a new understanding of the cultural and linguistic realities of a complex country.

One century after Prat de la Riba, only few Catalanists would claim that there is basically *one* national spirit underlying Catalan identity. The awareness of the complex identity patchwork that characterizes Catalonia today has become an important element in the ongoing debates on the status of Spanish in an independent Catalonia. Artur Mas, the current president of the *Generalitat*, declared in an interview given to the newspaper *La Vanguardia* (12.10.2012, own translation) that 'Castilian will keep being an official language' under independence. In a similar vein, Oriol Junqueras, the leader of the left Catalanist *Esquerra Republicana*, wrote in a press contribution – titled *La llengua dels meus amics, de la meva gent* ('The language of my friends, of my people'): 'In Catalonia, there is no language problem, and with an own state Castilian will be official' (*El Periódico*, 17.4.2014, own translation). Regardless of the reluctance that the 'Taliban' sectors within the sovereigntist block show towards granting Spanish a co-official status after achieving independence, such statements show that the key issue to be discussed with respect to language policy is not whether a sovereign Catalan republic should or should not be multilingual, but rather which institutional approaches towards multilingualism should be adopted at which level. An increasingly complex socio-linguistic setting eludes straightforward political formulas. In societies marked by diversity and migration, the very notion of a 'normal' language status seems to have become problematic. Thus, one may assume that Catalan will benefit from becoming the language of an independent state, but this should not lead to the expectation that linguistic 'normality' can be produced by political decree.

References

Ajuntament de Barcelona. Departament d'Estadística, 2010: *Informes Estadístics. La població estrangera a Barcelona. Gener 2010*, Barcelona: Departament d'Estadística. http://www.bcn.cat/estadistica/catala/dades/inf/pobest/pobest10/pobest10.pdf [last accessed: 25.11.2014]

Balcells, Albert, 1996: *Catalan Nationalism: Past and Present*, Houndmills: Macmillan.

Buch, Roger, 2014: *Asfixiant la llengua. Crònica dels atacs del PP contra el català*, Barcelona: Angle.

Calhoun, Craig, 2007: *Nations matter: culture, history, and the cosmopolitan dream*, London: Routledge.

fundacc – Institut d'Estudis Catalans, 2011: *Coneixements i usos del català a Catalunya el 2010: dades del Baròmetre de la Comunicació i la Cultura.*

http://www.fundacc.org/docroot/fundacc/pdf/dieta_llengua.pdf

[last accessed: 25.11.2014]

Generalitat de Catalunya. Departament de Cultura, 2011: *Informe de política lingüística 2011.*

http://www20.gencat.cat/docs/Llengcat/Documents/InformePL/Arxius/IPL2011.pdf

[last accessed: 25.11.2014]

Generalitat de Catalunya. Institut d'Estadística de Catalunya, 2009: *Enquesta d'usos lingüístics de la població 2008*, Barcelona: Institut d'Estadística de Catalunya.

http://idescat.cat/p/eulp2008

[last accessed: 25.11.2014]

Hall, Jacqueline, 1990: *Knowledge of the Catalan language (1975-1986)*, Barcelona: Publicacions de l'Institut de Sociolingüística Catalana.

Kraus, Peter A., 2007: 'Katalonien im demokratischen Spanien', in: Walther L. Bernecker, Torsten Eßer and Peter A. Kraus: *Eine kleine Geschichte Kataloniens*, Frankfurt a. M.: Suhrkamp, 149–247.

Kraus, Peter A., 2011: 'The Multilingual City: the Cases of Helsinki and Barcelona', *Nordic Journal of Migration Research*, Vol. 1, No. 1, 25–36.

Kraus, Peter A., 2012: 'The Politics of Complex Diversity: a European Perspective', *Ethnicities,* Vol. 12, No. 1, 3–25.

Moll, Aina: 1984: 'Els tràmits preliminars de la redacció de la Llei de Normalització Lingüística a Catalunya', *Revista de Llengua i Dret*, 3, 3–9.

Moreno Cabrera, Juan Carlos, 2014: *Los dominios del español. Guía del imperialismo lingüístico panhispánico*, Madrid: Euphonía Ediciones.

Linz, Juan J., 1975: 'Politics in a Multilingual Society with a Dominant World Language: the Case of Spain', in: Jean Guy Savard and Richard Vigneault, eds., *Les États multilingues: problèmes et solutions*, Québec: Les Presses de l'Université de Laval, 367–444.

Prat de la Riba, Enric, 1978 [1906]: *La nacionalitat catalana*, Barcelona: Edicions 62.

Requejo, Ferran, 2010: *Camins de democràcia. De l'autonomia a la independència*, Barcelona: L'Avenç.

Fiscal issues of Catalan independence

Elisenda Paluzie

1. Introduction

After a massive demonstration for independence on Catalan's national day in September 2012, and after the rejection by Madrid of a fiscal agreement proposed by the Catalan government, an early election of the Catalan Parliament was called. The parties proposing a self-determination referendum reached a majority of almost two-thirds in the Parliament and called for a referendum on independence that had to be held on November 9th, 2014. This referendum was suspended by the Constitutional Court in October 2014, and instead a symbolic consultation was held. Over 2.3 million Catalans went to the polls of which 1.9 million voted in favor of independence. But this symbolic consultation lacked guarantees as the electoral census was not used, and turnout rates were unavailable, leaving the question of Catalan independence open.

Although it is not the only issue at stake, economics has been considered key to understanding the growing support for independence in Catalan society, and the most conflicting of the economic issues is the fiscal relationship with the central government in Madrid. Here we analyze first the status quo in this relationship; second, we consider what a fiscal agreement, like in the Basque Country, would imply. And finally, we analyze the case for full independence before reaching our final conclusions.

2. The status quo

In Spain, fiscal decentralization is asymmetric: there are two systems, the "Common" and the "Foral" regimes, with the latest being instituted only for the Basque Country and Navarra. The "common" regime regulates the tax system of the other fifteen autonomous communities, including Catalonia, and is basically a decentralized unitarian model that has evolved over time, characterized by high degree of decentralization in expenditure, but a low degree in the revenues. Tax sharing and transfers are the keystones of this model.

In this regime, the regional financing model is channeled through a law called LOFCA ("Ley Orgánica de Financiación de las Comunidades Autónomas"), with a highly centralized fiscal structure. In fact, >90% of the taxes are collected by the central government. Redistribution is based on an equalization formula, based on "needs-assessment". On the other hand, the spending patterns of the central government, particularly on infrastructure, might also have regional effects. Overall under the Common regime, an important process of inter-regional distribution has taken place with time, Catalonia being one of the main contributors. As a result, the Catalan fiscal balance (its net fiscal flow) is highly in deficit. Let us examine first the Catalan fiscal balance in the context of interregional fiscal flows in Spain.

2.1 Interregional fiscal flows

The fiscal balance is a measure of the difference between the taxes levied in a territorial unit and the public services received by it. Hence it is a synthetic and global measure that includes all the relationships with the central administration, including Social Security. If a territory receives more expenditure than the income it raises, this territory would have a fiscal surplus; whereas if the income levied is higher than expenditure, it would have a fiscal deficit.

There are two standard methods to calculate interregional fiscal flows, the cash-flow approach and the benefit approach. Both are valid, but they respond to different objectives. The cash-flow method calculates the fiscal balance as the difference between the revenues generated in a region and government's direct spending in that region. This method is appropriate in estimating the economic impact of activity in the public sector in a given region. The benefit approach estimates the fiscal balance as the difference between the revenues supported by the residents of a region and the public expenditure that has benefitted its residents. Hence, this benefit could also be attained with expenditure that is not physically spent in the region. For instance, this method assumes that the expenditure of the central ministries (civil servants' wages, building maintenance, etc.) benefit equally all regions, regardless of the location of these ministries.

Table 1. Catalan Fiscal Balance, 1986-2011

	By Cash-flow	% Catalan GDP	By Benefit	% Catalan GDP
1986	-2,465	-6.8%		
1987	-2,868	-7.0%		
1988	-3,466	-7.5%		
1989	-4,056	-7.7%		
1990	-4,867	-8.3%		
1991	-5,174	-8.0%		
1992	-5,988	-8.6%		
1993	-7,263	-10.1%		
1994	-6,732	-8.8%		
1995	-6,416	-7.7%		
1996	-7,088	-7.9%		
1997	-7,018	-7.4%		
1998	-6,813	-6.8%		
1999	-8,124	-7.5%		
2000	-8,532	-7.2%		
2001	-8,565	-6.7%		
2002	-13,696	-10.1%	-10,225	-7.5%
2003	-13,036	-8.9%	-9,576	-6.6%
2004	-13,595	-8.7%	-10,101	-6.4%
2005	-14,186	-8.4%	-10,119	-6.0%
2006	-14,493	-7.9	-10,320	-5.7%
2007	-15,913	-8.1	-11,136	-5.7%
2008	-17,200	-8.6%	-11,860	-5.9%
2009	-16,409	-8.5%	-11,261	-5.8%
2010	-16,543	-8.5%	-11,258	-5.8%
2011	-15,006	-7.7%	-11,087	-5.7%
Average		-8.0%		-6.1%

Source: Departament d'Economia i Coneixement (2014 a)

The Catalan Government has calculated its fiscal balance for 26 years (1986-2011). This is the longest series available that uses both standard methods, although the benefit approach has only been available since 2002

143

(Table 1 gives this estimation). On average from 1986 to 2011, Catalonia had a fiscal deficit of 8% of its GDP, based on the cash-flow approach. In 2011, the last year in the series, it amounted to 15 billion euros. Regarding the benefit approach, the fiscal deficit was averaged 6.1% of Catalan GDP in the period 2002-2011, which amounted to 11 billion euros in 2011.

Note 1: The fiscal balance is calculated under the balanced budget hypothesis by adjusting revenues, ie in the case of a budget deficit, more revenues are imputed, and in the case of a budget surplus, revenues are detracted. The effect of variations in the financial situation of the public sector is therefore eliminated.

Note 2: In the series, there are two years that introduce methodological changes into the calculation. From 2002 onwards, investments of public firms have been included, and a share of the interest payments of the Central government debt has been considered as expenditure in the region. From 2011 onwards, a share of the Central government revenues obtained from the lottery and the dividends of the Bank of Spain are imputed to Catalonia.

Another way to express the fiscal balance is in relative terms compared to the total income and expenditure of the Spanish government. Thus, during the period 1986-2011, Catalonia provided 19.5% of all central government and Social Security income in Spain, but received only 14% of the expenditure. If personal redistribution is excluded, (mainly channeled through Social Security, ie social contributions, pensions, and unemployment benefits), the figures are more extreme. Catalonia contributed to 19.7% to central government income, and received only 11.1% of the expenditure. This means that for each euro paid in taxes to the central government, only 56 cents return to Catalonia, the other 44 cents being spent elsewhere in Spain.

However, we should place the Catalan fiscal balance in the context of Spanish regional fiscal flows. Is it, as many argue, the logical consequence of a higher income in Catalonia? Is Catalonia contributing more just because it is a relative rich region? Is this contribution meant to help compensate poorer regions? And do we have reliable estimates of the fiscal balances of these other regions?

In fact, we do not have a series for all regions comparable in length and methodological coherence to that of the Catalan government. Fiscal balances have not been systematically calculated using the same methodology. A more comparable estimation of the Catalan government is the one provided by the *Instituto de Estudios Fiscales* (Institute of Fiscal Studies), a research center linked to the Spanish Treasury. This institute calculated the fiscal balances of all regions for the year 2005, using both the cash-flow and the benefit approaches (Table 2).

Table 2. Interregional fiscal flows, Spain, 2005.

	Cash-flow approach (million €)	Cash-flow approach (in % GDP)	Benefit approach (million €)	Benefit approach (in % GDP)	Ranking GDP per capita
1. Balearic Islands	-3,191	-14.2%	-1,922	-8.6%	7
2. Catalonia	-14,808	-8.7%	-11,101	-6.5%	4
3. Valencia	- 5,575	- 6.3%	-3,192	-3.6%	13 (<average)
4. Madrid	- 8,911	- 5.6%	-14,201	-8.9%	1
5. Navarra	- 488	-3.2%	-232	-1.5%	3
6. Murcia	- 499	-2.1%	+36	+0.1%	15 (<average)
7. Basque Country	- 758	-1.3%	+112	+0.2%	2
8. La Rioja	+ 44	+0.7%	-99	-1.5%	6 (>average)
9. Canary Islands	+ 590	+1.6%	+2,200	+6.0%	14
10. Aragon	+ 510	+1.8%	-266	-0.9%	5 (>average)
11. Castile-la Mancha	+ 1,103	+3.5%	+1858	+6.0%	17
12. Andalusia	+ 5,729	+4.5%	+3,852	+3.0%	18
13. Cantabria	+ 571	+5.0%	+308	+2.8%	8 (>average)
14. Castile-Leon	+ 3,692	+7.6%	+2,164	+4.4%	11
15. Galicia	+ 3,807	+8.2%	+2,985	+6.4%	16
16. Asturias	+ 2,780	+14.3%	+1,980	+10.2%	12
17. Extremadura	+ 2,695	+17.8%	+2,274	+15.0%	19
18. Ceuta	+ 388	+28.6%	+96	+7.7%	9
19. Melilla	+ 421	+34.0%	+95	+7.7%	10

Source: Instituto de Estudios Fiscales (2008)

The Catalan fiscal deficit in 2005, according to the cash-flow approach, reaches almost 9% of Catalan GDP and amounts to 15 billion euros. According to the benefit approach, Madrid is the autonomous community with the highest deficit. This result is as expected, given that, under this approach, benefits of the capital region, which concentrates the ministries, are redistributed to all the regions in Spain. By the cash-flow approach, Madrid is the fourth region in fiscal deficit below the Balearic Islands, Catalonia and Valencia (the Catalan-speaking regions)

Catalonia is the fourth community in GDP per capita, the Balearic Islands the seventh, and Valencia the thirteenth, but these three autonomous communities occupy the top three places in the ranking by fiscal deficit, according to the cash-flow approach. There are regions with a GDP per capita higher than the Spanish average, including Aragon, Cantabria and La Rioja, which show fiscal surpluses. The system does not therefore seem to follow a rational pattern. Valencia seems paradigmatic in that it has a GDP per capita below the Spanish average (89%) and has a fiscal deficit that attains 6.3% of its GDP.

The figures show that regional fiscal flows cannot be attributed only to a redistribution policy; there are rich regions that do not have fiscal deficit (Basque Country and Navarre), and there are rich regions that have a fiscal surplus, ie they receive solidarity, - Aragon, Cantabria and la Rioja. And finally, there are poor regions that have a fiscal deficit (Valencia). Indeed, the fiscal balances of the regions do not seem to follow a strict solidarity path. In this respect, it is noteworthy that Lopez-Casasnovas and Pons (2005) established several principles that should inspire regional redistribution in any federation, and applied these principles to data from 1995 to 2003 from FUNCAS (*Fundación de las Cajas de Ahorro*), a private foundation that calculated fiscal flows for each of these years. They found that none of these principles was observed in Spain during that period.

Among these principles, we note in particular the following: a) No autonomous community should keep a positive fiscal balance if its primary income from the outset is above the Spanish average. This principle had been infringed for several years by Aragon, Castile León, Navarre, Basque Country, la Rioja and Melilla. b) Redistribution funds need to be established and allocated by a conditional spending procedure. The continuity of benefits of fiscal surpluses needs to be linked to an assessment of their effectiveness, a principle that has never been accomplished. Redistribution funds are neither limited in time nor evaluated. c) No regional fiscal balance should be greater than the difference in the relative participation in terms of income and its relative participation in terms of population. This principle has also been infringed.

Catalan fiscal deficit, therefore, exceeds standard solidarity funds. What, then, are the determinants of this fiscal deficit, and what patterns of expenditure lead to this result? Bosch and Espasa (2010) and Bosch (2013) carried out a decomposition analysis showing that the main reason for the Catalan fiscal deficit was regional funding from 2006 to 2009, which could explain 35% of it. Together infrastructure investment accounts for 10%, defense for 12%, security and jails for 10% of the deficit, with social protection and promotion expenditure accounting for a further 11%.

We will now look at the central government investment in infrastructure - a matter of heated debate in Catalonia - before moving to the analysis of the regional financing system, which is in fact mainly responsible for the Catalan fiscal deficit.

2.2 Spending on infrastructure

Figure 1 gives the percentage of central government investment in infrastructure in Catalonia from 1999 to 2015. This has been lower than the Catalan share of the Spanish GDP (18.8%) and the Spanish population (eg 15.4% in 1999, and 16% in 2014).

This situation led to the inclusion of a special provision in the 2006 Catalan Statute of Autonomy that forced the Central Government to ensure that for 7 years (2007-2013) investment in Catalan infrastructure should equal its share of the GDP. An agreement was reached between the Catalan and the Spanish Government on the method used to calculate these investments. This excluded some items of the infrastructure from the calculus, but also established an obligation of the Central Government to compensate the Catalan government 3 years later if the investments had not been delivered.

Figure 1. Central government investment in Catalonia (% of Spanish total), 1999-2015.

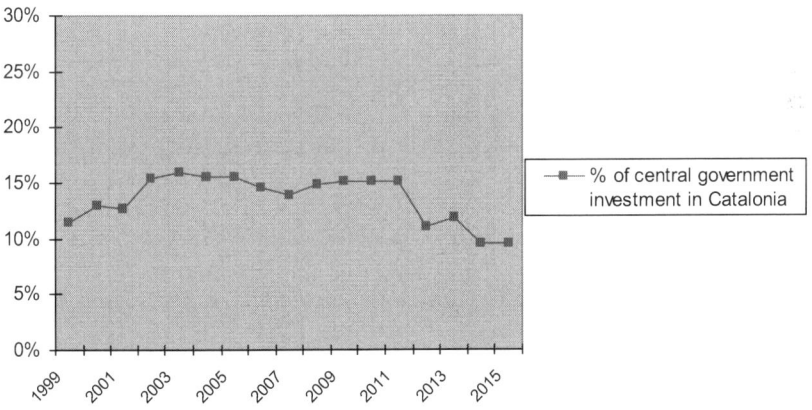

Source: Spanish national budget for the given years.

From 2012 onwards, the Spanish government has stopped including this special provision in its annual budget, and stopped paying the agreed debts originating from non-executed investments in previous years. This amounted to 3.967 billion € for 2008-2011. In 2014, special provision was no longer in force, but the Catalan government is trying to be paid in 2015 for the investments that were not executed in 2008, amounting to 759 million €! This experience is paradigmatic for the low credibility of the agreements signed with the Spanish government, including those that arise from the Statute of Autonomy, and are affirmed in a formal agreement between the governments. During the period of the special provision (2007-2013), investment in Catalonia never reached 18.8% of the Spanish total, and has since decreased to ~9.5%.

2.3 Regional financing system

The Catalan government, being responsible for providing education, health and social services, has systematically been underfinanced. One main objective of the reform of the Catalan Statute of Autonomy in 2005 has been a new financing system for the Catalan government. The project approved by the Catalan Parliament included a system similar to the Basque "Concierto", but the Spanish Parliament amended considerably the original project and maintained Catalonia in the "common" regime. The new Statute of Autonomy was approved in a Referendum by the Catalan population in June 2006, which led to the reform of the whole Spanish regional financing system in July 2009. Like previous reforms, the 2009 reform increased tax revenue sharing and kept the status quo, preventing any region from worsening revenues.

All regions increased their revenues, thanks to the additional funds contributed by the central government (11.408 billion €). The regional share of the personal income tax and the VAT increased up to 50% and that of the excise taxes up to 58%, but the tax sharing system did not transfer collection powers to the regions.

The equalization fund, formerly called the Sufficiency Fund, was split into two new funds: The *Essential Public Services Fund*, a horizontal transfer, the purpose of which was to guarantee the same resources per adjusted capita to all regions for the provision of health, education and social services; and the *Global Sufficiency Fund*, the purpose of which was to guarantee the status quo clause. The main novelty of the reform was indeed simply the creation of two further new funds; the so-called *Convergence Funds* were meant to compensate two very different types of regions: the *Cooperation Fund* for the poorest or less densely populated regions; and the *Competitiveness Fund* for the regions that would obtain less than average revenues per adjusted capita after the application of the redistribution system.

The gains obtained by Catalonia in 2009, the first year of the reform, amounted to 1.986 billion €, i.e. 0.96% of the Catalan GDP. Of this, 937 million € were obtained through the Competitiveness fund. In 2010, 863 million € came from this fund and a further 465 million € were provided through the Essential public services fund, an improvement totaling 1.328 billion €. These figures have to be seen in comparison to the results that would have been obtained under the former regime. In fact, the recession in 2009 (GDP down 4%) decreased revenues for all regions, but revenues would have been 2 billion less under the former system.

Thus, the reform did not significantly reduce Catalonia's fiscal deficit. Moreover, it failed to solve some of the problems of the regional financial system, namely the over-equalization problem. Equalization schemes are aimed at providing regions with the same services. Yet, the literature on political economy recently noted that complete equalization might induce richer regions to secede, while a system of partial equalization that reduces the gap between advantaged and disadvantaged regions without completely eliminating it guarantees the country's stability (Le Breton and Weber, 2003; Haimanko, Le Breton and Weber, 2005).

Table 3 shows regional fiscal capacity before and after equalization in 2011. The Spanish regional financing system clearly over-equalizes. Catalonia ranks third in regional fiscal capacity (taxes transferred to or shared by the region) before equalization and tenth after equalization. Moreover, not only is Catalonia's order in the ranking not maintained, it also received below-average funding.

Table 3. Regional fiscal capacity before and after equalization, 2011

	Before equalization	After equalization	
1.Madrid	134,2	1. Cantabria	124,4
2.Balearic Islands	121,7	2. La Rioja	120,7
3.Catalonia	119,1	3. Aragon	116,3
4.Aragon	114,6	4. Castile-Leon	116,3
5.Cantabria	114,4	5. Extremadura	114,5

6.Asturias	106,6	6. Asturias	112,6
7.La Rioja	103,2	7. Galicia	110,9
8.Castile-Leon	101,5	8. Castile-La Mancha	103,4
9.Valencia	93,7	9. Balearic Islands	100,8
10.Galicia	91,2	10. Catalonia	99,4
11.Castile-la Mancha	85,4	11. Madrid	95,4
12.Murcia	83,5	12. Andalusia	93,9
13.Andalusia	79,9	13. Valencia	93,6
14.Extremadura	76,2	14. Murcia	93,1
15.Canary Islands	42,2	15. Canary Islands	88,3
Average	100	Average	100

Source: Departament d'Economia i Coneixement (2014b)

Table 4 gives additional information on the regional financing system. In the first four columns, the total resources that the autonomous communities obtain from the regional financing System are given, as also what those resources represent in euros per inhabitant, the index relative to an average of 100, and an index adjusted to price differentials between regions. In the four last columns, other resources have been added that the regions obtained from the central government, eg the Inter-territorial Compensation Fund and the European Funds. In this way we can see the total resources in the hands of the regional governments, which are also calculated per inhabitant (indexed to the mean) and the index adjusted to price differentials.

In this global picture, Catalonia appears even worse than before. If indexes are corrected by price differentials, Catalonia's relative situation worsens because it is a region with higher price levels. The index of funding per inhabitant, adjusted by prices, falls to 90.9%. However, if we add the additional resources received by the autonomous communities, Catalonia's relative position also worsens, given that it is one of the regions that receives less European cohesion funds and does not benefit from the Inter-territorial Compensation Fund, a fund exclusively designed for the poorer regions that is not included in the regional financing model previously described. The relative index of resources per habitant of Catalonia is 95.4 (5 points below average) and the index adjusted by prices is only 87.7 (almost 13 points below average).

Table 4. Resources of the autonomous communities of the "Common Regime", 2011.

	Total resources of the regional financing model (million €)*	Resources per capita of the model (€/habitant)	Index of funding per habitant	Index of funding per habitant adjusted by prices	Total resources of the Autonomous Community (million €)	Total resources of the Autonomous Community per habitant (€/habitant)	Index of resources per habitant	Index of resources per habitant adjusted by prices
Catalonia	16.912	2.243	99,4	90,9	18.030	2.393	95,9	87,7
Galicia	6.999	2.504	110,9	113,6	7.985	2.856	114,5	117,2
Andalusia	17.855	2.120	93,9	96,6	20.805	2.470	99,0	101,8
Asturias	2.749	2.542	112,6	112,4	3.071	2.840	113,8	113,6
Cantabria	1.665	2.807	124,4	127,8	1.794	3.024	121,2	124,6
La Rioja	880	2.724	120,7	110,4	947	2.933	117,6	107,6
Murcia	3.090	2.102	93,1	93,6	3.424	2.329	93,4	93,8
Valencia	10.810	2.113	93,6	92,8	11.709	2.288	91,7	90,9
Aragon	3.535	2.626	116,3	120,4	3.794	2.818	112,9	116,9
Castile-.la Mancha	4.938	2.334	103,4	115,1	5.588	2.641	105,9	117,8
Canarias	4.236	1.992	88,3	102,8	4.886	2.298	92,1	107,3
Extremadura	2.868	2.585	114,5	130,9	3.421	3.084	123,6	141,3
Balearic Islands	2.532	2.275	100,8	95,5	2.678	2.406	96,4	91,3
Madrid	1.3978	2.154	95,4	91,0	14.779	2.277	91,3	87,1
Castile-Leon	6.715	2.625	116,3	123,2	7.365	2.879	115,4	122,2
Total or average	99.762	2.257	100	100	110.284	2.495	100	100

Source: Departament d'Economia i Coneixement (2014 b)

3. Fiscal agreement

In 2012, the Catalan Parliament approved a proposal for a system similar to the one enjoyed by the Basque Country and Navarre, known asthe Fiscal Agreement ("Pacte Fiscal"),which was proposed by the Catalan president to the Spanish Prime Minister at a meeting in Madrid in September 2012. The refusal of the Spanish government to negotiate an agreement of this kind lead the Catalan government to call for early elections under the new banner of the "right to decide", and the commitment to call a referendum on the political future of Catalonia. Let us now analyze what would have been the economic outcome for Catalonia of an agreement similar to the Basque "Concierto".

The Basque Country collects all taxes and pays annually a "cupo" to the central government, which is its contribution to the costs of the services provided by the central government. The "cupo" is calculated as the non-financial expenditure of the Central administration imputable to the Basque Country minus the share of the expenditure that could be financed from non-tax resources imputable to the Basque Country, and minus the public deficit imputable to the Basque Country.

The imputation coefficient was established in the early 80's as 6.4% and has never changed. This coefficient is similar to the share of the Basque Country GDP relative to the Spanish GDP, which now amounts to 6.2%. Hence, there is a small solidarity component in the Basque "cupo" because the relative GDP is higher than the relative population. In Table 2, the fiscal deficit of the Basque Country in 2005 is entered as 1.3% of its GDP, using the cash-flow approach.

In another publication (Paluzie, 2012), I simulated the results for Catalonia like the Basque "Cupo" for 2005-2009. By analogy, I used as an imputation index for Catalonia, its relative GDP of 18.7%. With a system like the Basque's, Catalan fiscal deficit would have been reduced to 4.492 billion € in 2005 (2.64% of Catalan GDP), and 5.449 billion € in 2009 (2.79% of Catalan GDP). The increase in resources for the Catalan government would have been 10-11 billion €.

In fact, the Catalan proposal of September 2012 was not exactly the Basque "Concierto", because the "cupo" had still to be negotiated and a larger contribution to solidarity was assumed. A similar proposal had been included in the Statute of Autonomy passed by the Catalan Parliament in September 2005. The Spanish Parliament had amended it in 2006, rejecting that Catalonia could collect taxes. In July 2010, the Constitutional Court's

decision made it virtually impossible because it ruled against a bilateral relationship between the Catalan and the Spanish governments.

4. Full independence

Bosch and Espasa (2014) and the *Consell Assessor per a la Transició Nacional* (2014) have estimated the public finance of an independent Catalonia
for 2006-2011. The calculation is equivalent to quantifying the additional
expenditure and revenue that the Catalan government budget would have
had, if Catalonia had become an independent Country The estimation assumes that Catalonia provided its public services, (those now provided by
the central government) at the same levels of public spending, and that it
would have imposed the same taxes and tax burden imposed by the central
government. Table 1 summarizes the results of this study. The series includes
two years of economic expansion (2006 and 2007) and four years of economic crisis (2008- 2011). The additional revenues for the Catalan government would have been higher in the first two years. Being reduced in 2008,
they would have reached their minimum in 2009 and started to recover in
2010. On average, the Catalan government would have had additional annual
revenue of 47.509 billion € (24.38% of Catalan GDP). As for the increase
in expenditure, this amounted to a yearly average of 36.311 billion € over
this period.

Hence, there is a net benefit of additional revenue once the additional
expenditure was linked to independence, as defence, pensions and unemployment benefits are subtracted. This net benefit amounted to 20 billion €
in the expansionary period and was reduced drastically during the crisis,
being of around 6 billion € at the end of the period. On average, the net annual
benefit would have been 11.198 billion € or 5.75% of Catalan GDP.

Table 5. Public finance in an independent Catalonia, 2006-2011.

	2006	2007	2008	2009	2010	2011	Average in 2011 constant euros	% over GDP
Additional revenues (in million €)	49.270	53.915	46.920	40.877	44.363	45.317	**47.509**	24,38%
Additional expenditures (in million €)	30.304	32.844	35.339	38.870	38.282	39.507	**36.311**	18,63%
Net benefit (in million €)	18.966	21.071	11.581	2.007	6.081	5.810	**11.198**	5,75%
Share in the surplus or public deficit of the Spanish Government (in million €)	-4.486	-5.249	5.624	15.618	10.708	7.184	**4.610**	2,37%
Total fiscal benefit (in million €)	14.480	15.822	17.205	17.625	16.789	12.994	**15.808**	8,11%
Net contribution to the EU (in million e)							**1.355***	0,69%
Net fiscal benefit maintaining contribution to EU							**14.453**	7,42%

*Average annual estimation for the period 2007-2013. Annual data on the fiscal balance with the EU are not available

Source: Bosch i Espasa (2014), CATN (2014) and Departament d'Economia i Coneixement (2013).

Until now, we have not been taking into account the proportional share of the Spanish public deficit that appears in 2008 and reaches a maximum in 2009. Hence, this is a net fiscal benefit in "cash" that assumes the hypothesis of zero deficit, ie the government is neither in debt nor surplus. In reality, the Spanish government had surpluses at the beginning of this period and huge deficits from 2008 onwards. We have to add to these figures the benefit of ceasing to contribute to the financing of the Spanish Government's budgetary deficit burden or detract the surplus in the years of expansion. The net fiscal gain would then average 15.808 billion € (8.11% of the GDP) for the period 2006-2011

A final adjustment that should be made relates to the contribution that Catalonia would have to make to international bodies (e.g. EU and IMF), to which it would belong. If an independent Catalonia remains in the EU, we should deduct from its fiscal gain the negative balance with the EU. The Catalan government estimated that during 2007-2013, its annual net contribution to the EU averaged 1.355 billion €. The fiscal gain from independence would then be of 14.453 billion € (7.42% of GDP), which is a very considerable figure.

5. Conclusions

Fiscal issues present a key issue in the Catalan conflict; they are not its only cause, but have nevertheless contributed significantly to the growing support for independence. Economic crisis has accelerated this process because it has made less tolerable the magnitude of transfers from Catalonia to other autonomous communities, given the huge budget cuts in education, health and social services imposed in the region, and also the growth of poverty and social inequalities within Catalan society.

Although the economic context is important, we have to bear in mind that the political crisis started before the economic crisis, with the failure of the new Statute of Autonomy to solve the political and economic conflicts between Catalonia and Central government. The endless discussions lasting from 2004 to 2010 and finishing with a decision by the Constitutional court that amended most of the Catalan Statute of Autonomy are at the heart of the problem.

The design of the system that generalized autonomy to all regions, regardless of their identity and will for self-government, makes reform extremely difficult. Identity differences are not easily understood in Spain, as shown by the impossibility to define Catalonia as a nation in the last reform of the Statute of Autonomy. The reluctance to accept difference and see devolution as an asymmetric process makes reform difficult because requires one to generalize them. The decision by the Constitutional Court on the Statute of Autonomy has made a fiscal agreement, such as with the Basque, virtually impossible from a legal standpoint. Moreover, any such agreement would imply a fiscal loss for the Spanish government similar to that of Catalan independence. A history of breaches in agreements makes it difficult to achieve a new one within the current legal framework.

References

Bosch, N. (2013): "Anàlisi econòmica del procés d'independència de Catalunya", Fundació Josep Irla, Barcelona.

Bosch, N. and Espasa, M. (2010): "Methodologies in Spain", in Bosch, N., Espasa, M. and Solé-Ollé, A. (2010) *The political economy of inter-regional fiscal flows*, Edward Elgar, Cheltenham, United Kingdom.

Bosch, N. and Espasa, M. (2014): "La viabilidad económica de una Cataluña independiente", *Revista de Economía Aplicada*, 64 (Vol. XXII), 135-162.

Consell Assessor per a la Transició Nacional (2014) "The fiscal and financial viability of an independent Catalonia", Report 18, Generalitat de Catalunya, Barcelona.

Departament d'Economia i Coneixement (2013) "Balança de Catalunya amb la Unió Europea", Generalitat de Catalunya, Barcelona.

Departament d'Economia i Coneixement (2014 a) *Metodologia i càlcul de la balança fiscal de Catalunya amb el sector públic central l'any 2011*, Barcelona.

Departament d'Economia i Coneixement (2014 b) *Anàlisi del model de finançament de les comunitats autònomes (2009-2012)*, Monografies núm. 15, Barcelona.

Haimanko, O., Le Breton, M. and Weber, S. (2005) "The stability threshold and two facts of polarization", CEPR Discussion Papers No. 5098, CEPR, London, UK.

Le Breton, M. and Weber, S. (2003) "The art of making everybody happy: how to prevent a secession", *IMF Staff Papers* Vol. 50, No.3.

Instituto de Estudios Fiscales (2008) *Las balanzas fiscales de las comunidades autónomes españolas con las administraciones públicas centrales 2005*, Ministerio de Economía y Hacienda, Madrid.

López-Casasnovas, G. and Pons, J. (2005) *Análisis de la redistribución entre las comunidades autónomas. Criterios de evaluación y propuesta de nuevos principios básicos*, Publicacions i Edicions UB, Barcelona.

Paluzie, E. (2012) "El concert econòmic: necessitat i viabilitat", *Idees* 34, 105-114.

Becoming more independent without independence?
Strong federalism with territorial autonomy as an alternative: the case of Belgium

Stephan Rixen

1. Introduction

Has independence no alternative? Are there no resorts should formal independence not become a reality? In other words, are there ways to become more independent without independence? My contribution does not immediately focus on Catalonia and Spain; it is about Catalonia's and Spain's future in a more indirect way. I want to look into the constitution of Belgium, which in many respects differs strongly from the situation in Spain and Catalonia. Nevertheless, my interest is to widen our perspectives, using Belgium as a case in point. First, I want to focus on the historical background, especially the rise of the Flemish politics of recognition. After this, I want to look at the complex constitutional framework. Finally, I will draw some conclusions; as a legal scholar, my main interest is to illustrate how constitutional law may help to organize cultural diversity and how this target may be reached with the aid of the political concept of federalism.

2. Historical backgrounds

Belgium is a country with a territory of about 30,000 square kilometers. The territory is a little bit smaller than that of Catalonia, and it is less than one-half of the territory of Bavaria. Belgium has about 11 million inhabitants, more than 6.3 million of them living in the Northern part of the country, i.e. Flanders. The dominant language is Flemish, a variety of Dutch, the language of the Netherlands (the linguistic difference is similar to the German spoken in Germany versus Austria). About 1.1 million live in the Brussels region which is placed, geographically, in Flanders, but is mainly French-speaking. About 3.5 five million live in the French-speaking South of the country, Wallonia. Thus, we have the Dutch-speaking Flemings in the North of Belgium, and the French-speaking Walloons in the South, with the Brussels region being a French enclave within Flanders.

When in 1830 Belgium declared its independence, the revolution was a product of French-speaking upper and middle class elites who fought against the predominance of the Dutch-speaking North, the Netherlands that Belgium at that time belonged to. In Napoleonic times Belgium was a part of France. After Napoleon's Waterloo and the Vienna Congress, Belgium became part of the newly-founded Netherlands. The predominance of the North of the Netherlands led to many restrictions that hindered the rise of the industries of the South (later Belgium). There was also a great cultural gap: the Roman Catholic Church was deeply rooted especially in the rural regions of Southern Netherlands –later Belgium – whereas the North of the Netherlands was mainly protestant.

It is a sort of ironic that the fight against the Dutch-speaking North of the Netherlands recurred in Belgian history in a modified manner. Now it was the Dutch-speaking people of the former South of the Netherlands that became opposed to the French-speaking elites. In Europe, the beginning and the middle of the 19th century was a time of cultural break-up, standardization of languages and invention of nations, not only in Catalonia. There was a kind of Flemish "Renaixença", which prepared the ground for political demands of the Flemings.

A number of painful events accelerated the willingness to accept Flemish demands, the most important probably being the conviction of two men in 1860, *Jan Coucke* and *Pieter Goethals*. They were unable to defend themselves properly in court because they did not speak French, and the judges and the advocates did not speak Dutch. They were later proven innocent, unfortunately after they had been beheaded. This story is a part of the collective memory of Flemings as well as the deaths of young Flemish soldiers during World War I, who died in the front line because they were unable to understand the orders of their French-speaking officers – which, as French-speaking activists say, is a Flemish myth without sufficient historical evidence. Nevertheless, after the war, a monument – the Yser Tower ("IJzertoren") – was built in Diksmuide in West Flanders in memory of the Flemish soldiers killed during the war. This monument was destroyed, presumably by French-speaking anti-Flemish nationalists, after World War II, and subsequently rebuild and reopened in 1965, a time the Flemish economy had become strong. At the top of the tower is an abbreviation that condenses the Flemish fight for recognition: "AVV-VVK" which means: "Alles Voor Vlaanderen – Vlaanderen voor Kristus" (All for Flanders – Flanders for

Christ). Although the Flemish society has become strongly secularized during the last decades, the Flemish authorities recognized the monument in 1992 as an official "symbool van de Vlaamse ontvoogdingsstrijd", a symbol of the Flemish struggle for liberation – an act both of identity politics and of the politics of the past.

What happened in the second half of the 19th and early 20th century was the beginning of a long process of granting recognition. Over decades the interests of the Dutch-speaking Flemings had to be accepted by the French-speaking economic and intellectual elite of the country. Events profoundly changed in favor of the Flemish interests in the beginning of the 1960 s. The decline of the traditional industries of the South (coal and steel) that slowly began in the 1950 s became obvious and the rise of the Flemish service industry received a tremendous push. Flanders became the "cash cow" of Belgium, Wallonia the poor house. The only "richdom" left today seems to be a language that one day represented national proudness, economic welfare and cultural predominance, the French language, which supposedly was superior to the "farmers' idiom", the Flemish. Together with the developing wealth of the Flemish, their political self-confidence grew, and the time of subtle retaliation came for some in Flanders, tamed by constitutional law.

Independence is an issue in Belgium, especially for Flemish politicians of the three Flemish nationalist parties *Nieuw-Vlaamse Alliantie*, *Vlaams Belang* and *Libertair, Direct, Democratisch (LDD),* which in total won nearly 30% of the votes in the federal elections of 2010. Even from a Flemish point of view, there are practical and symbolic obstacles on the way to independence, of which I will mention a few.

First, let us consider the status of Brussels. Although geographically Brussels is a part of Flanders, only 10% of its inhabitants use Flemish, and another 10% mainly Flemish-born inhabitants use both Flemish and French. The remaining 80% speak French, making Brussels a mainly French-speaking region. Most Flemish politicians, however, would be extremely unwilling to leave Brussels to the French-speaking part of Belgium (for comparison, no Catalan politician fighting for autonomy or independence would waive claims on Barcelona).

Second, what of the foreseeable consequences of the dissolution of Belgium? Who would take responsibility for the enormous state debt? Wallonia, living from fiscal transfers effectively coming from Flanders, would be unable to bear the burden. Similar problems had to be solved regarding the nation-wide social security system. Left-wing parties in Flanders fear that the universality of welfare could be undermined in a more right-wing Flanders after independence. And finally, independence would not stop economic migration of Walloons to Flanders not then resident in Flanders. Independence probably would augment the burden Flanders has to bear without any monetary compensation from a federal state that had ceased to exist. Under these circumstances, independence in Belgium seems to be a in dream rather than a reality. Is there an alternative?

3. Complex constitutional framework

Belgium's way to avoid the disadvantages of independence is a combination of strong federalism with territorial autonomy. Perhaps we should call this strategy some sort of hidden independence. Since 1993 and after the reform in 2001, Belgium has become a complex federal state. Federal states are models of government that distribute jurisdiction on at least two levels of power, which necessarily implies both a loss of power at the centre and a new balance between centre and periphery.

In a long process of devolution that started in 1970, new public bodies were created and given increasing competences. The Belgian Constitution separates the level of the federal state accurately from two other "sub-state" levels of political power, namely the communities and the regions. There are three communities – the Flemish Community, the French Community and, not so far mentioned, the German-speaking Community (in some regards an exceptional case, representing about 70,000 Belgians in the East of the country).

There are also three regions: the Flemish, the Walloon and the Brussels regions. Communities refer to "personalized" (person-centred) matters, especially cultural affairs (therefore, at first they were called "Cultural Communities"). Regions refer to more territory-centred matters. Although the communities' competences refer to "personalized" matters, they are territorial organizations. Communities do not realize a kind of personal autonomy, which refers permanently to the legal status of a person. Thus a Flemish-speaking person staying in Wallonia has to accept, for example, the language laws of the French Community. Speaking Flemish is not a kind of piggyback personal autonomy, although the Walloon side tried in the past to enforce this view without effect.

The main competences of the Flemish-, French- and German-speaking communities are:

- education,
- cultural matters (especially defense and promotion of language, arts, libraries, radio and television broadcasting, youth policy, leisure and tourism,
- development aid,
- use of language (but not for municipalities with a special status ["facilities"]),
- "personalized" matters (health prevention policy and social assistance to individuals, especially in the fields of family policy, disabled persons, senior citizens, youth, migrants, social assistance for prisoners),
- youth criminality justice.

The main competences of the regions of Flanders, Wallonia and Brussels are:

- economic affairs (especially export policy, economic policy [without monetary policy, price and income policy, labour law, social security]),
- employment policy,
- area development policy (e.g. town planning, monuments and sites),
- agriculture, chase, fishing, forestry (without food safety)
- environment (protection, waste policy),
- housing,
- water policy (production and supply, purification, sewerage),
- energy policy (without national infrastructure and nuclear energy),
- regulation and supervision of local and provincial authorities.

From a comparative point of view, it is a unique feature of the Belgian constitution that competences of regions and the communities cover all aspects of international cooperation within in the limits of the competences. This is combined with complex participation requirements when communicating with the European Union. With regard to question of fishery, for example, Belgium is represented solely by a Minister of the Flemish Region (the region is located in the North Sea). The competences of the regions and communities are exclusive, the federal state having no concurrent competences. The powers of the regions and communities are listed in a number of so-called special majority laws, i.e., laws that have been accepted by a two-thirds majority and a majority in each language group in the federal parliament.

What is left to the central level, the federal state, are some residual powers, especially:

- justice (the organization and functioning of the judicial system with a few exceptions, e.g. regions can set up administrative courts),
- social security (finance and organization, but not child allowances and not just social assistance),
- monetary policy (mostly transferred to the European Central Bank) and public debt,
- security and defence,
- civil law and civil status (especially marriages, contracts, nationality),
- foreign affairs (but not those matters devolved to regions and communities).

Nevertheless, the competences of the federal state are not completely clear. The Constitution says (according to the English version of the constitution): "The federal authority only has competences in the matters that are *formally* assigned to it by the Constitution and the laws passed by virtue of the Constitution itself." The official French version also uses "formellement"; the Flemish version uses "uitdrukkelijk", like the official German version "ausdrücklich", but there is a lack of norms in the Constitution (or special acts) that "formally" or "explicitly" distribute powers to the federal state. Although the intention was clear – distinct separation of competences between federal state and "sub-states" – it is, for example, difficult to differentiate exactly what "labour law" and "social security" (federal state) is, or what "employment policy" (regions) or "social assistance" (communities) covers.

Social security (social insurance) as a competence that remained federal has a strong redistributive element. In fact, social security is another mechanism to transfer money from Flanders to Wallonia. Therefore, questions of fiscal justice and constitutionality were raised when the Flemish side tried to implement a regular care insurance scheme as a form of "social assistance", which in fact only focuses on emergency situations. How to organize social security seems to be a specialist question, but it can emerge as a problem of constitutionality and can also challenge the legitimacy of the Belgian constitutional arrangement.

The entire regulation of fiscal transfers from the federation to the "sub-states" is documented in special majority laws of the federal parliament, which appear to be *the* preferred technique of piecemeal law-making in Belgium. Special majority laws do not require the long preparation of a constitutional change, but need to be accepted, as already mentioned, by a two-thirds majority in both houses of the federal parliament (Houses of Representatives and Senate) and by a majority in each language group in both houses. These laws, in effect, offer extra protection for the smaller French language group. Thus the 2011 reform of the financing system was implemented by these laws. It gave more competences for taxation to the regions which can now change the level of personal income tax. The new system has given the regions total fiscal autonomy for over 70% of their financial means (the communities are still predominantly financed by federal funds). Unfortunately, the economic situation of Wallonia will not allow a creative taxation policy. Therefore – as a typical compromise – financial compensation has been granted for 10 years, and will then gradually be abolished over another 10 years. Both sides know that there will surely be new opportunities to re-arrange fiscal justice over the next 20 years.

The Belgian federalism has a strong asymmetrical trait because the Flemish side has – in concordance with the constitution – merged its authorities of the region and the community. Therefore, in reality we have one Flemish sub-federal entity, "Het Vlaams Gewest", which has absorbed the level of "community" and normally does not use the denomination "community". The French-speaking side up to now has not merged the governing bodies because Wallonia fears a predominance of the Brussels region. Nevertheless, the Wallonians decided unilaterally – and without precise constitutional legitimacy – to call the French-speaking community "Federation Wallonia-Brussels" ("Fédération Wallonie-Bruxelles"). This is clearly a signal towards the Flemish side *and* to the Brussels region because most inhabitants of Brussels, according to polls, prefer in case of independence *not* to be part of an independent (mainly rural) Wallonia.

Different rules apply to the Brussels region because both communities have competences that refer to the territory of the Brussels region. Officially, Brussels region is bilingual, and thus all public services have to be granted in both languages, although only a small minority of Brussels' inhabitants is Flemish-speaking. No inhabitant of Brussels is obliged to choose one language; they have unlimited free choice to use services of one community, for example, the French-speaking community, although a client is Flemish-speaking (or vice versa).

Both sides, the Flemish and the French, have organized commissions in accordance with constitutional law and special majority laws that coordinate the activities mainly in the field of education, health care and social assistance. These commissions – in a complex interlocking with the authorities of the Brussels region – have asymmetrical competences. The VGC ("Vlaamse Gemeenschapscommissie"), which represents the Flemish community in the Brussels region, does not have any legislative power, but has to implement the decrees of the Flemish community. The COCOF ("Commission Communautaire Française") is a legislative body the French Community has delegated its Brussels-related competences to. The COCOM ("Commission Communautaire Commune") or GGC ("Gemeenschappelijke Gemeenschapscommissie") is the "Common Community Commission", which runs the bi-community institutions of the Brussels region for those inhabitants who do not want to choose an only-French or an only-Flemish institution, as in the field of health care.

To complete the official demands for bilinguality in significantly mixed areas of Belgium, there are some Flemish municipalities around the Brussels region that had to install so-called "facilities". Facilities allow the use of French in contacts with the administration, and in primary and secondary schools. These municipalities are officially called "faciliteitengemeenten", "communes à facilities" or "Fazilitäten-Gemeinden", the last being a special Belgo-German word that most Germans do not recognize (generally, the official German texts seem to be non-idiomatic, being strongly influenced by French and to a lesser degree by Flemish language use). There are also about 20 "facility" municipalities close to the language border between Flanders and Wallonia and along the language border in Wallonia to the German-speaking community.

4. Some Conclusions

Let me draw some conclusion after this broad picture of Belgium's endeavour to integrate its two diverging linguistic groups.

From a legal scholar's point of view, the Belgian case is appealing because we can learn a lot about the serving nature of law, in particular, the serving nature of constitutional law. The purpose of constitutional law is to regulate political power. Political power refers to the forces of a certain community with common grounds. It is the will of a certain people to give common grounds an organizational frame. If the images of what is common change, the common grounds have to be renegotiated. The only way, then, may be to divide the common grounds, to reduce them to the factors that are so fundamentally common that both sides will not – or not yet – pay the price of total separation. Federalism, therefore, can be *the* very model of organizing diversity up to the extreme of a minimum of common grounds and a maximum of autonomy, if so requested by the parties involved. International examples show that federations vary much between the poles of centralization and decentralization. Belgium places emphasis on radical decentralization to an extent that makes the federation a would-be-confederation.

Against this background, legal regulation, especially constitutional law, is more than a notarial act that sanctions the politically inevitable. Constitutional law is a technique of active configuration – not mere passive reaction – that gives form and direction to the instable stability (or the stable instability) of the political sphere. It may come unexpectedly, but the Belgian case is in fact the normal case (admittedly an unusual version); constitutional law has to cope with controlling and forming the dynamism of political power. The function of constitutional law is to temper extremes, facilitate compromises, and, most importantly reduce the notorious danger of any political power, which is to believe that the truth is only on one side. Constitutional law is not a "superstructure" energized by the political forces of a certain community; it is not (at least not for the main part) an intensifier of political moods and sentiments, but its purpose is to fix limits on moods and sentiments in order to moderate their overshooting potentials.

Despite the many differences between Spain and Belgium, my opinion is that we can learn from Belgium how to live permanently in a political situation that is preliminary, provisional and tentative, a situation characterized by severe conflicts with long traditions, followed by short-term solutions, followed by new severe conflicts, followed by new short-term solutions, i.e. a situation that, in other words, is a never ending story of permanent interim arrangements. What we can learn from Belgium is that living in an ongoing interim style may be (the only) viable way of solving political conflicts.

The Belgian constitution therefore installs a marriage of convenience, not a marriage of affection between the Dutch-speaking and the French-speaking. The constitution promotes and stimulates compromise, small-sized consensus, and enduring negotiations. It institutionalizes the art of incremental approach embedded into an open outcome procedure of piecemeal changes. Constitutional law gives a binding form to this process of permanent transition. Without any doubt this constitutional means of reducing problems to a viable level is technical, complex and sophisticated. It requires detailed and meticulous work that no one would take to heart – except lawyers. Would it not be much easier to go for the easy choice and realize independence?

Numerous Belgian politicians hesitate to answer bluntly this question. Rather, they focus on further questions that help to define the subject: Do we have compelling reasons for independence beyond desire and hope, frustration and comprehensible anger – even beyond money? Independence would be a new venture, but is it a hazard? Belgium has decided, at least for the time being, against independence and for a federation. A federation under multi-national circumstances is a second best type of government that allows far-reaching political change when fundamental change, separation, is not (or not yet) realizable. Strong federalism with territorial autonomy may be exit options. Belgium is not Catalonia, but Belgium can teach us that it is not only conceivable, but realizable to become more independent without independence. That federalism is a very flexible instrument if we want it to be so. In fact, it might be necessary to think about a more complex version of this federalism in Catalonia.

References

André Alen, Belgien: Ein zweigliedriger und zentrifugaler Föderalismus, Zeitschrift für ausländisches öffentliches Recht und Völkerrecht (Heidelberg Journal of International Law – HJIL) vol. 50 (1990), pp. 501-544

André Alen, Der Föderalstaat Belgien. Nationalismus – Föderalismus – Demokatie, Nomos Verlagsgesellschaft, Baden-Baden 1995

George Anderson, Henrik Scheller, Fiskalföderalismus. Eine international vergleichende Einführung, Verlag Barbara Budrich, Opladen/Berlin/Toronto 2012

Frank Berge, Alexander Grasse, Belgien – Zerfall oder föderales Zukunftsmodell. Der flämisch-wallonische Konflikt und die Deutschsprachige Gemeinschaft, Leske + Budrich, Opladen 2003

Frank Berger, Alexander Grasse, Föderalismus in Belgien: vom Bundesstaat zum Staatenbund?, Auslandsinformationen der Konrad-Adenauer-Stiftung (Auslandsinfo.) Nr. 6/2004, pp. 67-103

Charles B. Blankart, Föderalismus in Deutschland und in Europa, Nomos Verlagsgesellschaft, Baden-Baden 2007

Marleen Brans, Lieven de Winter, Wilfried Swenden (eds.), The Politics of Belgium, Routledge, London/New York, 2009, Paperback 2013

Matthias Chardon, "And now, the end is near". Die politische Dauerkrise in Belgien 2007/2008, Jahrbuch des Föderalismus 2008, pp. 287-303

Matthias Chardon, Und jetzt? Das Scheitern der belgischen Regierung an einem alten Problem, Jahrbuch des Föderalismus 2010, pp. 221-233

Matthias Chardon, Staat ohne Regierung: die belgischen Föderalwahlen 2010 und ihre Folgen, Jahrbuch des Föderalismus 2011, pp. 221-229

Kris Deschouwer, Belgien – Ein Föderalstaat auf der Suche nach Stabilität. Jahrbuch des Föderalismus 2000, pp. 97-119

Kris Deschouwer, Symmetrie, Kongruenz und Finanzausgleich: Die regionale Ebene in Belgien seit den Wahlen von 1999, Jahrbuch des Föderalismus 2001, pp. 203-216

Kris Deschouwer, Getrennt Zusammenleben in Belgien und Brüssel, Jahrbuch des Föderalismus 2002, pp. 275-287

Kris Deschouwer, The Politics of Belgium, 2nd edition, Palgrave Macmillan, Basingstoke/New York 2012

Jan Erk, Explaining Federalism. State, society and congruence in Austria, Belgium, Canada, Germany and Switzerland, Routledge, London/New York 2008

Stephan Förster, Karl-Heinz Lambertz, Leonhard Neycken, Die Deutschsprachige Gemeinschaft Belgiens – das kleinste Bundesland in der Europäischen Union, Jahrbuch des Föderalismus 2004, pp. 207-218

Bernard Fournier, Min Reuchamps (eds.), Le fédéralisme en Belgique et au Canada. Comparaison sociopolitique, Bruxelles 2009

Alain-G. Gagnon, James Tully (eds.), Multinational Democracies, Cambridge University Press, Cambridge 2001

Alain-G. Gagnon, Ferran Requejo (eds.), Nations en quête de reconnaissance. Regards croisés Québec-Catalogne, P.I.E. Peter Lang, Bruxelles 2011

Anna Gamper, Entstehung und Entwicklung des plurinationalen Mehr-Ebenen-Nationalismus, in: Christoph Pan, Beate Sibylle Pfeil (eds.), Zur Entstehung des modernen Minderheitenschutzes in Europa (Handbuch der europäischen Volksgruppen Bd. 3), Springer, Wien/New York 2006, pp. 267-299

Siebo M. H. Janssen, Belgien – Modell für eine föderal verfasste EU? Die Föderalisierung Belgien im Kontext der Europäischen Integration, Zentrum für Europäische Integrationsforschung, Bonn 2005

Bart Kerremans, Regieren im Mehrebenensystem und Bundesstaatlichkeit: Zur Mitwirkung der subnationalen Ebene Belgiens im Rat der EU und an der Regierungskonferenz 1996/97, Jahrbuch des Föderalismus 2000, pp. 479-509

Evelyne Mertens, Die Deutschsprachige Gemeinschaft im östlichen Belgien: Europa im Kleinen, Aus Politik und Zeitgeschichte Nr. 8/2008, pp. 3-5

Francesco Palermo, Rudolf Hrbek/Carolin Zwilling, Elisabeth Alber (eds.), Auf dem Weg zu asymmetrischem Föderalismus, Nomos Verlagsgesellschaft, Baden-Baden 2007

Patrick Peeters, Jens Mosselmans, Belgien – jüngste institutionelle Entwicklungen, Jahrbuch des Föderalismus 2007, pp. 295-303

Bettina Petersohn, Konfliktregulierung in multinationalen Demokratien. Föderalismus und Verfassungsreformprozesse in Kanada und Belgien im Vergleich, Nomos Verlagsgesellschaft, Baden-Baden 2013

Ferran Requejo (ed.), Democracy and National Pluralism, Routledge, London/New York 2001

Ferran Requejo, Klaus-Jürgen Nagel (eds.), Federalism beyond Federation. Asymmetry and Processes of Resymmetrisation in Europe, Ashgate, Farnham/Burlington 2011

Ferran Requejo, Miquel Caminal (eds.), Political Liberalism and Plurinational Democracies, London/New York 2011

Dirk Rochtus, Belgien vor dem Kollaps?, Aus Politik und Zeitgeschichte Nr. 8/2008, pp. 6-12

Dirk Rochtus, Belgien: Föderation mit Sollbruchstellen, in: Jügen Dieringer, Roland Sturm (eds.), Regional Governance in EU-Staaten, Verlag Barbara Budrich, Opladen & Farmington Hills, 2010, pp. 63-78

Caroline Sägesser, Introduction à la Belgique fédérale, Centre de recherche et d'information socio-politiques (CRISP), Bruxelles 2006

Wilfried Swenden, Föderalismus in Belgien 2003 – die Ruhe vor dem Sturm?, Jahrbuch des Föderalismus 2004, pp. 195-2006

Wilfried Swenden, Föderalismus lernen – 2004 als wendepunkt in der Entwicklung des belgischen Föderalismus, Jahrbuch des Föderalismus 2005, pp. 307-322

Wilfried Swenden, Belgischer Föderalismus 2005: getrennt zusammenleben oder zusammen auseinanderfallen?, Jahrbuch des Föderalismus 2006, pp. 303-317

Lieselot Van Herreweghe, Coucke en Goethals: Ware Martelaars van de Vlaamse zaak? Masterproef van de opleiding „Master in de rechten" (Stamnummer: 2005 3794), Faculteit Rechtsgeleerdheid Universiteit Gent, Academiejaar 2009-10, http://lib.ugent.be/fulltxt/RUG01/001/458/428/RUG01-001458428_2011_0001_AC.pdf

Vlaamse Gemeenschap, De Gemeenschapsminister van Verkeer, Buitenlandse Handel en Staatshervorming, Besluit van 10 november 1992, https://beschermingen.onroerenderfgoed.be/static/DOC2456.pdf

Vlaamse Gemeenschap (Vlaamse Overheid), Decreet houdende de erkenning van en de subsdidieregeling voor het Memoriaal van de Vlaamse Ontvoogding en Vrede van 15 Juli 2011, http://reflex.raadvst-consetat.be/reflex/pdf/Mbbs/2011/08/10/119447.pdf

Klaus von Beyme, Föderalismus und regionales Bewusstsein. Ein internationaler Vergleich, Verlag C.H. Beck, München 2007

Claudia Wasmeier, Erfolgskriterien föderaler Transition. Eine vergleichende akteursbasierte Prozessanalyse anhand Spaniens, Belgiens und Russlands, VS Verlag für Sozialwissenschaften, Wiesbaden 2009

Malte Woydt, in: Dissoziativer Föderalismus (1): Belgo-Föderalismus, in: Ines Härtel (ed.), Handbuch Föderalismus, Bd. IV: Föderalismus in Europa und der Welt, Springer, Berlin 2012, pp. 745-795

Devolution in the UK – a slippery slope or an alternative to independence?

*Markus Möstl**

1. Introduction

On Thursday, 18 September 2014, just 16 years after the process of devolution of powers to Scotland was initiated by the Scotland Act 1998[1], a referendum will be held in Scotland[2] on the question: "Should Scotland be an independent country?"

In the campaign leading up to this referendum, the position of the UK Government is that devolution is a better alternative to independence. A summary leaflet of the UK government argues: "Devolution gives Scotland the best of both worlds. It means decisions on issues like childcare, health and education can be made in Scotland, but that Scotland also benefits from being part of a larger UK with economic strength, national security and international influence."[3]

For the Scottish Government, on the other hand, successful devolution serves as an argument for greater independence. The publication "Scotland's future – Your guide to an Independent Scotland"[4] states that: "Through devolution, the people of Scotland have experienced some of the benefits of

---

* This article is based on a speech given before the Scottish referendum. The results and consequences of the referendum are not discussed in this paper.

1 http://www.legislation.gov.uk/ukpga/1998/46/contents; for an overwiew over British Devolution see Möstl, M., British Devolution und deutscher Föderalismus, BayVBl. 2013, 581.

2 Based on: The Scotland Act 1998 (Modification of Schedule 5) Order 2013, available at http://www.legislation.gov.uk/ukdsi/2013/9780111529881/pdfs/ukdsi_9780111529881_en.pdf; Scottish Independence Referendum Act 2013, available at http://www.legislation.gov.uk/asp/2013/14/pdfs/asp_20130014_en.pdf; Scottish Independence Referendum (Franchise) Bill 2013, available at http://www.legislation.gov.uk/asp/2013/13/pdfs/asp_20130013_en.pdf.

3 https://www.gov.uk/government/uploads/system/uploads/attachment_data/file/289195/Devolution_and_legal_implications_summary.pdf.

4 http://www.scotland.gov.uk/Publications/2013/11/9348/downloads, p. 16.

independence. The advantages of taking decisions for ourselves have been clear. (…) This guide lays out how we can complete Scotland's journey towards home rule and become a fully independent country." Devolution thus appears as an intermediary step towards independence, and the question of whether devolution is a safeguard against or a dangerous slippery slope towards the total break-up of the union is indeed as old as devolution itself.[5]

The problem, however, may be even more fundamental. Devolution may not only have created an appetite for greater independence (in as far as it is experienced as something positive), but may suffer from flaws that make it a rather unattractive alternative to independence. Devolution has been described as a "peculiarly British contribution to politics"[6], and indeed it seems to be a concept deeply rooted in peculiarities of British constitutional law and political thinking that finds no parallel in most models of federalism[7] or regionalism[8] seen in other countries and constitutional systems. Is British devolution in its present state a satisfactory, stable and sustainable constitutional arrangement or has it so far brought about piecemeal change suffering from inconsistencies and a completely unclear evolutionary potential[9]; is it a masterpiece of British pragmatism or does it need a fundamental principle-based rethinking?[10]

My presentation will try to answer these questions in three parts. In a first step, I will give a brief outline of the changes the process of devolution has so far brought about. In part two, I will explore certain specific characteristics

---

5 E.g. Hazell, R., The UK's Rolling program of Devolution: Slippery Slope, or Safeguard of the Union?, in: Docherty, D. and Seidle, L. (eds.), Reforming Parliamentary Democracy (2003) (p. 180 - 201), McGill-Queens University Press.

6 V. Bogdanor, cited by Parpworth, N., Constitutional and Administrative Law (2012), Oxford University Press, p. 160.

7 For the differences between federalism and devolution see Fenwick, H./Phillipson, G., Text, Cases and Materials on Public Law and Human Rights (2011), Routledge, p. 255.

8 Häberle, P., Der Regionalismus als werdendes Strukturprinzip des Verfassungsstaates und als europarechtspolitische Maxime, AöR 118 (1993), 1; Häberle, P., Föderalismus/Regionalismus – Eine Modellstruktur des Verfassungsstaates, JöR 54 (2006), 569.

9 Fenwick/Phillipson (fn. 7), p. 235.

10 See criticism by UK Changing Union partnership, A Stable, Sustainable Devolution Settlement for Wales (2013), p. 5, available at http://ukchangingunion.org.uk/en/wp-content/uploads/2013/02/A-Sustainable-and-Stable-Devolution-Settlement-UKCU-response-to-the-Silk-Commission-March-2013.pdf.

of British devolution. Finally I will try to draw some conclusions about the merits and the future of the concept of devolution.

2. The process of devolution to date

Let me begin with a statement from a recent book about constitutional reform in Britain: "...the old centralized British state has passed away..."[11] Indeed the process of devolution as initiated in 1998 has led to far-reaching constitutional change and has transformed Britain from a unitary state to a quasi-federal construction.[12] Before devolution, the situation was somewhat ambiguous:[13] On the one hand, Britain was clearly a unitary state[14] and the degree of centralization had even increased under the conservative governments of Thatcher and Major. On the other hand – despite some tendencies mainly in England to regard Great Britain as one common nation (dominated by England, of course), certainly in Scotland, but also in Wales. people had continued to think of Scotland and Wales as proper nations each with their own historical, cultural but also political and legal identity clearly distinguishable from that of England.[15] Despite the unitary nature of the constitutional arrangement, a considerable degree of legal diversity had also survived, as especially Scotland – due to guarantees in the Acts of Union 1707 – had been able to maintain its own legal system, church, education and local government systems, such that even before devolution, it was not unusual for the centralized UK Parliament in Westminster to pass laws applying only to Scotland (the so-called "Scotland-only legislation").[16]

Substantial devolution of powers to decentralized decision-making bodies in Scotland, Wales and Northern Ireland, however, after one unsuccessful attempt in Scotland in the 1970's, was only achieved in 1998 under the new

---

11 Brazier, R., Constitutional Reform: Reshaping the British Political System (2008), Oxford University Press, p. 121.
12 Bogdanor, V., The New British Constitution (2009), Hart Publishing, p. 89, 11 ff.; Fenwick/Phillipson (fn. 7), p. 258.
13 Hadfield, in: Jowell, J./Oliver, D., The Changing Constitution (2011), Oxford University Press, p. 213-214.
14 Leyland, P., The Constitution of the United Kingdom, A Contextual Analysis (2012), Hart Publishing, p. 243.
15 Bogdanor (fn. 12), p. 89, 99, 116, 118-119.
16 Parpworth (fn. 6), p. 158; Webley, L./Samuels, H., Public Law, Text, Cases, and Materials (2012), Oxford University Press, p. 297-298.

Labour government lead by Tony Blair. In Scotland and Wales, devolution had been preceded by referendums both yielding a majority for devolution (in Scotland the majority was 74%). From the beginning, devolution was asymmetric in the sense that Scotland was given substantially more independence than Wales (which initially did not receive powers of primary legislation). Northern Ireland is a very special case with particular problems and solutions of its own.[17]

Devolution is a process of decentralization that usually is defined like this: "Devolution involves the transfer of powers from a superior to an inferior political authority. More precisely, devolution may be defined as consisting of three elements: the transfer to a subordinate elected body, on a geographical basis, of functions at present exercised by ministers and Parliament. These functions may be either legislative ... or executive... . Devolution involves the creation of an elected body, subordinate to Parliament. It therefore seeks to preserve intact that central feature of the British Constitution, the supremacy of Parliament".[18] The supremacy of Parliament is a concept at the heart of the British constitution, which we will have to come back to shortly to understand its crucial meaning for the concept of devolution. In the meantime, let us look at what happened in the process of devolution.

The constitutional arrangement for Scotland is laid down in the Scotland Act 1998,[19] a piece of legislation passed by the Parliament in Westminster. The "subordinate elected body," which is necessary according to the definition of devolution, and to which powers have been devolved, is the Scottish Parliament that was recreated almost 300 years after it had been abolished and merged with the joint British Parliament in 1707.[20] Its 129 members are elected according to a mixed system of majority voting in constituencies and proportional representation by regional members chosen from regional party lists; i.e. the electoral system differs considerably from the simple majority voting system of the Westminster Parliament.[21] The Scottish Government[22] consists of the First Minister (the head of government) and the Min-

---

17 Leyland (fn. 14), p. 246-247.; Bogdanor (fn. 12), p. 91 f., 177; v. Andreae, Th. J., Devolution und Bundesstaat, Ein britisch-deutscher Verfassungsvergleich (2005), Boorberg, from p. 195.
18 Bogdanor, V., Devolution in the United Kingdom (2001), Oxford Paperbacks, p. 2-3.
19 http://www.legislation.gov.uk/ukpga/1998/46/contents.
20 www.scottish.parliament.uk.
21 Parpworth (fn. 6), p. 167; Hadfield, in: Jowell/Oliver (fn. 13), p. 216.
22 http://www.scotland.gov.uk/Home.

isters chosen by him plus the Lord Advocate and the Solicitor General for Scotland, and remains answerable to Parliament.[23]

The Scottish Parliament was, from the start, entrusted with considerable powers of primary legislation. Technically,[24] this was not achieved by defining a list of policy areas in which Scotland has the right to legislate, but, on the contrary, by giving it the right to pass laws unless certain reserved matters are concerned about which only the Parliament of Westminster may legislate. These reservations include constitutional questions, the status of Scotland as such, the foreign and military policy of the United Kingdom, the currency and fiscal policy, the common market (as well as certain clearly defined policy areas concerning the economy), infrastructure, home affairs, social and labour law.[25] The list of reserved matters is long, but it is equally clear that the legislative powers remaining for Scotland are considerable. What is surprising – from a German point of view, i.e. when you compare to the legislative powers of a German Land – is that the legislative powers of Scotland not only comprise autonomy in education, culture, local government, police and planning, but sensitive areas such as the civil and criminal law system. The Scottish Parliament has also been ambitious enough to try to pursue its own priorities as far as its health system and social problems are concerned.[26] The Scottish Parliament thus enjoys greater law-making autonomy than a German Land;[27] and, judging from the number of laws passed, it seems that it has also made an impressive use of its autonomy.[28] Regarding the budget of Scotland, at present between 25 and 30 billion pounds per year for a population of 5.25 Million is comparable to or even higher than the financial resources of a German Land.[29] These resources used to come from a block grant from London. Following the recommendation of the Scottish Calman Commission, the recent Scotland Act 2012

---

23 Fenwick/Phillipson (fn. 7), from p. 259.
24 As to these two techniques: Webley/Samuels (fn. 16), p. 293.
25 Sch. 4 and 5 of the Scotland Act, see Fenwick/Phillipson (fn. 7), p. 241-242.
26 Fenwick/Phillipson (fn. 7), p. 242; Bogdanor (fn. 12), p. 111.
27 Möstl, BayVBl. 2013 (fn. 1), 584.
28 Sutherland, E./Godall, K./Little, G./Davidson, F., Law Making and the Scottish Parliament: The early years in context, in: Sutherland/Godall/Little/Davidson (eds.), Law Making and the Scottish Parliament, 2011, from p. 3; for an overview over Scottish legislation see http://www.legislation.gov.uk/asp.
29 Möstl, BayVbl. 2013 (fn. 1), 584.

devolved considerable tax-raising powers to Scotland, which in future will partly replace the block grant.[30]

3. Characteristics of British devolution

After this brief outline of some basic facts about devolution, especially as far as Scotland is concerned, the second step is to turn to the analysis of some characteristic features of devolution in Britain to understand that concept better.

3.1 Parliamentary Sovereignty and constitutional conventions

We must begin with the consequences of that central notion of British constitutional law, which we mentioned earlier on: Parliamentary Sovereignty or, in other words, the supremacy of Parliament (Parliament meaning the Parliament in Westminster)[31]. It is due to that very concept of Parliamentary Sovereignty that we must take note of one of the first characteristics of British devolution, that of a striking and sharp contrast between legal construction and political reality.[32]

"The Principle of Parliamentary Sovereignty", according to the classic definition by Dicey,[33] "means neither more nor less than this, namely, that Parliament... has, under the English Constitution, the right to make or unmake any law whatsoever, and, further, that no person or body is recognized by the law as having a right to override or set aside the legislation of Parliament". Parliament, therefore, can neither bind itself nor can it be bound by any higher source of the law, and its laws have absolute validity that cannot be set aside by any judge. As a result, there cannot be a written constitution claiming overriding force over simple legislation; on the contrary, it is the essence of the British constitution that Parliament can change the constitution at any time by simple legislation. This principle of parliamentary

---

30 See   https://www.gov.uk/government/policies/maintaining-and-strengthening-the-scottish-devolution-settlement.

31 Bradley, in: Jowell/Oliver (fn. 13), p. 35.

32 Webley/Samuels (fn. 16), p. 293.

33 Dicey, A. V., An Introduction to the Study of the Law of the Constitution (10th Ed. 1959), edited by Wade, E. C., p. 39-40.

sovereignty has, as a result of recent developments (EU-membership, Human Rights Act, and devolution), encountered a number of modifications and political and practical restraints. From a legal point of view, however, it remains intact and still lies at the heart of the British constitution.

If devolution is to keep the notion of Parliamentary Sovereignty intact, its legal construction must be characterized by two important features:[34] First, devolution can only be construed as a unilateral top-down decision of the Westminster Parliament to delegate certain powers that can, at least theoretically, be reversed at any time. Second, even in areas that have been devolved to a regional parliament, Westminster must (again theoretically) retain its power to legislate for that region with overriding force over regional legislation. Consequently, s. 28 (7) of the Scotland Act states that the provisions on devolution do "not affect the power of the Parliament of the United Kingdom to make laws for Scotland".

If this legal construction is taken literally, the devolved powers of Scotland would seem extremely weak, and fully reversible with a permanent threat of overriding legislation from London. It is obvious that political reality is different. Theoretically the Westminster Parliament may have the right to repeal its decision to devolve powers, practically; one must not forget, however, that this decision was prepared by referendums in Scotland and Wales that are and must be seen as an expression of "popular sovereignty" in Scotland and Wales, which London cannot normally set aside.[35] On the contrary, the recent practice of deepening devolution to Scotland, according to the recommendations of a Scottish commission,[36] have led to a kind of "devolution on demand",[37] which clearly shows, that from a political perspective, devolution is by no means a unilateral development. And, in particular, the fact that Westminster has even been ready to make possible a Scottish referendum on independence[38] demonstrates the extent to which the central Parliament respects the expression of self-determination in Scotland. Similarly, the residual right of the Westminster Parliament to continue to legislate for Scotland, even in devolved areas, must not be taken too seriously. From the beginning, the understanding has been that Westminster

---

34 Möstl, BayVBl. 2013 (fn. 1), 582; Webley/Samuels (fn. 16), from p. 283.
35 Hadfield, in: Jowell/Oliver (fn. 13), p. 214, 218, 233; Bogdanor (fn. 12), p. 117.
36 See https://www.gov.uk/government/policies/maintaining-and-strengthening-the-scottish-devolution-settlement.
37 v. Andreae (fn. 17), p. 563.
38 Cf. fn. 2.

would normally not legislate for Scotland in devolved matters without the consent of the Scottish parliament, and it has stuck to that understanding since 1998. It is therefore regarded as a politically binding constitutional convention, the so called Sewel convention.[39] As in other areas of British constitutional law, the real distribution of powers may therefore not be measured according to theoretical legal rights, but according to what would be practically feasible in the light of recognized and binding conventions. Judging on the basis of constitutional reality instead of legal construction, it is clear that the notion of parliamentary sovereignty has, as a consequence of devolution, – survived only in a very modified and diminished form.[40]

3.2 Asymmetric structure

Let us turn to a second characteristic feature of British devolution, its strikingly asymmetric shape and structure.[41] Devolution in Britain does not reflect a grand and coherent constitutional design aiming to give all parts of the country an equal status. It is rather to be seen as an attempt to find very pragmatically a tailored special solution for each British nation that suits their different traditions and political ambitions.[42] As a result, Scotland enjoys greater autonomy than Wales, whereas Northern Ireland is a very special case, and the biggest British nation, England, most strikingly, has no constitutional status and no autonomy at all, but is still fully governed by the centralized UK Parliament and Government. Very often, namely in all policy areas that have been devolved to the Parliaments or regional assemblies of Scotland, Wales and Northern Ireland, the UK Parliament of Westminster will therefore have to make laws that apply only to England; the deeper devolution becomes, the more apparent it is going to be that the central Parliament of the UK is or acts at the same time as a regional Parliament for England. Two problems arise from this:

---

39 See Memorandum of Understanding and Supplementary Agreements Between the United Kingdom Scottish Ministers, the Cabinet oft he National Assembly for Wales and the Northern Ireland Executive Commitee, Cm 5240 (2001); Fenwick/Phillipson (fn. 7), p. 52, 256-257.; Hadfield, in: Jowell/Oliver (fn. 13), p. 217.

40 Bogdanor (fn. 12), p. 113 f., v. Andreae (fn. 17), from p. 519 , 633-634.

41 Leyland (fn. 14), p. 247, 292; Fenwick/Phillipson (fn. 7), p. 234-235, 266; Bogdanor (fn. 12), p. 93, 98; v. Andreae (fn. 17), from p. 275, each with further references.

42 v. Andreae (fn. 17), p. 563.

The first one may appear to be a minor side-effect with little relevance, but it might nevertheless turn out to be a potentially harmful development. In a "multi-national" United Kingdom, both numerically and historically dominated by the English, the fact that the British Parliament serves as the English Parliament at the same time, even increases the existing confusion over the concepts of "English" and "British," which are very often not sufficiently distinguished and kept apart in everyday language, but identified with one another. The feeling that Great Britain and the United Kingdom is essentially an English enterprise (with some autonomy for Scotland and Wales) may thus be increased and lead to some resentment in Scotland and Wales.

The second problem arising from the fact that the UK Parliament is the Parliament for England at the same time, is a much more fundamental one, a major unresolved question at the heart of the construction of British devolution. It is usually called the "English Question" or the "West Lothian Question" (because it was first addressed by a Scottish MP from the constituency of West Lothian). It deals with the problems of unequal representation in the UK.[43] Is it fair that, when the UK Parliament passes laws that apply specifically to England only, all UK MPs, i.e. not only the 528 MPs from England, but also the 118 MPs from Scotland, Wales and Northern Ireland can vote, whereas the English have no say in devolved matters that are decided only by Scottish, Welsh or Irish representatives in their regional Parliaments or assemblies? The West Lothian question has been debated for a long time without a clear resolution. The obvious solution would be to create a devolved English Parliament, and to leave to the UK Parliament only matters of the Union that have not been devolved to the regional assemblies. This, however, is a solution that the English dislike, perhaps because they still regard the Parliament in Westminster – despite some MPs from the regions – as essentially their own Parliament, so that creating an extra Parliament for England seems unnecessarily complicated and costly, perhaps also, because such a step would inevitably turn Westminster into some sort of federal Parliament with limited powers. This would be is the exact opposite of the sovereign Parliament it used to be and which the English prefer (it seems that the English might prefer a Parliament which at

---

43 See: Bogdanor (fn. 12), p. 98-110; Webley/Samuels (fn. 16), from p. 317; Leyland (fn. 14), from p. 272; Fenwick/Phillipson (fn. 7), from p. 288; v. Andreae (fn. 17), from p. 310, each with further references; cf. also http://en.wikipedia.org/wiki/West_Lothian_question.

least for England, keeps its original omnipotence, even if it involves the participation of non-English MPs for England-only matters).

An alternative might therefore be to leave the powers of the Westminster Parliament unchanged, but to change the way it functions by making sure that for England-only matters, the right to vote is held by the English MPs ("English votes for English laws"). This, however, would lead to a kind of split Parliament with possibly different political majorities for the entire UK and for England only (because the Conservatives are traditionally much stronger in England than in the rest of the country, whereas Labour draws disproportionate support from Wales and Scotland). A split Parliament – in a parliamentary system of government like the UK – would inevitably render a coherent creation of a government more complicated. English insistence on "English votes for English laws" may also threaten the Union and enhance separatist movements in the regions. In 2012, the UK government formed a Commission to consider the West Lothian Question, which reported in March 2013. The commission suggested a typically British solution, a compromise by a new constitutional convention, namely a principle to be enshrined by a Parliamentary resolution that a decision with separate and distinct effect for England should normally be taken only with the consent of the majority of MPs sitting for constituencies in England. English MPs would thus get a conventional possibility to delay laws; yet the legal right of all MPs to pass a law for England only would remain unaffected.[44] The government said it would give the recommendations in the report serious consideration, but it is unlikely that a decision will be taken quickly. The "English question" thus remains unresolved, and perhaps cannot be resolved, To accept that Scottish and Welsh MPs participate in votes on English laws may well be the price the English have to pay to keep the Union intact, despite the English dominance and the widespread identification of "English" and "British".[45]

3.3 Evolutionary potential

The last characteristic feature of British devolution, which I would like to look at, and which also has to do with the fact that devolution delivers prag-

---

44 http://webarchive.nationalarchives.gov.uk/20130403030652/http://tmc.independent.gov.uk/.
45 Bogdanor (fn. 12), p. 107-108.

matic and flexible solutions rather than being the expression of systematic constitutional design or of a long-lasting constitutional settlement, is its highly dynamic nature and its evolutionary potential that is currently difficult to grasp.[46] In both Scotland and in Wales, the 1998 legislative settlement seems to be only a starting point for ever more devolution. Wales – after a successful referendum in 2011 – was entrusted with an enumerative list of legislative powers; and Scotland – following the recommendations of the Calman Commission – was given more tax raising powers by the Scotland Act 2012. In both cases, therefore, devolution has been accelerating.[47] What is most striking is that even complete independence is a possible option, which may not be intended, but which, nevertheless, is principally inherent in the concept and process of devolution. For Northern Ireland, for example, it was from the very beginning of devolution that the Good Friday Agreement in 1998 laid down certain conditions under which termination of the Union would be possible.[48] And for Scotland, too, the British government has accepted the right of the Scottish people to hold a referendum on independence, which will take place on 18 September.[49] The right of secession and self-determination for the comprising parts of the Union – a right denied by many federal constitutions – thus has, in principle, come to be politically accepted in the United Kingdom.[50]

4. Conclusion

From what I have said, it will have become obvious that the question addressed in the title of my talk – of whether devolution will eventually turn out to be an alternative or a slippery slope to independence – is a question that simply cannot be answered at the present moment. Let me nevertheless

---

46 Fenwick/Phillipson (fn. 7), p. 235.
47 Hadfield, in: Jowell/Oliver (fn. 13), from p. 219 and 225; Möstl, BayVBl. 2013 (fn. 1), 583.
48 See Fenwick/Phillipson (fn. 7), p. 274-275; Hadfield, in: Jowell/Oliver (fn. 13), p. 214.
49 Agreement between the United Kingdom Government and the Scottish Government on a referendum on independence for Scotland, available at http://webarchive.nationalarchives.gov.uk/20130109092234/http://www.number10.gov.uk/wp-content/uploads/2012/10/Agreement-final-for-signing.pdf; see also fn. 2
50 Bogdanor (fn. 12), p. 116.

try to come to some conclusions about the future as to the merits and dangers of devolution.

First, devolution is a flexible process that can respond to the varying aspirations of the different parts of the UK and has not reached its limits. It can cope with more decentralization and is theoretically open for maximum autononomy ("devo-max"[51]), which should be able to satisfy the political ambitions even of the Scottish people. It is, therefore, certainly possible that devolution is a lasting alternative to independence. The more devolution there is, however, the more Westminster will become a Parliament for England, the more its legitimacy as the Parliament for the entire UK may be weakened, and the more it will become obvious that the "English question" has not been solved.

Second, British devolution is built around the concept of Parliamentary Sovereignty, and its success, therefore, depends on the trust, that – by respecting constitutional conventions – Westminster will not make use of the legal powers it still has. So far, this trust still seems to be there, but it seems equally possible that the continuous political unrest over independence may destroy that trust on which the constitutional arrangement depends. Likewise the present arrangement depends on the readiness of the English to accept that "their" Parliament – from a political, but not a legal, point of view – is no longer sovereign. The debate over the English question may be a sign that this readiness can no longer be taken for granted.

Third, however much autonomy Scotland may have gained in the process of devolution (an autonomy even bigger than that of a German Land), there is and remains one important difference with a federal country like Germany:[52] Scotland as a political entity has no independent say at the central level in London. German Länder – in the Bundesrat, the second chamber – take part in federal decision-making; important constitutional decisions depend on a qualified majority amongst the German Länder. The UK lacks all these structures, and as the political majority in Scotland is frequently different from that of England and Scottish MPs in Westminster form only a small minority, this lack of independent influence on the central level matters.[53] It is – as I would say from the German point of view – the wisdom of federal systems to give their components some sort of say on the central level

---

51 Hadfield, in: Jowell/Oliver (fn. 13), p. 216.
52 Möstl, BayVBl. 2013 (fn. 1), 586-587.
53 Scotlands Future, Your guide to an independent Scotland, p.61, available at http:// 82.113.138.107/00439021.pdf.

and, thus, to make it clear, that the central state has not only devolved some powers from the top to the lower level, but that the central state is also composed by and legitimized through its parts. Any step in that direction – like giving Scotland veto-powers on certain questions of union-wide importance (exit from the EU, for example, should England want it) – would, of course, be a far-reaching departure from characteristic features of British constitutional law. It would turn Britain into a kind of truly federal country with a real written constitution in which Parliamentary sovereignty is no longer the fundamental constitutional principle. And I know very well that it is highly unlikely that any such a step will ever be considered. The fact that the British nations are of such unequal size – England alone makes up more than 80% of the UK population – and that adequately balanced federal structures would indeed be difficult to imagine for the UK, makes it even more understandable that the English in particular, but probably also the Scottish, are reluctant to consider any step in that direction.[54] The widespread reluctance to consider such fundamental constitutional change and to think in terms of real federalism (instead only of devolution) – as I would answer – increases however the risk that an even greater constitutional "earthquake" may occur, the total break-up of the UK in its present form. According to recent opinion polls on the Scottish referendum[55] such an outcome still seems unlikely, but it is obvious that Scottish independence, virtually unthinkable until recently, is becoming a more and more realistic option.

Finally, is British devolution an example that can and should be copied in other countries? What is certainly an example is the incredibly civilized manner in which the debate on devolution and even independence is led in Britain, the unmatched ability of the British to keep calm even when questions are being discussed that might undermine the very existence of the British Union. British devolution is also an example which proves that giving autonomy to regions with great political aspirations (as in Scotland) may be a way to abate separatist tendencies; nevertheless there is no guarantee that separatist tendencies will not prevail. Apart from that – one has to admit – the construction of British devolution is so deeply rooted in peculiarities of British constitutional law, tradition and history that it cannot and should not be copied easily in other countries and constitutional contexts.

---

54 Fenwick/Philipson (fn. 7), p. 290 -291. quoting from a report of a Royal commission 1973: "A federation of four parts…would be so unbalanced as to be unworkable".
55 http://whatscotlandthinks.org/opinion-polls.

Scottish independence in Europe – a model for others?

Florian Becker

A. Introduction

This article scrutinises the consequences in international and European law of Scottish independence from the United Kingdom (UK) and examines whether this process can serve as a model for other independence movements. In this regard, we need to consider the following questions: How would the process of Scottish independence work? What desirable and undesirable consequences does independence have on the international and European obligations of the parties concerned? The latter question is of particular importance as undesirable implications and consequences of the process might form the basis of a political argument against independence, a deterrent for other regions.

Although the referendum did not result in Scottish independence, lessons from the process that led to the referendum, and from all the work that has been written to discuss its conditions and consequences might still be of help to others. However, I submit that the historical as well as the constitutional background is highly relevant, particularly when analysing Scottish independence from the perspective of international and EU law. Accordingly, the transfer of insight depends upon the existence of comparable conditions.

B. Historical and constitutional background

I. The Union

The legal foundation of the Union between Scotland and England consists of a number of legal acts. In 1706 representatives of both Parliaments signed the Treaty of the Union which was ratified – again by both Parliaments – in 1707. This constituted an international treaty between two (at that time) independent states in the sense of international law. However, according to popular doctrine, its provisions can be altered or amended through legislation of the UK Parliament in Westminster[1]. The legal consequences of the treaty and its ratification have been controversial. While some UK courts argued that the Union resulted in the emergence of an entirely new state, others took the view that England simply expanded to the North in the sense that Scotland acceded to England. This view is supported by the fact that the English constitutional bodies subsisted and were joined by the Scottish. In any event, Scotland was extinguished as a state in 1707[2].

II. Development towards a referendum

It is impossible to present the entire development of the Scottish-English relationship since 1707. The most notable recent aspect, however, was the process of devolution that led to the establishment of a Scottish Parliament which has delegated powers known as "devolved matters". Within this framework, there are issues upon which only the UK Parliament can make laws, referred to as reserved matters (Schedule 5 of the Scotland Act 1998): "The following aspects of the constitution are reserved matters,… (b) the Union of the Kingdoms of Scotland and England." These issues remain exclusively the responsibility of the UK Parliament. Accordingly, the Scottish Parliament cannot pass any legislation other than on a non-binding and merely consultative referendum regarding independence.

III. Constitutional arrangements for the referendum

To avoid constitutional difficulties resulting from the limited jurisdiction of the Scottish parliament set out above, the governments of the United Kingdom and Scotland reached the Edinburgh Agreement (2012), resolving ex-

---

1 *James Crawford / Alan Boyle*, Annex A. Opinion: Referendum on the Independence of Scotland – International Law Aspects, in: UK Government, Scotland analysis: Devolution and the implications of Scottish independence (2013), 64-108, 76 (para. 45-46), available at:
https://www.gov.uk/government/uploads/system/uploads/attachment_data/file/79417/Scotland_analysis_Devolution_and_the_implications_of_Scottish_Independan...__1_.pdf (accessed on 28 October 2014).
2 *James Crawford / Alan Boyle*, Annex A. Opinion: Referendum on the Independence of Scotland – International Law Aspects, in: UK Government, Scotland analysis: Devolution and the implications of Scottish independence (2013), 64-108, 75 (para. 37).

actly these constitutional problems of the referendum and its consequences[3]. Both governments agreed that the referendum should have a clear legal base legislated for by the Scottish Parliament and deliver a fair test as well as a decisive expression of the views of people in Scotland, leading to a result that everyone would respect. The agreement illustrates that the United Kingdom respects the democratic will of the people of Scotland and that, in the event of an affirmative vote, it will accept that Scotland should become independent.

Thus, it is essential to understand that the Scottish independence referendum was initiated as a consensual process between the parties concerned rather than a process of (unilateral) secession, which might be considered illegal (or, at least, unwelcome) under public international law as long as it takes place outside the process of decolonisation[4].

C. Consequences of a "Yes"-vote

The referendum took place on 18th September 2014. It asked the electorate the following question: 'Should Scotland be an independent country? Yes/ No.' Had the majority voted "Yes", this would have resulted in several problems that would have had to be considered, including constitutional

---

3 Agreement between the United Kingdom Government and the Scottish Government on a referendum on independence for Scotland, Edinburgh, 15 October 2012, available at:
http://www.scotland.gov.uk/Resource/0040/00404789.pdf (accessed on 28 October 2014).

4 *Antonio Cassese*, International Law (2nd ed. 2005), 60-64, 68; *James Crawford*, Brownlie's Principles of Public International Law (8th ed. 2008), 141-142; *Hans-Joachim Heintze*,Völker im Völkerrecht, in: Knut Ipsen (ed.), Völkerrecht (6th ed. 2014), 316-377, 353-357; *Marcel Kau*, Der Staat und der Einzelne als Völkerrechtssubjekt, in: Wolfgang Graf Vitzthum / Alexander Proelß, Völkerrecht (6th ed. 2013), 131-235, 178; *Susanna Mancini*, Rethinking the boundaries of democratic secession: Liberalism, nationalism, and the right of minorities to self-determination, IntJConstL 6 (2008), 553-584, 556-557; *Daniel Thürer / Thomas Burri*, Secession (June 2009), MPEPIL, available via: http://www.mpepil.com (accessed on 28 October 2014); *Stephen Tierney*, In a State of Flux: Self-Determination and the Collapse of Yugoslavia, IJMGR 6 (1999), 197-233, 203-204; *Christian Tomuschat*, Secession and self-determination, in: Marcelo G. Kohen (ed.), Secession. International Law Perspectives (2006), 23-45, 23-25; *Malcolm N. Shaw*, International Law (7th ed. 2014), 183-188.

difficulties concerning Scotland's transition to independence and its consequences in international and European law. It is important to note, however, that any interpretation of the transition process and its consequences from an international and European law perspective would have depended on how transition had actually taken place.

I. Statehood

The answer to the most significant legal question lies at the heart of all the other problems, and naturally it also has strong political relevance. How can Scotland become a state in the sense of public international law? Achieving (full) statehood is an important political objective, particularly when assessing the desirability of independence from a Scottish point of view. There is no doubt that Scottish statehood should be the outcome. However, so far it remains open how that can be achieved and therefore how a new independent Scotland would be linked to "old Scotland", to the new "UK" (without Scotland) and its relationships with the EU and the world community.

Different scenarios have different implications on Scotland's status under international law. In turn, Scotland's status under international law (and how it would be achieved) can have an impact on the assessment of it being within the EU.[5]

The following roles have to be assigned in the process[6]: At the end, there would have been a predecessor state, i.e. a state that has lost some parts of its territory and/or population. It would have been a continuing state or continuator that had retained its legal identity and existence despite a significant change in its circumstances (i.e. this loss of territory and/or population). There would also have been either a successor state, i.e. a state that has acquired a territory, or an entirely new state that comes into existence following a change of sovereignty.

It has rarely been disputed that the result of the independence would have been the existence of two states (though not necessarily new ones). The

---

5 *Stephen Tierney*, Legal issues surrounding the referendum on independence for Scotland, ECL Review 9 (2013), 359-390, 382-289.

6 *Anthony Aust*, Handbook of International Law (2nd ed. 2010), 361; *James Crawford / Alan Boyle*, Annex A. Opinion: Referendum on the Independence of Scotland – International Law Aspects, in: UK Government, Scotland analysis: Devolution and the implications of Scottish independence (2013), 64-108, 72 (paras. 22.4-22.6).

former UK either would have ceased to exist as a legal person and two entirely new entities would have emerged (dissolution) or it would have persisted (as "residual UK", rUK) and Scotland would have emerged as an entirely new state separated from the rUK. It seems quite unrealistic that the rUK would have been regarded as the new state.

In case of a dissolution, the UK as predecessor state would have ceased to exist[7]; this consequently would have led to the emergence of two new states[8] (Scotland and the rUK). The basic assumption is that both of them would be free of the majority of international treaty obligations (including memberships in international organisations), and both states would have to reorganise these obligations under international law[9]. There have been some examples of dissolution with consequences deviating from this basic assumption. Czechoslovakia dissolved into the Czech Republic and Slovakia. Both states reached agreement to the effect that Czechoslovakia would cease to exist and that neither would claim to be the continuator state.[10] They were consequently recognised by the international community as new states having to build their international obligations from scratch.[11] After the collapse of the Socialist Federal Republic of Yugoslavia (SFRY), the Federal Republic of Yugoslavia claimed to be the continuator state,[12] but its claim was

---

7 *James Crawford / Alan Boyle*, Annex A. Opinion: Referendum on the Independence of Scotland – International Law Aspects, in: UK Government, Scotland analysis: Devolution and the implications of Scottish independence (2013), 64-108, 83 (para. 71); *James Sloan*, The international law implications for an independent Scotland: findings of an expert legal opinion requested by the UK Government, Edinburgh Law Review 2013, 224-229, 226-227; *Stephen Tierney*, Legal issues surrounding the referendum on independence for Scotland, ECL Review 9 (2013), 359-390, 371.

8 See *David Edward*, EU Law and the Separation of Member States, Fordham International Law Journal 2013, 1151-1168, 1156.

9 *Antonio Cassese*, International Law (2nd ed. 2005), 78-79; *Malcolm N. Shaw*, International Law (7th ed. 2014), 710.

10 *Anthony Aust*, Handbook of International Law (2nd ed. 2010), 370-371; *Anthony Aust*, Modern Treaty Law and Practice (2nd ed. 2007), 381-383; *Jan Klabbers*, An Introduction to International Institutional Law (2nd ed. 2009), 104-105; *Stephen Tierney*, Legal issues surrounding the referendum on independence for Scotland, ECL Review 9 (2013), 359-390, 371.

11 *Jiří Malenovský*, Problèmes Jurisdique Liés à la Partition de la Tchécoslovaquie, AFDI 39 (1993) 305-336.

12 *Malcolm N. Shaw*, International Law (7th ed. 2014), 710; *Anthony Aust*, Handbook of International Law (2nd ed. 2010), 369.

rejected by the international community and consequently the SFRY was considered to have dissolved.[13]

The key factor in the decision of the consequences of dissolution of the states concerned is the own perception, and their views of and the recognition by third parties (mainly states and international organisations). A "general predisposition of international law is to favour state continuation where possible"[14].

Another possibility is to interpret Scotland's independence as a case of separation as there would be one continuator state retaining the legal identity of the UK and one new state that has to reorganise its relationships under international law.

3. The case of the UK and Scotland

It was quite unrealistic that Scotland would have been perceived as the continuator state so that this role would have been assigned to rUK[15]. If Scotland had become independent, rUK would have retained the majority of territory (more than two-thirds) and population (about 92%) as well as its principal governmental institutions on its territory (London)[16]. The views of the parties concerned (Scotland and the rUK), and the international community as

---

13 *Anthony Aust*, Handbook of International Law (2nd ed. 2010), 370; *Anthony Aust*, Modern Treaty Law and Practice (2nd ed. 2007), 379-381; *Photini Pazartzis*, Secession and international law: the European dimension, in: Marcelo G. Kohen (ed.), Secession. International Law Perspectives (2006), 355-373, 364-367; *Malcolm N. Shaw*, International Law (7th ed. 2014), 152-153; *Stephen Tierney*, In a State of Flux: Self-Determination and the Collapse of Yugoslavia, IJMGR 6 (1999), 197-233; *Marc Weller*, The International Response to the Dissolution of the Socialist Federal Republic of Yugoslavia, AJIL 86 (1992), 569-607.

14 *Stephen Tierney*, Legal issues surrounding the referendum on independence for Scotland, ECL Review 9 (2013), 359-390, 371.

15 *David Edward*, EU Law and the Separation of Member States, Fordham International Law Journal 2013, 1151-1168, 1155; *James Sloan*, The international law implications for an independent Scotland: findings of an expert legal opinion requested by the UK Government, Edinburgh Law Review 2013, 224-229, 225-226; *Adam Tomkins*, Scotland's choice, Britain's future, The Law Quarterly Review 2014, 215-234, 231.

16 *James Crawford / Alan Boyle*, Annex A. Opinion: Referendum on the Independence of Scotland – International Law Aspects, in: UK Government, Scotland analysis: Devolution and the implications of Scottish independence (2013), 64-108, 83 (para. 69).

a whole, would probably have confirmed this approach. The rUK would certainly have claimed continuity. Contrary to Yugoslavia, there is no reason to contest this claim, which probably would have been accepted finally by Scotland.

Scotland would not have re-emerged as the state existing before 1707[17], but as an entirely new state[18]. There have been cases of re-emergence (e.g. the Baltic states after the end of Soviet occupation), but the underlying fact of state continuity is only in cases of illegal, but effective annexation. In any event, Scottish reversion would not be relevant to questions of membership of international organizations and the EU as the corresponding international institutions had not existed in 1707[19].

II. Membership of international organisations

Territorial changes of the continuator state do not lead to the loss of membership of international organisations (IO)[20]. However, the question of membership for a new state can have significance, particularly if it is not entirely clear whether all current members of IO sympathise with the cause of independence. This could lead to difficulties if the new state would not be a member of IO automatically[21]. Accordingly, it would have been a cru-

---

17 *James Crawford/Alan Boyle*, Annex A. Opinion: Referendum on the Independence of Scotland – International Law Aspects, in: UK Government, Scotland analysis: Devolution and the implications of Scottish independence (2013), 64-108, 90 (para. 109); *James Sloan*, The international law implications for an independent Scotland: findings of an expert legal opinion requested by the UK Government, Edinburgh Law Review 2013, 224-229, 228-229.

18 *Stephen Tierney*, Legal issues surrounding the referendum on independence for Scotland, ECL Review 9 (2013), 359-390, 390: "a territory aspiring to new statehood".

19 *James Crawford/Alan Boyle*, Annex A. Opinion: Referendum on the Independence of Scotland – International Law Aspects, in: UK Government, Scotland analysis: Devolution and the implications of Scottish independence (2013), 64-108, 91 (para. 113).

20 *Antonio Cassese*, International Law (2nd ed. 2005), 77; *Hans-Joachim Heintze*,Völker im Völkerrecht, in: Knut Ipsen (ed.), Völkerrecht (6th ed. 2014), 316-377, 352; *Malcolm N. Shaw*, International Law (7th ed. 2014), 696.

21 *Anthony Aust*, Modern Treaty Law and Practice (2nd ed. 2007), 370; *Antonio Cassese*, International Law (2nd ed. 2005), 80; *Volker Epping*, Internationale Organisationen, in: Knut Ipsen (ed.), Völkerrecht (6th ed. 2014), 197-307, 211; *Malcolm N. Shaw*, International Law (7th ed. 2014), 713-714.

cial question for the new state of Scotland, whether a "clean slate rule" applies and Scotland enters into the international community completely free of contractual relationships and obligations with regard to membership positions, or whether the new state could remain on the same level as the predecessor, basically choosing to inherit its position (or better, splitting it into two). There are some obvious difficulties with this approach, which become evident when, for example, scrutinizing UN membership of the UK. Nobody would have argued that the rUK *and* Scotland would both have had a permanent seat in the UN Security Council. Similar concerns become evident regarding the opt-out privileges that the UK (and probably rUK) enjoy in its relation to the EU. Apart from all legal arguments, it was politically undesirable and thus contested by the UK and the EU that the new Scottish state should automatically succeed to all of the UK's rights and responsibilities in these respects.

Concerning contractual obligations in general, the Vienna Convention on Succession of States in Respect of Treaties (1978) (VCSST) establishes as a basic principle that of the continuity of treaty obligations, but Articles 34(2) (b) and 35(c) provide exceptions to this rule, which would apply here, because in a case of automatic succession, the constitution of the IO would have be radically changed regarding voting rights, financial obligation, etc., as confirmed by Article 4 VCSST. This provision states that the Convention is not applicable to succession to a treaty that is "the constituent instrument of an international organization without prejudice to the rules concerning acquisition of membership and without prejudice to any other relevant rules of the organization". Beyond this, these provisions merely offer some guidance in our case as the UK is not a party to this convention,[22] and it is highly questionable whether it contains rules of customary law[23].

Against this background, it is worthwhile scrutinizing the relevant treaties for explicit or implicit rules about acquisition and/or loss of membership.

---

22 *James Crawford / Alan Boyle*, Annex A. Opinion: Referendum on the Independence of Scotland – International Law Aspects, in: UK Government, Scotland analysis: Devolution and the implications of Scottish independence (2013), 64-108, 93 (para. 124).

23 *Anthony Aust*, Modern Treaty Law and Practice (2nd ed. 2007), 369.

1. UN membership

Article 4 of the UN-Charter sets conditions for the admission of a state to the UN. It is the task of the Security Council and General Assembly to apply them, although in practice political considerations are also significant. In connection with Pakistan's application for membership, the General Assembly adopted several principles which included the following: If a new state emerges, it will never automatically succeed to membership, but always has to be formally admitted to membership[24]. This happened in the case of Russia that succeeded as continuator state to all international treaties of the USSR[25]; the new successor states had to reapply for membership[26] (except Ukraine and Belarus, which had been original members under the political agreement at the San Francisco Conference in 1945[27]). Consequently, the rUK would retain the UK's membership, whereas Scotland would have to apply for new membership.

2. ECHR/Council of Europe membership

Membership of the ECHR and the Council of Europe (CoE) presents a similar case. Although these are two distinct questions, the legal positions are closely linked as only members of the Council of Europe may accede to the ECHR, and approval to the ECHR depends on membership in the Council of Europe. Article 7 of the Statute of the Council of Europe (Statute CoE, cf. also Articles 2; 3; 4 and 16 Statute CoE) clearly states that withdrawal is possible after notification and lapse of a deadline. However, there is no explicit rule for state succession. In the case of Serbia-Montenegro, Serbia continued the membership of Serbia and Montenegro, while the latter had

---

24 Admission of Pakistan to membership in the United Nations: Question raised in the First Committee by the representative of Argentina (documents A/399, A/C.6/145, A/C.6/146, A/C.6/156 and A/C.6/162), reprinted in: GAOR, 2nd Session, 6th Committee, 42nd meeting (6 October 1947), 37-38, 38.

25 *James Crawford*, Brownlie's Principles of Public International Law (8th ed. 2008), 427.

26 *Anthony Aust*, Handbook of International Law (2nd ed. 2010), 373; *Volker Epping*, Internationale Organisationen, in: Knut Ipsen (ed.), Völkerrecht (6th ed. 2014), 197-307, 212-213; *Jan Klabbers*, An Introduction to International Institutional Law (2nd ed. 2009), 104; *Malcolm N. Shaw*, International Law (7th ed. 2014), 696.

27 *Anthony Aust*, Handbook of International Law (2nd ed. 2010), 187.

to apply for new membership[28]. The ECHR continued to be applicable to Montenegro because of the self-commitment of Montenegro[29].

The Scottish situation would have been similar[30]: The rUK would have remained a member of the ECHR and the Council of Europe (CoE), whereas Scotland would have had to apply for new membership. Scotland would probably have followed the example of Montenegro by committing itself unilaterally to respect the rules of the convention until new membership had been approved (if this was not going to happen *before* independence had been achieved). A different scenario would have arisen only if Scotland had not wanted to join the ECHR/CoE; however, that would have had a negative knock-on effect on the desired EU-membership.

3. EU membership

Prospective EU membership and the relevant conditions had probably been the most important aspects for an independent Scotland. One might question up to which point the presented state practice with regard to other IO is relevant for the EU. The application of general international law to the EU

---

28 Council of Europe, Committee of Ministers, 967th Meeting, 14 June 2006, Decisions adopted (CM/Del/Dec(2006)967), State Union of Serbia and Montenegro (Item 2.3 a, Item 2.3 b), available at: https://wcd.coe.int/ViewDoc.jsp? id=1010947&Site=CM&BackColorInternet=C3C3C3&BackColorIntranet=ED-B021&BackColorLogged=F5D383 (accessed on 28.10.2014); *Tanja E. J. Kleinsorge*, Council of Europe (2010), part of: Jan Wouters (ed.), International Encyclopaedia of Laws / Intergovernmental Organizations, 147-148.

29 *Tanja E. J. Kleinsorge*, Council of Europe (2010), part of: Jan Wouters (ed.), International Encyclopaedia of Laws / Intergovernmental Organizations, 148.

30 *James Crawford / Alan Boyle*, Annex A. Opinion: Referendum on the Independence of Scotland – International Law Aspects, in: UK Government, Scotland analysis: Devolution and the implications of Scottish independence (2013), 64-108, 98 (para. 140).

is often seen as problematic[31] since the EU constitutes a "new legal order of international law"[32]. However, the creation of the EU was achieved with instruments of international law and the "questions of whether a state is a member of the EU has hitherto been treated as a matter of international law (just as the question of the territorial extent of a state has been)"[33].

Priority must be given to the treaty law governing the organisation in question. Article 52 TEU and Article 355 TFEU describe the territorial scope of the application of EU law: only in those territories mentioned EU law is applicable. The EU itself does not have any territorial sovereignty; this is only derived from its Member States. In cases of enlargement of the territory of Member States, the principle of territorial variability of treaties applies. Thus, the territorial scope of the treaty expands in accordance with the enlargement.

For the first time, Article 50 TEU provides the possibility of withdrawal of Member States from the EU. A notification to the European Council and the passage of two years are required. In contrast, the Treaties do not provide for independence of any parts of territories. Only Article 52 TEU comprises an indirect statement.

So far, there is no clear precedent in EU law. Algeria was a part of France and constituted the majority of its territory. When it became independent in 1962, it left the EEC. Despite its size, its withdrawal did not affect France's membership because Algeria was in effect a French colony that the EEC

---

31 See e.g. *Albert Bleckmann*, Die Rechtsnatur des Gemeinschaftsrechts. Zur Anwendbarkeit des Völkerrechts im Europäischen Rechtsraum, DÖV 1978, 391-398; *Hans-Joachim Cremer*, Art. 48 EUV, in: Christian Calliess / Matthias Ruffert (eds.), EUV / AEUV (4th ed. 2011), paras. 19-21; *David Edward*, EU Law and the Separation of Member States, Fordham International Law Journal 2013, 1151-1168, 1162; *Jörg Philipp Terhechte*, Artikel 47 EUV, in: Jürgen Schwarze *et al.* (eds.), EU-Kommentar (3rd ed. 2012), paras. 18-21; *Ramses A. Wessel*, Reconsidering the Relationship between International and EU Law: Towards a Content-Based Approach?, in: Enzo Cannizzaro / Paolo Palchetti / Ramses A. Wessel (eds.), International Law as Law of the European Union (2012), 7-33, 5-16.

32 ECJ, Judgment of 5 February 1963 (Case 26/62) Van Gend & Loos, ECR 1963, 1-16.

33 *James Crawford / Alan Boyle*, Annex A. Opinion: Referendum on the Independence of Scotland – International Law Aspects, in: UK Government, Scotland analysis: Devolution and the implications of Scottish independence (2013), 64-108, 98 (para. 142).

never recognised as part of its territory, but treated it as a dependency[34]. Greenland gained autonomy from 1979 onwards, but it remained part of Denmark[35] (and therefore of the EC). When its people voted for leaving the EC in 1985, this did not affect Denmark's membership[36]. However, since Greenland has not become independent, this case is of limited relevance.[37]

At the outset, it "seems unlikely that anyone would suggest that the UK's EU membership could somehow have lapsed as a consequence of the loss of population and territory due to Scottish independence."[38] "Member State's territory depends on that Member State's own constitution, not on the EU treaties. No treaty amendment is therefore required simply as a result of a change to the borders of a state's territory"[39]. A withdrawal as defined in Article 50 TEU would also have to be explicitly requested. However, institutional adjustments would be necessary because of the reduction in its territory and population, resulting in smaller representation in the institutions with knock-on effects on the financial contributions.

---

34 *James Crawford / Alan Boyle*, Annex A. Opinion: Referendum on the Independence of Scotland – International Law Aspects, in: UK Government, Scotland analysis: Devolution and the implications of Scottish independence (2013), 64-108, 99 (para. 146.1).

35 *Claus-Dieter Ehlermann*, Mitgliedschaft in der Europäischen Gemeinschaft. Rechtsprobleme der Erweiterung, der Mitgliedschaft und der Verkleinerung, EuR 19 (1984), 113-125, 123; *Meinhard Schröder*, Artikel 299 EGV, in: Hans von der Groeben / Jürgen Schwarze (ed.), Kommentar zum Vertrag über die Europäische Union und zur Gründung der Europäischen Gemeinschaft (6th ed. 2003), paras. 43-44.

36 *James Crawford / Alan Boyle*, Annex A. Opinion: Referendum on the Independence of Scotland – International Law Aspects, in: UK Government, Scotland analysis: Devolution and the implications of Scottish independence (2013), 64-108, 99 (para. 146.2).

37 James Crawford / Alan Boyle, Annex A. Opinion: Referendum on the Independence of Scotland – Inter-national Law Aspects, in: UK Government, Scotland analysis: Devolution and the implications of Scot-tish independence (2013), 64-108, 99 (para. 146.2).

38 *James Crawford / Alan Boyle*, Annex A. Opinion: Referendum on the Independence of Scotland – International Law Aspects, in: UK Government, Scotland analysis: Devolution and the implications of Scottish independence (2013), 64-108, 99 (para. 145).

39 *James Crawford / Alan Boyle*, Annex A. Opinion: Referendum on the Independence of Scotland – International Law Aspects, in: UK Government, Scotland analysis: Devolution and the implications of Scottish independence (2013), 64-108, 101 (para. 159), referring to ECJ, Judgment of 10 October 1978 (Case 148/77), Hansen v Hauptzollamt Flensburg, ECR 1978, 1787-1810, 1805 (para. 10).

With regard to Scotland as a new state, an automatic membership might not have been completely inconceivable, but was highly unlikely as it would require too many institutional adjustments.

Any Scottish membership – no matter how it happens – would have required amendments to the constitutional framework of the EU as regards, for example, financing and representation. These changes always require negotiation between the parties concerned. The position of rUK would also have required the amendment of the provisions. On any account, considerations with regard to an automatic membership would have depended on the course of events, as well as the opinions and declarations of the parties involved. Against that background, it seems safe to say that neither the rUK nor the EU would have assumed an automatic membership of the new state.

This might have resulted of only the rUK as the continuator state remaining a member of the EU (including all its privileges); (new) Scotland would not have received automatic membership in the EU and would have had to apply for it. Sticking points of the negotiation would have been a possible membership of Scotland in the Schengen area, because Scotland would have had to leave the Common Travel Area with the UK and Ireland[40]. A similar problem would have arisen with regard to an expected Euro membership, as Scotland would have had to abandon the pound, which it was not inclined to do[41].

A new state needs to apply for EU membership. Article 49 TEU sets out the rules of applying for membership (formal accession). And while European institutional bodies have to be involved in the process, the crucial point is that all other Member States have to agree. On the face of it, no (new) state has a legal entitlement to accede. To avoid political problems that could have arisen in the course of negotiations for a fresh Scottish membership, the Scottish government had brought the ordinary revision procedure as a fast-track option into the discussion (Article 48 TEU)[42]. Although the more complex procedure of Article 49 TEU appears to be the *lex specialis*, the

---

40 Scottish Government, Scotland in the European Union, 27 November 2013, 13, available at: http://www.scotland.gov.uk/Resource/0043/00439166.pdf (accessed on 28 October 2014).

41 Scottish Government, Scotland in the European Union, 27 November 2013, 12-13, available at: http://www.scotland.gov.uk/Resource/0043/00439166.pdf (accessed on 28 October 2014).

42 Scottish Government, Scotland in the European Union, 27 November 2013, 12,86, available at: http://www.scotland.gov.uk/Resource/0043/00439166.pdf (accessed on 28 October 2014).

new composition of the organs has been negotiated in the context of the Eastern enlargements through the ordinary revision procedure for the treaties, and not through membership process. In any event, the situation of Scotland would evidently not have been comparable to that of any other accession candidate, notably because an adjustment of its domestic legal order to EU law would have been unnecessary. Accordingly, an amendment of the treaty with regard to an accession, as referred to in Article 48 TEU,[43] would have been more likely than an accession process as defined in Article 49 TEU[44].

No matter which of the two routes would have been chosen, both options would have led to a certain time pressure as it was questionable whether the timespan between the referendum and the (prospective) independence in 2016 would have been sufficient for the conclusion of negotiations. During an interim period, Scotland could have committed itself to unilaterally respecting EU law as a purely national solution, which would have eased problems that arise from any period of non-membership (or even an interim period) affecting the legal status of EU citizens living in Scotland. However, Scottish people would have – at least for a certain period – seen their legal positions (e.g. fundamental freedom) compromised had these states been unwilling to cooperate.

Against this background, it was argued that any negative impact on individuals could be avoided by using the concept of citizenship as an argument for an automatic membership[45]. In *Rottmann*,[46] the ECJ held that "a Member State must exercise its powers to withdraw an individual's nationality compatibly with the principles of EU law"[47], otherwise the privileges of EU membership would be taken away from the individual. Using the *fortiori argument* of Article 50 TEU[48] would mean that a failure of negotiations

---

43 See above.

44 See above.

45 See *Aidan O'Neill*, A Quarrel in a Faraway Country?: Scotland, Independence and the EU (posted on 14 November 2011), available at: http://eutopialaw.com/2011/11/14/685/ (accessed on 28.10.2014).

46 ECJ, Judgment of 2 March 2010 (Case C-135/08), Rottmann v Bavaria, ECR 2010, I-1449-I-1492.

47 *James Crawford / Alan Boyle*, Annex A. Opinion: Referendum on the Independence of Scotland – International Law Aspects, in: UK Government, Scotland analysis: Devolution and the implications of Scottish independence (2013), 64-108, 107 (para. 178.1).

48 See above.

should result in an automatic membership to avoid individuals being deprived of their status under EU law. However, Article 20(1) TFEU states that European citizenship is based on of the Member States' citizenship; using this derivative concept as an argument against the possibility of a state withdrawing from the EU would simply be a circumvention of an explicit sovereign right enshrined in the treaty. Accordingly, this automatism could not have been employed to argue in favour of automatic membership.

David Edward had developed a slightly different approach to ease Scotland's way (back) into the EU[49]. From his point of view, the obligation to negotiate as defined in Article 50 TEU[50] might resolve this complex situation. "Looking to the presumed intention of the Treaty-makers, they cannot reasonably be supposed to have intended that there must be prior negotiation in the case of withdrawal but none in the case of separation."[51] This would have amounted to all the parties involved being obliged to negotiate in good faith. This, however, results at best in a procedural right or obligation.

D. Scottish independence in Europe – model for others?

Is the discussion about Scottish independence in Europe and its outcomes a role model for other independence movements? It *can* be for several reasons: because Scottish independence would have come about in an amicable way and in the form of an agreement between the UK and Scotland, each appreciating its respective constitutional arrangements. In case of a unilateral secession, however, the legal consequences would be entirely different and not in any way be comparable to the Scottish case.

---

49 *David Edward*, EU Law and the Separation of Member States, Fordham International Law Journal 2013, 1151-1168, 1160-1168.
50 See above.
51 *David Edward*, EU Law and the Separation of Member States, Fordham International Law Journal 2013, 1151-1168, 1167.

The consequences of an independent Catalonia for the German foreign policy

Mario Kölling

1. Introduction

Although the debate on the independence of Catalonia is primarily a Spanish domestic affair, it has many European dimensions that could also have consequences for German international and European policy. Germany´s foreign policy is in fact more commercially-driven than those of other EU countries, so economic interests are very important in analyzing the consequences of an independent Catalonia for German foreign policy. According to worst case scenarios, permanent hostile relations between Catalonia and the Spanish government, or an escalation of the conflict, could have a disastrous shock on the economy of the Iberian Peninsula or at least affect the economic recuperation and fiscal consolidation of Spain. This topic has until now been mainly discussed in political terms and has shown no economic impact. In this sense, the German Chancellor underlined on several occasions that the problem is a Spanish domestic affair, although Chancellor Merkel expressed at the same time her support for the territorial integrity of Spain.

There are several variables that might determine different scenarios and the consequences of an independent Catalonia for German foreign policy, although most are uncertain. Besides the debate among domestic actors, the scenario most likely to take place during the following months depends on external actors or massive citizen´s movements, which could move decision-makers in one direction or another.

There is no historical precedent for dealing with Catalan independence, and every reflection on this topic is highly hypothetical. Nevertheless, if we assume for the purpose of this contribution that Catalonia will be an independent state, there are also many questions that should arise at the beginning of an analysis of the consequences of an independent Catalonia for German foreign policy:

Would Catalonia be a viable state? Would Catalonia be a member state of the EU? What will be the EU policy of the Catalan government regarding its role in the policy process or its power resources? What would be the relationship with the Spanish government? What might be the consequences of the secession of one of the most prosperous regions for the economy and stability of the rest of Spain? Will the rest of Spain be a viable member state? What would be the consequences for other member states?

Depending on how these questions are answered, several hypothetical scenarios can emerge. Here we will analyse two scenarios related to possible developments within the next few months, and one related to the role of Catalonia as an independent state and its relation to the EU. These scenarios are built on each other, considering a theoretical chain of preferences of the German government: 1. Improved status quo, if not possible; 2. Negotiated secession; 3. Transition period to association agreement or (maybe) full EU membership.

To explore these scenarios, we have to analyse German European policy and its goals on a long-term and short-term perspective, as well as German-Spanish relationships. Tt will also be analysed if there are some specific interests of Germany in Catalonia and how the German government faces the current situation in Spain. We will not discuss all the theoretical or prac-tical paths for Catalonia's disintegration from or (re)integration into the EU, and put only forward those that more likely accord with the preferences of the German government.

At the time of writing, the question of whether the government of Cat-alonia will continue the path towards independence remains open, and we will only assume here that Catalonia will continue this path to be in the near or more distant future its own nation state.

2. Characteristics and interests of German EU policy

Germany was very important in EU integration. "Germany has historically been a major – probably *the* major – demander of EU policy solutions and therefore of integration itself." (Bulmer and Paterson 2010:1052). Also Ger-man reunification and the German interest in the Eastern enlargement of the EU represent in some ways the prevalence of the idea of integration in the German domestic and European policy.

Moreover, Germany's industrial and commercial interests drive its for-eign policy more strongly than is case in Britain or France. A common mar-ket without barriers is clearly an advantage for the German export-oriented policy, which has been pushed forward and defended by all German governments.

Germany is also the largest net contributor in absolute terms to the EU budget, but solidarity is also important. Nevertheless, there are increasing fears that the EU could become a "transfer union" in which a growing EU budget is redistributed from richer to poorer member states.

Already the Schröder government brought a more overt stand of 'national interest' into policy debate and defended more openly German commercial interests in EU negotiations. Chancellor Merkel has assumed a much more assertive position and foreign policy became more cautious. During the euro crisis, however, German European policy changed and Germany became Europe's leader in making its economic policy. Before the European Council in March 2010, Chancellor Merkel raised the idea of excluding states from the common currency if they put in danger the future of the eurozone. This has been considered an example for a new approach of Germany's traditionally solidaristic relation to EU partners and set a different tone towards greater unilateral and unpredictable action. It has been argued that "Germany is tempted to go it alone in the multipolar world: they are the biggest economy with global competitiveness, a stable social structure, good relations with Eastern Europe and Russia, and a global reputation for being the world's biggest exporter of machine tools" (Guérot and Leonard, 2011). Apart from the geographical reorientation, one of the key changes in German European policy since the 1990 s has been the emergence of compelling demands. The need to take into account the views of the *Länder* governments and of the *Bundestag* and remain in compliance with the judgments of the Federal Constitutional Court enables the federal government to present to EU partners non-negotiable demands. In this sense different compelling demands, such as constraints arising from domestic public finances, adverse public opinion and fear of a Constitutional Court ruling, were key in identifying solutions to the eurozone crisis. The German government ignored communitarian comments related to domestic affairs; in this sense, not only since the financial crisis, the German European policy has become more intergovernmental-oriented, and both the Commission and the European Parliament have been criticised as lacking economic expertise by the German government (Grant 2013). German considerations as how to enhance cooperation within the eurogroup also show its preferences for an ongoing integration with fewer member states. Instead of joint institutions, the government expressed its preferences for self-responsibility of each member state for its agenda on reform.

Nevertheless, the German government has a clear understanding that it cannot lead Europe on its own, and after several months of misunderstandings, German-French relations improved. Poland has also become a very trusted European partner. Much more important for the purpose of this study, the German government has an in-depth interest in a very close relationship with the British government, and has tried during the past to accommodate British interests within the EU. Apart from traditional coalitions since the Eastern enlargement of the EU, ad hoc coalitions among member states have become increasingly important. In this sense, the German government maintains a close relationship with all EU member state governments, especially during the recent cleavage between member states opting for continuing austerity measures and those favouring economic incentives for growth.

Besides the above, in the German European policy of non-conflict orientation, bargaining and sidepayments are important policy tools, as well as the German foreign policy characterised by the strongly-held principle that any problem can be solved through negotiation (Grant 2014).

Finally, uploading of domestic institutional settings to the European level was one of the main preferences of the German government in negotiating several treaties. In its constitutional practice, the EU emulated the approach to political integration typical of a federal nation-state like Germany, where there is a clear constitutional hierarchy and a sense of common destiny amongst its constituent parts (Börzel 2002; Engel and Parkes 2012). In this sense, the German federal model is seen by the political class as a successful instrument for multi-level policy-making and post-conflict management as well as a tool for the management of different and diverse societies. In a similar way, German elites also tend to see the German economic and monetary model as the only solution for solving the euro crisis (Guérot and Leonard 2011).

3. What are the relations between the German government and Spain?

3.1 Economic relations

German-Spanish relations have traditionally been very good and are fostered by the positive basic attitude of each country's population towards the other. However, cultural and economic relations remain asymmetric. While there are approximately 130,000 Spaniards living in Germany, there are well over 500,000 German citizens living permanently in Spain and nearly 10 million

German tourists visit Spain each year. Since the beginning of the economic crisis, an increasing number of Spaniards are moving to Germany seeking job opportunities or professional education.

Germany is Spain's second largest trading partner, after France, and ranks first among suppliers of Spanish imports and second for Spanish exports. Spain's exports to Germany have traditionally been worth less (EUR 23.7 billion in 2013, 10% of all exports) than its imports from Germany (EUR 31.3 billion in 2013; 11% of all imports). According to the German-Spanish Chamber of Commerce figures, some 1,200 German companies have subsidiaries or holdings in Spain, many with their own production facilities. However, in the statistics on German export for 2013 Spain is, only at 12th and 13th for imports (Statistisches Bundesamt 2014). The German GDP per capita is 31,500 EUR (2012), well above the Spanish GDP per capita of 22,700 EUR. In particular, Spain's motor industry, the world's 8th-largest producer of cars, and its chemical sector closely intervene with the German market.

Nevertheless, this asymmetry is even bigger with regard to German-Catalan relationships. Catalonia represents 1/5 of Spanish GDP and ¼ of Spanish exports. The GDP per capita of Catalonia is higher than the European Union average. According to the Catalan government, there are 6.000 multinational companies established in Catalonia. Although the economic and financial crises have also affected the region (employment is similar to the Spanish average, with Catalonia is one of the ACs with the highest public debt), Catalonia is one of the most prosperous industrialised regions of Spain, with a very diversified and innovative economy intertwined with the German economy (chemical sector, motor industry, etc.). In this sense, there are over 500 German firms established in Catalonia. Catalonia has a well-developed infrastructure (harbour; airport, highways, etc.). According to recent figures published in 2014 by the Spanish Ministry of Economics, the foreign direct investments in Catalonia have grown between 2011 and 2013 by 15.0% and Catalonia remains, after Madrid, the second most important region in Spain for German direct investments (Ministerio de Economía y Competitividad 2014).

The European Union (63%), and especially France (17%) and Germany (11%), are the main markets for Catalonian companies; although the demand from these markets helped to overcome the crisis, recently there has been a reduction in exports because of the lack of growth within the Eurozone. On the other side, imports from Germany (16.5% of all imports) have been growing during the past months, which underlines both the relevance of the

Catalonian market for German companies and the lack of impact of the political debate on their economic relations.

3.2 Political relations

Traditionally, party affiliation has a minor role in German-Spanish governmental relations. There have been very strong relations between Kohl and (Felipe) González; however, since then the relation has been weaker. José María Aznar had closer relation with the British Prime Minister, Tony Blair, than with his German Counterpart, whereas José Luis Rodríguez Zapatero was bereft of close allies. Due to the economic policy differences, his successor, President Rajoy, failed to revive the formerly close partnership with Germany.

During the economic and financial crisis, Spanish-German relations became even more complicated and stereotypes have created a new divide that burdened their bilateral relationship. While in Germany the negative image of the *Südländer* increased distrust, the German government was held responsible in Spain for the drastic cuts in social welfare programmes. Chancellor Merkel was called "Madame No" or "Angela the Faint-hearted" in Catalonia and the rest of Spain broadly by public opinion, but also within the academic elite. The German approach towards budgetary consolidation and austerity was seen as the opposite of the Spanish demands towards investments for growth and job creation. The German government, among others, has pushed the so-called Euro Plus Pact in 2011, which forced Spain to translate European fiscal rules into national legislation and reduce public spending at the national level, but also to ensure budgetary discipline among the Autonomous Communities (ACs). Budgetary constraints have been a strong motivation for adopting control mechanisms that led to the recent recentralisation in Spain. The German government was also crucial in supporting the new EU initiative against youth unemployment, which will also become a policy managed by the central government. The Spanish government already linked the transfer of resources for this policy to several macroeconomic conditions that the ACs have to fulfil. In this context, it could be argued that the secessionist aspirations in Catalonia, which have been growing since the beginning of the Euro crisis, have also been accentuated by the German austerity dictate.

Nevertheless, due to crisis management and reforms of the Spanish government, as well as the need to form stable coalitions at the European level, the relation has grown closer. Although the German government acknowledged the efforts made by the Spanish government to reform the Spanish economy, the focus of German interests is clearly in other parts of the world.

Even though there have not been formal institutional relations between the German government and the *Generalitat*, several important political links between Catalonia and many of the German Länder have been established. The German federal state of Baden Wuerttemberg's special cooperation with Catalonia within the four Motors of Europe[1] provided an important institutional framework for economic cooperation and external representation for the Catalan government. In this context, the role of Jordi Pujol has been crucial. The former President of the Catalan government had excellent relations with German institutions, was German speaking and had a great knowledge of the German political system; he has been frequently invited to many German political institutions. Nevertheless, these close relations were related to him personally and since he finished his mandate, the relations have been weaker. The recent scandal around his family business has also been followed by the German press.

4. What is the German government's position in the current situation in Spain?

When the EU is discussing sensitive policies and important reform steps as the Banking Union and an EU wide tax, an increasing number of actors and diversity seems to be a synonym for more complexity. In general terms, the German government may find the prospects of Scottish, Catalan or Flemish independence particularly worrying.

In analysing the approach of the German government towards Catalonia, we can see a trend from first ignorance to increasing awareness, and finally towards clear support for the Spanish government. As already mentioned, the Catalan government has been receiving German support for a long time, including formal co-operation at the Länder level. In 2007, Catalonia was invited to the Frankfurt Book Fair as "Partner Nation," which was a very welcomed occasion for the Catalan government to increase its international

---

1 The regions of Catalonia, Lombardy (Italy), and Rhône-Alpes (France) had signed the "Four Motors for Europe" cooperation agreement in 1988 with the German federal state Baden Wuerttemberg.

presence. In 2012, the German Consul General in Barcelona, Bernhard Bra-
sack, said: "…in other parts of the world, there has been no problem to switch
overnight from German consulate to German embassy". However, since
2013 the government seemed to be more aware of avoiding involvement in
the issue. There was no official answer to the official letter sent by the Catalan government to the German government in December 2013. Government
representatives only referred to the official statements made by representatives of the European Commission or Council saying that the question is an
internal affair of Spain, and that the territorial integrity of EU member nations is indispensable. The German government was also neutral in the debate among Catalonia-based German business leaders[2] and the territorial
debate in Spain was not an issue that came up in official statements related
to crisis management. Finally, at a press conference in July 2014, the German
Chancellor made the first statement underlining that the question is an internal affair of Spain, but that she supports the opinion of the Spanish government regarding the territorial integrity of Spain: "We defend the territorial
integrity of all states, which is something totally different from a situation
in which regions become independent. I agree on this point with the position
of the Spanish government."[3] During an official visit of the Chancellor to
Spain at the end of August 2014, she confirmed the Spanish government's
opposition to the Catalan demand for independence, saying: "This is a matter
of Spanish domestic politics, but the Spanish government position on Catalonia is logical and should be supported, but I say that with reservations
being a head of government of another country."[4]

5. Hypothetical scenarios

After this short empirical analysis, we will come back to the scenarios put
forward at the beginning of the text: (1) Improved status quo, if not possible;

---

2 In a document entitled 'The Barcelona Declaration' 60 German businesspeople working in Catalonia warned against "the dreadful consequences" that independence would
   bring for the Catalan economy. Nevertheless the German-speaking Business Leaders
   group (KDF), has completely disavowed any relation with the document.
3 Merkel sobre la consulta catalana: "Opino como el Gobierno español", El Pais,
   18.07.2014.
4 Merkel respalda el rechazo de Rajoy a la consulta independentista en Cataluña, El
   Pais, 25.08.2014.

(2) negotiated secession and afterwards; (3) transition period to association agreement or (maybe) full EU membership.

As already underlined, German European policy is very economic interest driven; however, there are also strong political goals towards European integration and commitments rooted in its Europeanist tradition and own history, along with hard facts related to a calculus of the voting power and majority building in the Council. In this sense, the German government will continue being reluctant to comment sensitive Spanish domestic affairs, Berlin will also try not to get unilaterally involved and will avoid any escalation of the conflict in order to maintain a close relation with the Spanish government at the EU level, and to reduce possible conflicts in the future. Considering the lack of specific political relations and the pro-integration approach of German European policy, it could be assumed that economic calculus will be dominant in German preferences. Nevertheless, the economic impact of an independent Catalonia is hard to estimate, and estimations vary considerably according to its authors. However, there seems to be a common understanding that Catalonia and the rest of Spain would suffer economically from secession. Hence it could be assumed that independence will have some clear negative effects for Germany and European Union, and thus pose a potential risk or obstacle for recovery of the Spanish economic, and also result in greater complexity in European crisis management. In this sense, the best solution would be to end the conflict in a way that will not (economically or financially) affect the EU. If the domestic actors could not find a solution, diplomatic contacts of the German government, together with other member states, to the Spanish Government could be offered to help negotiate a solution. Taking into account that member states will not get involved in direct consultation with the Catalan government, only the Spanish government could be asked to offer an improved status quo for Catalonia that comfortably accommodates Catalonia in Spain. Within the existing options, the "Federal model" would be the best approach for the German government. However, during negotiations the German government would closely monitor possible financial agreements and insist that any agreement that could improve the status quo for Catalonia within Spain should be taken within the Treaty on Stability, Coordination and Governance in the Economic and Monetary Union (TSCG).

Concerning our second scenario, if we consider that there is no possible agreement and Spain could be threatened by paralysis and political stability that is no longer granted, German economic interests and preferences regarding the European integration process are going to be much more affected. Although, as already mentioned, there is a common understanding that secession would be bad for all, the status quo could have further negative consequences. Nevertheless, Germany in this case would not encourage secession but favour cooperation on both sides, as well as trying to "de-escalate" the crisis between the Spanish and the Catalan governments. In this context from a German perspective, a negotiated separation is preferable to permanent instability. Nevertheless, Germany will not act unilaterally or promote separation. This approach is based on several assumptions; first from the lessons from the past, German concerns could be related to the damage of its image towards other European countries, and be suspicious of the fact that Germany would have unilaterally chosen to promote separation again, as previously with regard to Yugoslavia. Second, Germany concentrates traditionally on multilateral strategies within the EU, thus it could accept a controlled move towards secession if this is also supported by other member states. In any scenario, a hostile separation has to be avoided. Berlin would stand for a rapid secession and a transitional regime that would allow businesses to operate.

With regard to the third scenario, and assuming that Catalonia will become an independent state, there are strong arguments for Berlin maintaining close relations to Barcelona, as also between Catalonia and the EU. With regard to the economic relations, Catalonia has important commercial relations with Germany. An independent Catalonia within the EU could build on this relation and become an important trade partner for Germany. If secession obliges Catalonia to leave the European Union, which might lead to economic isolation, the German government would vote for a flexible and pragmatic solution, and prefer that European law continue to be applied to the new state. The highest possible number of economic relations with the EU should continue, along with the rights and obligations of businesses operating in Catalonia. These measures would allow German companies to maintain their activities with Catalonia.

With regard to the political relations, Germany could support in the long-term the full membership of Catalonia. Although secession would be a step back in the integration process, the German governments have always been open to enlargements and adhesion of new member states. Taking into account that Catalonia and its citizens have belonged to the EU since 1986, this fact would place the new country quite close to other candidate countries. This is not only because of the economic relations and existing implementation of the *acquis communautaire,* but because it is based on political calculus. Catalonia would be a partner of Germany with similar interests in

Council negotiations. Considering the current economic data, Catalonia would become a net payer to the EU budget.

However, if full membership requires a long transition period and a painful reform of the EU treaties, as well as making the way back to economic recovery more complicated, the German government would not push for EU membership. If the relations towards Spain should remain hostile and the Spanish government would insist on its status quo with regard to its voting power in the Council, Commission and European Parliament, Berlin would not insist on the entry of Catalonia into the EU. This position could be underlined by the fact that a successful move of an independent Catalonia towards EU membership might destabilize several other European countries, e.g. secession movements could gain new input, and regionalist-nationalist parties would have to push for referendums in their own countries.

6. Conclusions

An analysis of the consequences of an independent Catalonia for German Foreign policy can only be hypothetical, there being too many open questions. First there are many questions relating to its economic solvency, but also questions relating to the political projection of the new state, since existing experience is only based on its role as an EU region.

In general terms, an increasing number of EU member states, both through external or internal enlargement, adds greater complexity to day-to-day European decision-making. Conflicts and resentments among former unitary states might even increase complexity. This seems contrary to German interests, especially in the current debates on reform.

Nowadays there is no perception of political instability in Spain with regard to its territorial unity. The conflict between the Spanish and the Catalan governments is not a priority, since economic reforms and recovery are more crucial issues. The conflict could become more decisive if it interferes in economic reforms. Only when the political (or economic) stability is no longer guaranteed in Spain, Germany (as part of the EU) will try to reduce the conflict and support arrangements that keep Catalonia as part of Spain. If there are signals indicating that Spain is threatened by paralysis, Germany could act more decisively. Germany will not encourage separation, but would insist on negotiations that lead to an agreement and cooperation on both sides. Uncontrolled or hostile secession as well as secondary effects of moving borders, or the difficulties that might arise from EU-membership renegotiations, are clearly seen as negative.

Finally, after the debate on the independence of Catalonia became less intensive, the German government may be more concerned with the raise of populist anti-austerity movements like "Podemos" which could become an important political actor in 2015 and which, together with Syriza openly demand the restructure of the county's debt.

References

Börzel, Tanja (2002), "Member State Responses to Europeanization", *Journal of Common Market Studies*, vol. 40, pp. 193-214.

Bulmer, Simon; Paterson, William E. (2010), "Germany and the European Union: from 'tamed power' to normalized power?," *International Affairs*, vol. 86: 5, pp. 1051–1073.

Engel, Arno; Parkes, Roderick (2012), "Accommodating an independent Scotland: how a British-style constitution for the EU could secure Scotland's future", *European Policy Centre, policy brief*, 24.10.2012.

Grant, Charles (2014), "What is wrong with German foreign policy?", *Centre for European Reform, policy brief*, May 2014.

Guérot, Ulrike; Leonard, Mark (2011), "The New German Question: How Europe can get the Germany it needs", *ECFR policy brief*, no 30, April 2011.

Ministerio de Economía y Competitividad (2014), "Flujos de inversiones exteriores directas 2013, Registro de inversiones exteriores", Dirección General de Comercio e Inversiones.

Statistisches Bundesamt (2014), "Ranking of Germany's trading partners in foreign trade 2013".

Independent Catalonia – a viable new European state?

Klaus-Jürgen Nagel

1. Small states and liberal democracy

The independence of small nations is often rejected, questioning their viability and/or the quality of their democracy. Since Madison[1], liberals fear that factions, either economically based or based on "passion" (religion or political ideology), may become more oppressive in smaller polities. John Stuart Mill[2] particularly recommended Bretons not to sit sulking on their rocks, but to assimilate into the burgeoning culture of France. In Germany, liberals and social democrats may be particularly critical with *Kleinstaaterei*. Marxists more often agreed than not. Karl Marx advocated the unity of Germany, and Rosa Luxemburg rejected even Polish independence on grounds of the bigger markets of Russia. Friedrich Engels, in the Hegelian tradition, wished to send "peoples without history" (stateless peoples) into the dustbin of history.[3]

Even Austromarxists, like Renner or Bauer, while arguing that only under socialism Nations could reach the most developed and inclusive expression of their cultures, initially stood against a break-up of the Austro-Hungarian Empire.[4] Contemporary Marxists, like Eric Hobsbawm, fear that small states may easily fall prey to the interests of big companies, as politicians may be more easily "captured" by economic interest.[5] In the same line of thought, ecologists may fear ecological dumping or "races to the bottom".

In fact, independence has not everywhere improved human rights or liberal democracy. Most of the new states of interwar Europe started as democ-

---

1 See Madison in Cooke, Jacob E. (ed.): The Federalist, Middletown, Conn. (3)1989, p. 56-65.
2 Considerations on Representative Government, ch. 16, London 1861.
3 See Avineri, Shlomo: Marxism and Nationalism, Journal of Contemporary History 26, 1991, 637-657.
4 See Nimni, Ephraim (ed.): National Cultural Autonomy and its Contemporary Critics, London/New York 2005.
5 See Hobsbawm, Eric: Some Reflections on "The Break-Up of Britain", New Left Review 105, 1977, 3-23.

racies but quickly changed to authoritarian regimes, took oppressive measures against their minorities, and/or waged war against their neighbours. More recently, independent South Sudan and Eritrea have failed as states. On the other hand, Norway seceded from Sweden in 1905 by parliamentary declaration, afterwards confirmed by referendum. Iceland seceded from Denmark in 1944 by a referendum for dissolution. Singapore's independence in 1965 may be considered an expulsion from the Malaysian Federation, but the terms were agreed upon by both governments. Slovakia's independence came in the form of a "velvet divorce" of the Czechoslovakian federation in 1993, formalized by an Act of the Federal Assembly. Montenegro won independence from Serbia in 2006 by a referendum ruled by Montenegrin law, but making use of a right to secede established in the federal constitution. In Kosovo, an overwhelming majority of the elected members of the parliament declared the country's independence from Serbia in 2008. Independence has been confirmed in an advisory opinion by the International Court of Justice in 2010, stating that there was nothing in International Law that prohibited Kosovo's independence. We may conclude that human rights or democracy have not suffered - at least in those among the aforementioned cases that occurred years ago.

This chapter is about hypothetical Catalan independence. With the help of data on the present situation, we assess the "viability" of Catalonia. Now "viability" can be affirmed as simply the state of living, the capacity to survive, or, as in business administration, providing greater benefit than the current situation. We understand that it is not only economic viability that is at stake, but also viability as a liberal democracy. Would Catalan independence according to present data endanger democracy, individual and minority rights, and international peace, and should it therefore be avoided or even outlawed?

2. Secession theories

In international law, and excluding colonial situations, new states are more easily accepted if they are created by mutual agreement, particularly when they result from the dissolution of a federation by mutual agreement (Czechoslovakia) or even using a constitutionally existing right to secede (Montenegro). But Spain is not a federation; in addition, there seems to be no way of an agreed dissolution - at least at the time of writing. What is more, the Spanish government, parliament, constitutional court and the majority of its public opinion and the population itself are not only opposed to Catalan independence, they also defend that there is no Constitutional right to secede, not even a right to hold a referendum in Catalonia on the issue.

However, there may be conditions legitimising independence, even unilateral independence. Liberal approaches that accept such cases may broadly be grouped into two schools. "Remedial right" theories accept secession if there is a just cause and no other remedy can be found.[6] The onus of proof lies with the secessionists. Causes for legitimate secession that are widely accepted among the defenders of such approaches include re-establishment of a state that had previously existed, protection against a real and immediate menace of physical extermination or genocide, and defense of the principle of "no taxation without representation". Cultural oppression, while sometimes accepted as a legitimate cause under very restricted conditions, is mostly rejected by scholars who only recognize a right to culture, but not to any particular culture.

However, there is no blood running through the streets of Barcelona. The Catalan language may today be used in the public space as more, it is also an official language, together with Spanish, at least within the region, and without any obligation to know it.[7] Catalonia's former independence is either doubted or considered to have ended a long time ago (1714). Autonomy, as an alternative solution, is available and even has been accepted under circumstances in 1978 when the vast majority of the Catalans said "yes" to the Spanish Constitution. With these arguments, legitimacy for secession is often denied by international public opinion. Catalan independentists, if at all using "remedialist" arguments to legitimize their claim, believe they have a just cause because of the lack of fairness of existing accommodation, the central states' continuous rejection of negotiations, and/or the lack of compliance of the central state with solutions it had previously agreed to, e.g. provisions of the statute of 2006 that are theoretically in force, but have not been obeyed.

However, as other chapters to this book have shown, Catalan independentists now generally prefer arguments coming from "choice" theories of secession.[8] These approaches conceive self determination as a primary right,

---

6 For ex. Buchanan, Alan: The Morality of Political Divorce from Fort Sumter to Lithuania and Quebec, Boulder 1991.

7 All Spaniards have a constitutional obligation to know Spanish.

8 The classical text is Beran, Harry: A liberal theory of secession, Political Studies 32, 1984, 1, 21-31.

a right that also includes, in principle, secession. The holders of the right are either Nations (with the corresponding problem to define what a Nation is, and the need of an arbiter to decide on doubtful cases), or individuals. If liberal democracy sees citizens as individuals with the widest possible right to choose, then frontiers should also be open to such choices. However, the territory for the new state may be a problem. What if the outcome is a map that looks like a Swiss cheese or is extremely small? What if the separatists are sitting on a mineral resource or occupy a territory that would allow them to blackmail the citizens of the "rest of" the previous state or third parties? What if they secede to oppress minorities? Choice theories therefore usually include more or less large lists of exceptions, cases where self determination may only take place inside the state, excluding the option of independence, in order to avoid encroaching upon the rights of the citizens of the rest-of-State or third parties, or lead to serious economical mischief.

Let us look at whether any of the excluding conditions of a right to decide, including the independence option, are to be found. Let us particularly look at whether the new state would be viable to assess the probability of its falling into the hands of evil interests, or to practice social or ecological dumping. Let us try to analyze whether any oppression of new minorities or nested communities is intended or probable, and whether independent Catalonia would have any unfair blackmailing capacity (for example, by the appropriation of any strategic resource, control of essential harbors or the like), that, if not controlled, could affect the viability or the rights of the rest-of-state and its citizens.

Sometimes arguments of a utilitarian character (more people will be better off or feel better after independence) or on welfare (with a higher degree of common identity, social redistribution will be more acceptable and probable)[9] are also presented as justifications for separation, but are generally too difficult to prove and weigh up in this article. The argument that the people of the seceding territory only have to demonstrate consistently to have different policy preferences may also work under choice theories, while there surely has to be an additional argument to be acceptable as a legitimate cause for secession in the context of "remedial right" approaches.

In any case, our assessment has to consider that the existing road-maps towards self determination in Catalonia (as in Scotland) do not include a

---

9 For the use of such arguments, see Miller, who, generally, uses them against secession, however; Miller, David: On Nationality, Oxford 1995.

total breakaway. The continued existence of treaty based relations with the respective rest-of-state, even including fields of shared sovereignty, and in particular the maintenance of social and economic unions (currency in Scotland and Catalonia, monarchy in Scotland), and of international treaties (NATO, EU), may be seen as guarantees against many of the dangers of secession.

3. Independent Catalonia: an evil state?

Would an independent Catalonia be more oppressive towards its minorities than current-day Spain? "Choice" theorists like Brenan (1984) exclude communities from the right if the purpose of secession is to oppress minorities. One such minority could be immigrants; however, Núria Franco's chapter stresses the efforts of the Catalan independentists towards inclusion and against the prejudice of an "ethnic" blood-based Nation. In regards to autochthonous linguistic or ethnic minorities, only the people of the Vall d'Aran may qualify as such. In this small Pyrenean valley that enjoys a high per capita income as consequence of its booming tourism, a version of the Occitan language is spoken. Although the linguistic rights of this community are far reaching and are secured by the Catalan statute of autonomy, inhabitants of the valley may feel aggrieved by the planned Catalan law for territorial reorganization, which includes the valley (today a "comarca"/county with a special status) into a wider district ("vegueria"), where its tiny population would no longer be decisive. Choice theorists like Brenan, in these situations, demand the independence seekers grant such a community a right to secede of their own, a right that Catalan nationalists are happy to grant.

A much larger community in question is the Spanish-speaking Catalans, who are no minority. In today's Catalonia, Spanish is the more widely spoken language, particularly in the capital region. Any possible campaign for secession either by referendum or as a result of an election to Parliament has to address this community if it is to win. It is difficult to argue convincingly that independence, once achieved, would lead to discrimination of Spanish speakers, who are in the majority. Most likely, Spanish would enjoy official status. However, Catalan, as the weaker of the two languages, would probably be favoured by the continuing of existing policies of linguistic immersion in schools, which today enjoy the overwhelming support of the Catalan population.[10] Existing imbalances that still disfavour Catalan will probably be abolished.

The case of a possible discrimination of those that principally or totally identify as Spaniards is of a somewhat higher concern. The solution provided by choice theorists (redrawing of frontiers according to local majorities) will probably not be available in the Catalan case, where such identifiers (and voters in an election on independence or a referendum) might win majorities in counties (p. E. Baix Llobregat) located at the centre of Catalonia. And choice theorists are generally opposed to "Swiss cheese" solutions, as they may encroach on the rights and well-being of the surrounding territories, leading to potential blackmailing circumstances. Dual citizenship (Spanish and Catalan) after secession seems an acceptable solution, and has repeatedly been accepted by prominent Catalan nationalists, following the Scottish model. It provides consular protection and protects people with double identities. This should not be too difficult to achieve, particularly if independent Catalonia is allowed to stay inside the EU.

In sum, permission for third parties to separate may apply for the Vall d'Aran, while no exploitation of immigrants or (under democracy) of the Spanish speaking majority may be envisaged. As in all political questions, those that have politically "lost" are at risk of suffering retaliation by the winners, particularly if the way towards independence was difficult, thorny and conflictive. However, means of lowering the risk are available and their use is probable, if (as assessed later) Catalonia remains a liberal democracy. While the discussion on Catalan secession has often focussed on groups inside Catalonia (Spanish speakers and Spanish identifiers), the fate of the numerous Catalan speakers (and sometimes identifiers) in the rest-of-state (Valencia, Balearic Islands, Aragon) has rarely been worthy of comment. They may, in a conflict scenario, become objects of distrust or retaliation policies; for example, an even more discriminating treatment against their language. In a scenario of a negotiated separation, the minorities on both sides may be protected by mutual agreements, eventually with the help of intermediaries (like the EU), in the interest of both sides.

---

10 See Nagel, Klaus-Jürgen: Unabhängigkeit und Sprachpolitik in Katalonien, in *Vasco da Silva/Andrea Rössler (eds.): Sprachen im Dialog*, Berlin 2015, forthcoming.

4. Independent Catalonia: a failed state? A loss in the quality of democracy?

History has shown that independent states may fail, or at least that democracy may fail in newly independent states. After the First World War, all states created in Europe started as democracies (except Hungary) and became non-democratic before the Second (except Czechoslovakia). Many post-soviet states became democracies, but often of low quality. However, European states created by secession or dissolution of formerly democratic states are often enjoying a high quality democracy (Norway, Iceland, Slovakia, to name but a few). Again, much depends on how the process leading to independence was conducted.

Constitutional debates in an independent Catalonia will have to face problems as everywhere else. But actors probably would compromise on constitutional essentials (parliamentary democracy, rights and freedoms) as there already is a long lasting and broad agreement on these values and institutional forms. The role of the city and metropolitan area of Barcelona in contrast to its hinterland may be one of the issues at stake, particularly in relation to establishing the electoral system. However, the very active civil society is already organized inside the territory, and where this is not the case (as in the Catholic Church), already existing plans and schemes may be quite easily activated.[11]. In spite of recent volatility of electors, and always supposing that the process towards independence runs smooth, the long established Catalan party system will continue. Its leading parties are non-state wide. Probably, the Catalan nationalist parties of the right (CiU), of the left (ERC) and eventually the extreme left (CUP), as well as the Greens (ICV), may stabilize, while PP and PSC-PSOE probably will lose influence because the losers in the process may more easily vote for Ciutadans (C's) because the party is not involved (at least until today) with Spanish "mother parties". The new "Podemos" party, in spite of defending the Catalan right to decide, is more likely to follow the Syriza way to insisting of state sovereignty against "troika" and/or European encroachment.

Spanish politicians (including some Catalans opposed to secession) have sometimes argued that a smaller state, like an independent Catalonia, may

---

11 See Nagel, Klaus-Jürgen: Religion and the political accommodation of Catalonia. A non-relation?, in *Ferran Requejo/Klaus-Jürgen Nagel (eds.): Politics of Religion and Nationalism. Federalism, consociationalism and secession*, London/New York 2015, 194-210.

be captured by the interest of powerful economic actors, e.g. multinational companies. However, the country is not at all small by EU standards, and more importantly its economy is quite diverse in relation to its size, which makes the predominance of a small group of actors more improbable. Recently, drawing also on the many scandals of corruption, Spanish media have sometimes implied that an independent Catalonia would become an unusually immoral state. While it is obvious that tax evasion, illegal party financing, and even outright buying of favours (or intending to do so) have proliferated during the years of autonomy, it is also clear that the importance of the shadow economy is lower in Catalonia in comparison to Spanish standards.[12]

Again, nobody has questioned the future of democracy in the rest-of state. And it may well be that the problem would be more salient there - without Catalonia, the PP might from time to time have a better chance to obtain an absolute majority there, while the multi-party system of Catalonia would be more competitive.

5. An economically viable state?

Catalonia represents about 6% of the Spanish territory, 16% of its population, nearly 20% of its GDP, over 25% of Spain's industrial investments and some 25% of its R&D, as well of 20-24% of its income from tourism. However, Catalonia has no relevant mineral resources, and though its harbours are important for Spanish exports, it is not cutting off Spain from the sea, as Eritrea's independence did in the case of Ethiopia. If we consider the arguments provided by "choice" secession theories, we find that Catalan independence does not take away essential zones of the original state in economic, military or cultural affairs. This is not to say that economic losses for Spain would not be considerable. However, until now, the discussion has centred on the economic viability of Catalonia, while it may well be a bigger problem for the rest-of state.

In fact, the discussion on whether an independent Catalonia would be viable is one of the most developed topics of the debate on independence. It is in this context that the two possible definitions of viability (capacity to

---

12 According to Derichsweiler, Cornelia: „In Spanien blüht die Schattenwirtschaft", Neue Zürcher Zeitung 7.2.14, the percentage of shadow economy on general GDP in Catalonia reaches 24.6%, while Extremadura stands at 31.3%.

survive/profitable project) most often clash. For many academic economists at Catalan universities, for a great part of the *Col.legi d'Economistes de Catalunya*[13], for the Small and Medium Employers (PIME), and particularly for the academics that gathered under the significant name of *Col.lectiu Wilson* (6 professors working at renowned universities including Princeton, Harvard, Columbia and the London School of Economics and Political Science), independence means more money for Catalonia and the Catalans, maybe after a short period of adaptation.[14] For these economists, the end of the fiscal deficit outweighs in the long or even the short run the costs of getting the new state going. For the other side represented by economists working at Spanish universities, and also by the *Instituto de Estudios Económicos* (the think-tank of the Spanish Employers Federation CEOE)[15], the Catalan section of the Spanish employers' association CEOE (*Foment de Treball*), the smaller, influential employers clubs Círculo de Empresarios, Puente Aéreo employers club[16], or the Círculo Ecuestre of Barcelona, independence would inflict severe damage on the Catalan economy, if not outright catastrophe.[17] Some particularly influential leaders, like Manuel Lara of the Planeta editorial group (which includes also the main houses that publish in Catalan), Josep Oliu (Banc de Sabadell), Isidre Fainé (La Caixa savings bank), former Spanish PP minister for Foreign Affairs and Vueling company head Josep Piqué, and Josep Lluís Bonet (Freixenet sparkling wine) are particularly outspoken in fighting independence.[18]

In the scenarios designed by anti-independentists, Spanish boycott, losses in export, moving out of foreign investors, and higher administrative and credit costs cumulate to produce lower welfare for more than a generation of Catalans, rendering the Greek drama insignificant in comparison with the

---

13 See Col.legi d'Economistes de Catalunya: Economia de Catalunya. Preguntes i respostes sobre l'impacte econòmic de la independencia, Barcelona 2014. See also El Periódico de Catalunya 12.2.14.

14 See an example for a "Wilsonian" scenario in Ara 21.3.2013. See also Xavier Cuadras in Diari de Tarragona 27.10.13.

15 See Instituto de Estudios Económicos (ed.): La cuestión Catalana, hoy, Madrid 2013. This publication was widely commented in the Spanish press, for example Diario de Navarra 15.3.13, Diari de Tarragona 15.3.13, La Gaceta de los Negocios 18.3.13, Levante 31.3.13.

16 See El País 2.2.14.

17 This is not to say that all aforementioned actors reject a referendum on the issue.

18 Lists of employers sharing this standpoint may be found in El País 2.2.14 and ABC 2.2.14.

Catalan apocalypse[19], converting Catalonia into another Somaliland[20], and even producing GDP losses higher than those suffered by Germany in 1945, which was not a particularly good year for its economy. The message is that, as independence makes people suffer, independentism is not only stupid but immoral.

The first "battlefield" of the discussion on economic viability is the amount of Catalonia's fiscal deficit. This important topic is dealt with in Paluzie's chapter of the present book. The current PP administration has continuously contested the Catalan figures, although they were based on the methods that had been agreed with the former socialist Spanish government. Recently, the current Rajoy government introduced its own method of calculation.[21] Not surprisingly, this gives lower figures of the Catalan deficit (3.6% average between 2006 and 2010, according to foreign minister Margallo).[22]

A second field of contention is the effect of the boycott on Catalan goods that everybody expects to occur if Catalan becomes independent or even before. Spanish economists often considered such a boycott to have devastating consequence, as Catalan GDP is heavily dependent on exports (over 50%), of which more than half goes to Spain. However, such goods were boycotted in 1932 and 2005 without in general too much effect, "cava" (sparkling wine) being the only exception. Catalan economists do not admit the probable effect of 1.7-4% of Catalan GDP to be devastating, and assure that even this effect will soon pass by; probably only direct consumers (and not companies) will participate, and only goods that can clearly be identified as Catalan will suffer. Catalan producers may look for alternatives inside and outside the country. Some Spanish producers, bereft of Catalan products or markets, may also effectively protest against the backfire effect that the

---

19 See Antonio Porta, of the Círculo de Empresarios, in giving support to the conclusions of the Instituto de Estudios Económicos, cited in El País 15.3.2013.

20 See Francesc Granell in Ara 14.2.14.

21 See Ara 1.2.14; the CSIC and Angel de la Fuente are in charge of the calculation according to the new method. See Ara 1.2.14; El País 1.5.14; El Mundo, El Periódico de Catalunya, and El País 16.5.14; Diari de Tarragona 17.5.14.

22 Still a high quota, but considerably lower than the 6-8% that the method agreed by both sides yielded; see Núria Bosch in Ara 6.1.14.

boycott would have on the Spanish economy.[23] Catalan minister for the economy, Mas Colell, shares these views.[24]

Regarding the importance of the Spanish market for the Catalan industry, anti-independentists argue that Murcia is more important a market than the US, and Aragon more than Germany.[25] After independence, Catalan goods would have to pay tariffs. The other side contends that the importance of these markets is dwindling away steadily[26], and that even if Catalonia finds itself outside the EU, free trade is likely to continue as it does with several other countries outside the EU, like Iceland, Norway and Switzerland. Even more important is the issue of foreign investment; Catalonia today receives an over proportional share of foreign investment in Spain. German and American interests are said to have already protested against independence and threatened to move out, and some have already done so.[27] On the other hand, this seems improbable as investment is planned many years in advance, and costly installations will not be given up easily. Catalonia, according to the latest numbers, continues to receive an over proportional share (22.2%) of Spain's inward investments, which has even increased during 2013.[28] Several companies have already announced they will stay in the case of independence.[29]

In fact, most important investors do not forward any comment on their position. As far as public sources admit, the alleged protest of German investors consisted of a document signed by some managers and an oral statement by a Spanish member of the Kreis deutschsprachiger Führungskräfte

---

23 The standard work from a pro-independence standpoint is Guinjoan, Modest/Cuadras Morató, Xavier: Sense Espanya. Balanç econòmic de la independència, Barcelona 2011.

24 See El Periódico de Catalunya 14.9.11; El País 14.9.11; Público 15.9.11; Expansión Cataluña 4.10.11; La Gaceta de los Negocios 18.3.13; Xavier Cuadras in Diari de Tarragona 27.10.13; El País 1.5.14.

25 See La Gaceta de los Negocios 18.3.13.

26 According to Oriol Amat only slightly more than 1/3 of all transactions go to Spain; see Levante 31.3.13.

27 Joaquin Trigo mentioned Procter and Gamble; Sur 22.9.13.

28 Recent investments were provided by Grimaldi, Nissan, Novatis, Ikea, Booking, BTG and Ferrari. See Ara 3.7.13 and El Punt Avui 19.4.14..For the numbers given by president Artur Mas in parliament, see La Vanguardia 13.2.14; for more numbers, El Punt Avui 19.4.14 (title: "L'estranger té fe en Catalunya").

29 See La Vanguardia 18.11.12, referring to BASF and Dow Chemical.

(KdF) on occasion of a speech delivered by a Catalan minister.[30] The alleged protest of American investors seems to have been the opinion of one anti-independentist Catalan. It stands to reason, however, that investors prefer continuity of the present situation to political insecurity. A prolonged and conflictive process may scare new money away from Catalonia; while a quick and peaceful process, particularly if ending in continued EU membership of Catalonia, can be expected to have only minor effects, if any. Obviously, neither foreign investors to Catalonia nor to other parts of the current Spanish State, have any interest in expelling Catalonia from the Common Market, which applies to the Spanish economy as a whole. In particular, big companies like Nissan, Solvay, BASF, and Volkswagen, as well as the Spanish Repsol, Telefónica, Santander and BBVA banks, or retailers like El Corte Inglés or Mercadona, would have to suffer losses if Catalonia remained outside the EU.[31]

Another conflictive issue is the Spanish debt. Adversaries of independence hold that Catalonia has to pay its share of the current debt. Initially, many independentists agreed; however, it was far from clear on what basis a fair share should be calculated (inhabitants? GDP? tax volume?). During 2013-2014, when the rejection of any Catalan referendum by Spain became increasingly clear and Spanish actors used the threat to veto Catalonia's membership of the EU in the case of a declaration of independence, independentists more often rejected to pay any part of the debt[32], or at least linked

---

30   KdF associates some 200 managers and employers, lead by BASF, Bayer, Air Berlin, and Bertelsmann, among others. The mentioned protests by some KdF members are highlighted in elEconomista.es, Negocios.com, Diàlogo.Libre, all 28.1.14, elEconomista.es and eldiario.es 9.2.14, as well as in the written press, La Vanguardia 28.1.14, Diari de Girona ABC 29.1.14, El País and ABC 2.2.14; Ara and El País 9.2.14; Expansión 10.2.14. Some 60 members signed a manifest against Catalan independence, if Leo Wieland (FAZ 13.2.14) is to believed. Wieland, in a sensationalist way, saw an "Aufstand" (revolt) of German employers in Catalonia. For a more moderate statement, see the interview with the president of this club, Andrés Gómez Núñez, in L'Econòmic 6.12.13. It seems that at least two German Staatssekretäre (junior ministers of the departments of finance and foreign affairs, respectively) visited Barcelona to talk with representatives of German investors in Barcelona during the last months of 2013.

31   See Xavier Cuadras in Sur 22.9.13 and in Diari de Tarragona 27.10.13; see L'Econòmic 5.10.13.

32   See David Ros and Roger Fatjó in Ara 14.2.14.

their disposition to a Spanish waiving of the veto.[33] They argue that sharing the debt of an original state is neither mandatory for nor customary of new states, and that the partition of the debt should be bargained against EU membership, maintaining of open frontiers, and/or sharing social security funds. Against arguments that an independent Catalonia could not shoulder the accumulated debts (the original debt of the Autonomous Community, the share of the Spanish debt, and the new debts to be contracted to set up the new Catalan state), they contend that, if the current situation continues, Catalans would also have to pay as Spanish citizens, and that they have been adjusted unfair charges so far.

Spanish social affairs minister, Fátima Báñez, recently argued that it was Spain that paid Catalan pensions and unemployment subsidies in 2013, financing Catalonia's deficit with Spanish Social Security.[34] However, this deficit was higher in the rest of Spain, and it is financed from the reserve funds, into which Catalonia had contributed in previous years, in fact over proportionally (an average of 29% for the years 2006-2009). Catalan independentists increasingly argue that, should independence come, they should get this money back, but sometimes threaten to reject paying any part of the Spanish debt or not paying back regional fund loans[35] should their claim be not answered.

The most catastrophic scenarios see independent Catalonia outside the European common currency, the euro. They prophesize that Catalonia's new currency would be quickly devaluated (at least 50%)[36], its debt interest rates would escalate, a spiral of devaluation drive capital out[37], leading Catalan banks into bankruptcy (or take-over by Spanish houses) as no European

---

33 Liberal radical economist Sala i Martin, in Diari de Tarragona, 6.4.14: "si los españoles se ponen burros y nos mandan fuera del sistema solar y del Universo, pues que se coman ellos la deuda. Y ya se encargarán los europeos de que aquí no se ponga ni una sola frontera."

34 According to Ara 29.4.14. See López Casasnovas, L'Econòmic 17.5.14.

35 Loans granted to Catalonia as an emergency help to pay providers, for example, consist an ever more important argument against viability. They seem to prove that Catalonia cannot even manage its tasks as an Autonomous Community, far from those of a state. However, Catalan independentists see these loans as a way to get back the money that an unfair fiscal system has taken away from their Community. These loans, until 2015, had to pay interest. See L'Econòmic 17.5.14.

36 Lluís Feito according to El País 15.3.13.

37 Joaquin Trigo, according to Levante 31.3.13.

Central bank or funds would be available to bail them out.[38] Most Catalan economists hold that Catalonia, like some other European states outside the EU, may keep the euro currency if absolutely necessary outside the European Central Bank, even in the undesirable case of the country's exclusion from the EU.[39] They hold that Catalan banks will have access to ECB credits even in the worst case, if need be by branch plants in member states of the Union[40]. They remind us that Spanish banks have about 20% of their market in Catalonia[41] and do not have any interest in losing it for the sake of an act of political retaliation against a previous declaration of independence. For the College of Catalan Economists, Catalan debts would rise between 52% and (worst case scenario) 103% of its GDP in case of such an event[42], that is, to the current situation of Germany (under 60%), or Spain (about 100%).

To sum up, if we exclude the most extreme scenarios presented by Spanish anti-intependentists, numbers underline the viability of an independent Catalonia in economic terms. For its survival, the country would not depend on economic, social or ecological dumping. However, the real balance of costs and benefits of independence depends on the political handling of the process.[43] Scenarios designed to scare people away from independence usually assume a low fiscal deficit of Catalonia, on the one hand, and an independent Catalonia that finds itself outside international organizations like EU or OECD on the other, and assume that this situation holds on for years. Scenarios designed to make independence popular tend to assume the contrary. Other chapters of this book deal with the issue of EU membership of a territory that separated from a European member state. A reasonable conclusion shared by Catalan economists may be that independence is neither apocalyptic nor a panacea.[44]

---

38 La Gaceta de los Negocios 18.3.13.
39 See El Periódico de Catalunya 21.9.13; Sur 22.9.13.
40 According to Jaume Ventura; see Ara 6.10.13 and Guillem Lòpez Casasnovas, La Vanguardia 16.10.13.
41 This number was given by Artur Mas in an interview with La Repubblica, and was referred to by the Catalan press; see La Vanguardia 28.12.13.
42 Numbers given by David Ros and Roger Fatjó in Ara 14.2.14.
43 See Col.legi d'Economistes 2014, and Ara 14.2.14.
44 "Ni apocalipsi, ni panacea. Els economistas catalans neguen els vaticinis catastròfics de Margallo, però reconeixen que un estat propi hauria d'enfrontar-se a un elevat deute i un posible boicot comercial", El Periódico de Catalunya 14.3.14.

6. By way of a short conclusion

It must be said that the current situation of rejecting the Catalan referendum also hinders a reasonable discussion taking place between those that argue for a secession and those that argue for a "better together"; the defenders of the latter position do not feel the same pressure to win a debate on a hypothesis that, according to their interpretation of the Spanish Constitution, cannot really occur. But it seems fair to say that, the Spanish Constitution apart, an independent Catalonia would probably be a quite normal European state, without the threat of imminent dangers to liberal rights, democracy and peace. It would have an economic capacity that assures its survival and, together with its developed civil society, party system and other institutions, protects the country from state failure.

Some conclusions and final reflections

Klaus-Jürgen Nagel / Stephan Rixen

Neither the Scottish nor the Catalan "process" have been concluded, making it difficult to present conclusions. This book will have shown that their history and present situation are different. The Scottish National Party was founded in 1934. In Scotland, ethnic and linguistic issues have at least in the long run, been of minor importance. Its first electoral success only happened during the 1970 s, in the context of the crisis in Great Britain on the one hand and the discovery of the North Sea Oil on the other. It was later, fuelled by the long years of Conservative government of Prime Ministers Thatcher and Major, when Scotland was bereft of any significant influence in London. Scotland became nearly a "Tory-free" zone, with policy preferences systematically opposed to those defended by a majority in England. Endowed with autonomy (devolution) under Tony Blair (1997), its initial Labour majority nevertheless could not become pro-secessionist, as the remaining English state would – for the time being – be governed by Conservatives or others. It needed the victory of the SNP, a rival left party, to bring Scotland closer to independence. SNP's true bid may have been for an enlarged autonomy (devo-max), the third option that Alex Salmond wanted to include in the referendum. Cameron, still on his high horse, forced the SNP to accept a "yes or no", calculating that this would assure a unionist victory without establishing a need to negotiate for further autonomy. Ironically, when the majority of the "better together campaign" backed by all major British parties started to wither away, Cameron and his allies had to step back and promise greater autonomy to prevent independence.

In many aspects, the Catalan independence movement features a different, in some aspects, an opposite development. Its history is rooted in a national movement with a political history that started already at the end of the 19th century, when a movement based on language and culture (but not on ethnic origin) became politicized. The party system of Catalonia was quickly dominated by non-state-wide parties, but unlike Scotland, there always was a plurality of left and right parties standing for Catalan Nationalism. Catalonia, without any major natural resource, became the first industrialized region of the Spanish state with a class-based society and a recognized capital,

Barcelona. While taken together, the majority of the forces that represented Catalan Nationalism was usually more convincing than in Scotland, they were always divided and had to struggle against a Spanish state, and (under democracy) Spanish political parties that stopped well short of accepting the existence of a Catalan "Nation". Contrary to the UK, Spain tried to adopt the French model of a nation-state during good part of its history up to present times. While the United Kingdom could recognize the Scots as a (junior partner) Nation without any major problems and treat them differently, Spain did not do something similar for the Catalans. In a state where, according to the Constitution and widespread public opinion there exists only one Nation, Catalonia cannot be recognized as such, and the self-governing rights that the one and only existing Nation in use of its sovereignty may hand down to part of its population, are not grounded in the recognition of any previous historical or federal rights. When the forces that had campaigned for a referendum won the Catalan elections in 2012, there was therefore no issue for the Spanish government to negotiate a change in the rules of the "game". And when a majority of the Catalan parliament declared its sovereignty and in 2014 asked the Madrid Parliament to pass a law to empower the Catalan institutions to hold a referendum emulating the British model, this was rejected. Instead of acknowledging a justified claim for negotiations, the Catalan bid for a referendum was interpreted as a challenge to the base of Spain's constitutional order. In a country that has seen a very turbulent history, there was no practice of mutual respect and trust, nor a Constitutional Court that, like in Canada in the case of the Quebec opinion, could provide a way towards independence. Not as a unilateral process or by recognition of a unilateral right, but as a right to be taken seriously and have negotiations in good faith, i.e. if a clear majority of the Quebec demos so decided. While in the UK all major state wide parties accepted to grant Scotland a referendum (and then campaigned against it), all major Spanish parties opposed the right to hold a similar referendum. This decision led to the passing of a law on consultations by the Catalan parliament in summer 2014 that was outruled by the Spanish Constitutional Court. Next was the attempt to start a process of democratic participation on the issue led by the Catalan government, the prohibition by the Court of this involvement, the celebrating of the vote, and the start of a prosecution against the Catalan Prime Minister, his deputy, and the Minister of Education in the first place for disobedience to the Court. Rejecting serious negotiations on how to allow the Catalans to decide, even if eventually restricting the immediate consequences of a positive vote on independence, the Catalan actors were by-and-by driven to decide either to abandon or break the rules.

It is still not clear at the time of writing (January 2015) which decision they will take. After these experiences, it is clear however that no bilateral negotiation on rule changes will take place now, and that if Catalan independentists want to continue and start to break rules, they will have to look for a higher legitimacy. Rule changes, like constitutional reforms of considerable character, are politically improbable, given that they can only be passed with the support of the major parties of Spain, and that at least one of these parties, the Conservative Partido Popular, is not only opposed to secession, but also to confederalism, and federalism. While the repeated Socialist claim for a basically symmetrical federation, even if taken seriously today, would not accommodate the claims of a Catalan majority. As a referendum is impossible (and the Quebec or Scottish ways are therefore excluded), a Kosovo scenario with a declaration of independence by a Parliamentarian majority becomes more probable. This would then have to be followed or preceded by taking control of the territory to achieve the international recognition of what would amount to a *de facto* Catalan state. Before such challenges, a breakdown of the process, maybe as consequence of the loss of the social majority for independence or the inner divisions of the movement (for example, along the right-left cleavage line of the party system), is possible, particularly when the organized civil society loses its grip on the Catalanist parties.

But differences apart, Catalan, Scottish as well as Flemish and Quebec independentist movements challenge the stability of their host states, albeit not of the state system. All of them see themselves as "stateless nations". In some cases, even non-nationalistic or post-national independentism can be found, stressing the civic character of the demos. However, these territories have all enjoyed the status of a member state of a federation or at least enjoy devolved or autonomous institutions for some time. That means that they do not have to be created *ex nihile*. Their political actors have gained administrative experience, and institutional practices and routines have been developed. They feature plural party systems and leading elites. Their civil societies have developed along the frontiers of their Nation or demos. They question the legitimacy of existing frontiers, which at least in Europe usually are the product of dynastic decisions, wars or marriages of rulers, not of democratic decision. They criticize the eternal status of states and frontiers, more or less sacralized by the correspondent state nationalisms (and the international state system, which they see as unfairly biased in favor of existing states). It remains to be seen whether they are going to copy the history of existing states if the possibility arises. However, all aforementioned territories could be bases for politically viable liberal democracies, at the same level of liberal and democratic rights as their host states. Catalonia, and perhaps the others, would probably be economically viable, thereby not falling into the hands of evil interests or becoming failed states. While questioning the frontiers of existing liberal democratic states, they are striving for less independence than many separatist movements of the past. They look for peaceful and at best negotiated ways out of their host state, and they do not appeal to other states for political or military intervention, as do many national minorities trapped in states dominated by adverse majorities. Their future relation to the former host state after independence is envisaged as peaceful, even as a partnership. Dual citizenship has been announced by Scottish and Catalan independentists. They do not question existing international security systems or the confederal agreements and treaty systems of their host state; on the contrary, they wish to continue with these international organizations and treaties, participating as equals. According to the mainstream of the respective independentist movements, independent Quebec would continue to be within NATO and NAFTA; independent Scotland and Catalonia, in NATO and in the EU. Scotland even would keep the Queen. Catalonia would surely maintain the Euro, even in case of (temporary?) exclusion from the EU.

Neither the EU Treaties nor international law seem to be prepared for those cases. Perhaps existing state boundaries should not be excluded from democratic decision processes when there is no tangible threat to international peace and security. While no unconditional right to secession might be granted or encouraged, it seems unfair to put the future of a minority into the hands of a majority, tolerating even the plain rejection of negotiations, even when the new pretenders to statehood are at least as "civic" and inclusive in regards to membership than the existing states and their nations.

To some observers, setting up new states in a time when globalization makes states less souveraign than ever before seems anachronistic. However, it may also be that the alternatives to independent statehood - autonomy, federalism and consocialism, which so often have been propagated - proved unworkable, insignificant, insufficient, biased, or discriminatory, at least in territories where majorities for an alternative statehood might be found. In particular, the Europe of the Regions that has been advertised so often, has crystalized in little more than a Committee of the Regions that cannot satisfy nations or *demoi* that strive for recognition as equals, or, for that matter, regions with legislative powers. A certain return to the idea of a Europe of member states may have occurred. The turn towards independence, therefore, can also be seen as the failure of potential alternatives. Independence, in the cases we have dealt with, may not be portrayed correctly as the return to a cosy homeland of folk dances and songs, disentangled from Europe and/or global processes. It may mean quite the contrary. When the only way to influence or control globalization processes that seems worthwhile is the control of a state, working alone or, like in Europe, together with other states, striving for statehood may be all but anachronistic. It may be a logical conclusion, at least in territories where corresponding majorities may be found because existing accommodations have failed or alternative proposals of such accommodation have been rejected. In the EU, where the European promises of the demise of the member states are no longer believed by many actors, the status of a member state seems a logical objective, a way to take responsibility, and not to eschew it.

Authors

Yasser Abdelrehim, Postdoctoral Researcher, Law, Universität Erfurt

Antoni Abat Ninet, Professor, Law, Københavns Universitet (University of Copenhagen)

Florian Becker, Professor, Law, Christian-Albrechts-Universität zu Kiel

Hermann-Josef Blanke, Professor, Law, Universität Erfurt

Núria Franco Guillén, PhD Candidate, Political Science, Universitat Pompeu Fabra, Barcelona

Jaume López Hernández, Adjunct Professor, Political Science, Universitat Pompeu Fabra, Barcelona

Mario Kölling, Senior Researcher, Political Science, Fundación Manuel Giménez Abad, Zaragoza

Peter A. Kraus, Professor, Political Science, Universität Augsburg

Markus Möstl, Professor, Law, Universität Bayreuth

Klaus-Jürgen Nagel, Associate Professor, Political Science, Universitat Pompeu Fabra, Barcelona

Elisenda Paluzie, Associate Professor (Tenured University Lecturer), Dean of the Faculty, Economy, Universitat de Barcelona

Hans-Jürgen Puhle, Professor emeritus, Political Science, Johann Wolfgang Goethe-Universität Frankfurt am Main

Stephan Rixen, Professor, Law, Universität Bayreuth

Ivan Serrano Balaguer, Postdoctoral Researcher (IN3 Fellow), Political Science, Universitat Oberta de Catalunya, Barcelona